D0072592

First Amendment Freedoms

Books in the **Contemporary World Issues** series address vital issues in today's society such as genetic engineering, pollution, and biodiversity. Written by professional writers, scholars, and nonacademic experts, these books are authoritative, clearly written, up-to-date, and objective. They provide a good starting point for research by high school and college students, scholars, and general readers as well as by legislators, businesspeople, activists, and others.

Each book, carefully organized and easy to use, contains an overview of the subject, a detailed chronology, biographical sketches, facts and data and/or documents and other primary source material, a forum of authoritative perspective essays, annotated lists of print and nonprint resources, and an index.

Readers of books in the Contemporary World Issues series will find the information they need in order to have a better understanding of the social, political, environmental, and economic issues facing the world today.

First Amendment Freedoms

A REFERENCE HANDBOOK

Michael C. LeMay

ABC-CLIO®

An Imprint of ABC-CLIO, LLC
Santa Barbara, California • Denver, Colorado

Library of Congress Cataloging-in-Publication Data

Names: LeMay, Michael C., 1941- author.
Title: First amendment freedoms : a reference handbook / Michael C. LeMay.
Description: Santa Barbara, California : ABC-CLIO, [2021] | Series: Contemporary world issues | Includes bibliographical references and index.
Identifiers: LCCN 2020035782 (print) | LCCN 2020035783 (ebook) | ISBN 9781440869297 (hardcover) | ISBN 9781440869303 (ebook)
Subjects: LCSH: United States. Constitution. 1st Amendment. | Freedom of speech—United States. | Freedom of the press—United States.
Classification: LCC KF4770 .L46 2021 (print) | LCC KF4770 (ebook) | DDC 342.7308/5—dc23
LC record available at https://lccn.loc.gov/2020035782
LC ebook record available at https://lccn.loc.gov/2020035783

ISBN: 978-1-4408-6929-7 (print)
      978-1-4408-6930-3 (ebook)

25 24 23 22 21   1 2 3 4 5

This book is also available as an eBook.

ABC-CLIO
An Imprint of ABC-CLIO, LLC

ABC-CLIO, LLC
147 Castilian Drive
Santa Barbara, California 93117
www.abc-clio.com

This book is printed on acid-free paper ∞

Manufactured in the United States of America

Contents

Preface

The Bill of Rights, the first ten amendments to the U. S. Constitution, is one of the most important features of the American system of government. And the First Amendment is, arguably, the most important, contested, controversial, and consequential amendment of the Bill of Rights. The First Amendment consists of a bundle of rights crafted in several clauses: the freedom of religious expression, antiestablishment of a national religion, the freedom of assembly and the right to protest and to petition the government for redress, the freedom of the press, and the freedom of speech. Each of these clauses is stated rather simply, and they were originally interpreted to only apply to the federal government. Over more than two hundred years, the meanings and the constraints on government implicit in the First Amendment have been expanded upon, applied to all levels of American government, and been hotly contested in American politics.

Through adjudication involving a sizable number of federal cases, and particularly key—landmark—Supreme Court case decisions, the First Amendment prohibitions against government have been clarified. Actions taken by federal, state, and local authorities have been challenged and often found to be unconstitutional on the basis of First Amendment rights. The U.S. Congress has passed subsequent legislation expanding the meaning of those First Amendment freedom rights. The issue has also been impacted by executive orders and by U.S. treaty provisions, which have the force of law.

As the United States grew in size and power and its stature and influence in world politics expanded, the country became increasingly diverse in its population demographics. Those developments led to many issues and problems that had to be addressed and resolved with respect to the meaning of the prohibitions established by the First Amendment. Solutions to some problems appropriate to a given time and place had, on occasion, unintended consequences resulting in new problems that had to be resolved anew.

First Amendment Freedoms examines the politics of those fundamental freedoms. Like all volumes in the Contemporary World Issues series, this one is aimed at general readers and high school, college, and university students. It follows an established format for all volumes in the series.

Chapter 1 discusses the history and background of the establishment of the First Amendment and traces the conflicts that the amendment generated in American politics and how those conflicts expanded and changed the understanding of those fundamental rights and privileges, first with regard to citizens and then to persons residing within the United States. The chapter provides a thorough examination of the economic, political, and social contexts surrounding American society's sense of what freedoms are guaranteed by the First Amendment and how those guarantees impact and limit the actions of government at all levels. It presents the discussion in a comprehensive and unbiased manner, allowing readers to reach their own judgments on the issues.

Chapter 2 outlines some of the more problematic concerns related to the First Amendment's guaranteed freedoms. It discusses why those issues arose and why they pose such difficulty for effective policy making to ensure those fundamental rights. It addresses the efforts taken at all levels of government to cope with the problems. It details specific actions taken to date and discusses some proposed solutions to those problems that are on the agenda of government, especially at the national government level.

Chapter 3 is composed of original essays contributed by scholars and activist stakeholders involved in the politics of First Amendment–based fundamental freedoms. The chapter brings together voices from diverse disciplinary perspectives to examine many sides of the topic and to enrich the perspectives that the book's primary author is able to provide.

Chapter 4 briefly profiles key organizations and people who are political stakeholders in the issue. Both governmental and nongovernmental organizations and people are highlighted. They are participants in the search for solutions to the problems raised by the need to expansively ensure the fundamental freedoms enshrined in the First Amendment.

Chapter 5 offers some key primary source data and documents gathered by the author, principally from government sources. These data are presented in line, bar, and pie chart formats; in tables; and in excerpts and summaries of primary source documents.

Chapter 6 is a comprehensive list of annotated books on the subject, important scholarly journals that present original scholarly research on the subject, and films and videos that portray aspects of the subject. These sources provide the reader with a fairly comprehensive review of the discourse on the fundamental freedoms guaranteed by the First Amendment. Hopefully, they direct the reader to further research on the topic.

A chronology of key events in the history of the issue is then provided. Finally, a glossary of key terms and concepts is presented in an easily accessible format. The glossary is followed by a comprehensive index.

1 Background and History

Introduction: Why the Bill of Rights Established the First Amendment's Freedoms

From colonial times to the present day, the fundamental freedoms in the United States, especially those guaranteed by the Bill of Rights, have been a beacon, a contentious issue, and an ever-evolving yet fundamental aspect of American society and politics. This became increasingly so as the United States grew in size and became more diverse in its demographic composition—ethnic, racial, and religious. These fundamental and foundational freedoms are enshrined in the United States Constitution and the Bill of Rights, but the meaning of those lofty ideals had to be clarified and agreed upon.

Throughout its history, the United States has struggled with tension caused by the practical meanings of these fundamental freedoms. That struggle is well illustrated in a variety of court decisions concerning the First Amendment to the Constitution and those freedoms it guarantees. The First Amendment had to be defined and clarified, and it was increasingly expanded upon by further legislative action, by court decisions, and by developments in national government policy and political party positions taken with respect to those freedoms. As an increasingly diverse polity, government and society more generally coped on

The Constitution of the United States, "The Signing." Howard Chandler Christy, artist, ca. 1900. In its First Amendment, the Constitution provides for the fundamental freedoms, especially freedom of religion. (Library of Congress)

1

a regular basis with the practical meaning of the First Amendment, which is generally considered to be the most sacred of the Bill of Rights and the most important amendment to ensure constitutional democracy and the basic rights of citizens.

The First Amendment states that, in regard to the freedoms of religion, speech, press, and assembly and petition,

> Congress shall make no law respecting an establishment of religion, or prohibiting the free exercise thereof; or abridging the freedom of speech, or of the press, or the right of the people peaceably to assemble, and to petition the Government for a redress of grievances.

In the following sections, each of these four First Amendment freedoms will be discussed, with a focus on how landmark Supreme Court decisions clarified the meanings of each freedom guaranteed by the amendment and the extent to which the behavior of all three levels of government in the United States were impacted by its fundamental principles.

Freedom of Assembly

Clarification was needed regarding precisely what the word "assemble" meant. Did it concern parades and marches? Did it cover behavior taking place in public places only, or did it protect assembly in private spaces? Could a government body, through laws, ordinances, or regulations, limit the right to assemble to govern or protect other societal values? Who is included by the term "person"? Does it protect noncitizens as well as citizens? Can those persons assembling be required to obtain a permit or license of some sort in advance of their doing so? What precisely is meant by "peaceably to assemble"? Can people so assembling simply advocate violence without actually behaving in a violent manner be considered "peaceably" assembled or not?

This right was considered so fundamental to the founders because they had experienced a lack of that right during the colonial period leading up to the Revolutionary War fought to free themselves from an autocratic regime in distant England that used colonial governors to restrict their right to assemble. They were asserting a "right" of English citizens recognized in English common law to assemble to petition the government to redress a grievance. The founders wanted to assure that the common-law "right to assemble" would apply to the government of their newly established republic going forward.

Between 1876 and 2011, the U.S. Supreme Court issued a dozen decisions regarding the freedom of assembly/association issue. Most of those decisions concerned the actions of state and local governments after ratification of the Fourteenth Amendment; the Supreme Court interpreted its due process clause as incorporating the First Amendment freedoms to state and local government as well as the national government.

In *United States v. Cruikshank* (92 U.S. 542, 1876), in a 5–4 decision, the Supreme Court ruled that neither the First nor the Second Amendment applied to state governments or individuals. By its narrow interpretation of the Fourteenth Amendment, that both reflected and justified a diminishing role of the federal government after the Reconstruction period, the *Cruikshank* ruling left African Americans in the South at the mercy of increasingly hostile state governments and groups of private individuals—such as the Ku Klux Klan—to use paramilitary force to suppress black voting. The majority opinion was written by Chief Justice Morrison Waite and concurred in by Justices Noah Swayne, Samuel Miller, Stephan Field, and William Strong. The four dissenters were Justices Nathan Clifford, David Davis, Joseph Bradley, and Ward Hunt. *Cruikshank* was later overruled, in part, by *DeJonge v. Oregon* in 1937.

In *DeJonge v. Oregon* (299 U.S. 353, 1937), the court invalidated as unconstitutional the Criminal Syndication Law of Oregon. The court held that the rights of free speech and peaceable assembly are fundamental rights that are safeguarded against state interference, incorporating those rights by the Due Process Clause of the Fourteenth Amendment to state governments. The case concerned the imposition of criminal punishment under a state statute for participation in the conduct of a public meeting, otherwise lawful, merely because the meeting was under the auspices of an organization—in this case the Communist Party of the United States—that teaches or advocates the use of violence or other unlawful acts.

Can unions hold a political meeting in a public park without first getting a permit? That was the right of assembly at issue in *Hague v. Committee for Industrial Organization* (307 U.S. 496, 1939). By a 5–2 decision, the Supreme Court ruled that banning a group of citizens from holding political meetings in a public place violated the group's freedom of assembly under the First Amendment. The decision set the precedent for the "public forum doctrine" of the court. The CIO was backed by an amicus brief of the ACLU. Justice Owen Roberts wrote the majority opinion, joined by Justices Black, Stone, Reed, and Hughes. Justices McReynolds and Butler dissented. In the majority opinion, Justice Roberts wrote that streets, parks, and public places belonged to citizens and must be protected as public forums. In his concurring opinion, Justice Harlan Fiske Stone found that the Due Process Clause of the Fourteenth Amendment provided this to citizens and noncitizens alike. The case was a landmark decision for labor organizations over the use of public spaces.

In *Thomas v. Collins* (323 U.S. 516, 1945), in its 5–4 decision, the Supreme Court held that a State of Texas law violated the First and Fourteenth Amendment rights to free speech and assembly. The issue was a Texas law requiring an organizer's card before soliciting members. A state judge convicted a labor organizer of contempt for speaking at a labor rally without a permit. In the decision, the court announced its "clear and present danger to public welfare" doctrine. In his majority opinion for the court, Justice Wiley Rutledge argued that the "preferred position doctrine" of the court previously found that restraint can only be justified by "clear and present danger."

The civil rights era initiated several challenges to state and local laws on freedom of assembly grounds for unpopular groups on both sides of the civil rights movement, and Chief Justice Earl Warren's Supreme Court issued seven landmark decisions on the matter.

In *NAACP v. Alabama* (357 U.S. 449, 1958), the court ruled an Alabama law unconstitutional on First Amendment and Fourteenth Amendment grounds. Alabama sought to prevent the NAACP from conducting business in the state. After the circuit court issued a restraining order, the state issued a subpoena for various records, including the NAACP's membership lists. A unanimous U.S. Supreme Court, in an opinion written by Justice John Harlan, ruled that Alabama's demand for the lists had violated the right of due process guaranteed by the Fourteenth Amendment to the Constitution.

Similarly, in *Bates v. Little Rock* (361 U.S. 516, 1960), the court rendered another unanimous decision, written by Justice Potter Stewart, on the issue of freedom of association to advocate ideas and air grievances protected by the First and Fourteenth Amendments' Due Process Clause. The court barred state actions that might suppress that principle, holding for Daisy Bates, president of the Arkansas NAACP, who had refused to turn over the organization's membership list to the state.

In *Edwards v. South Carolina* (372 U.S. 229, 1963), the Supreme Court held that the First and Fourteenth Amendments forbade state government officials to force a crowd to disperse when they were otherwise legally marching in front of a statehouse. The court ruled 8–1, in its majority opinion by Justice Potter Stewart, that the Due Process Clause of the Fourteenth Amendment extends the free petition clause of the First Amendment to the states as well as to the federal government. Petitioner Edwards had been arrested and convicted for the "breach of peace," and the court ruled that the South Carolina law infringed on free speech, free assembly, and the freedom to petition for redress of grievances. Only Justice Thomas Clark dissented.

In *Cox v. Louisiana* (379 U.S. 536, 1965), by a 7–2 vote, the court struck down a Louisiana law defining breach of peace as being unconstitutionally vague and overly broad in scope. The majority opinion, written by Justice Arthur Goldberg, held that the Louisiana law had no "uniform, consistent, and nondiscriminatory" standard for granting exceptions to the general law and ruled for the petitioner, the Reverend Elton Cox, who had led a peaceful protest group of twenty-three students from Southern University, a local black college, against a segregated restaurant in Baton Rouge. Rev. Cox had been arrested and convicted of breach of peace when the protest riled up a group of whites against them. The sheriff arrested Rev. Cox for disturbing the peace rather than anyone from the mob of unruly whites.

The rights of protestors on the other side of the civil rights movement were upheld in *Carroll v. President and Commissioners of Princess Anne* (393 U.S. 175, 1968). In the *Carroll* case, by a unanimous decision in the majority opinion written by Justice Abe Fortas, the court struck down a ten-day injunction by a Maryland court against the National States Rights Party, a white supremacist group.

In *Gregory v. City of Chicago* (394 U.S. 111, 1969), the court unanimously upheld the right of comedian and civil rights activist Dick Gregory and a group of civil rights protestors against the overzealous actions of the Chicago Police Department in its attempts to quell an "anticipated civil disorder." In the majority opinion, written by Chief Justice Earl Warren, the conviction was overturned because the march was demonstrably "peaceful and orderly."

In a similar ruling, in *Shuttlesworth v. City of Birmingham* (394 U.S. 147, 1969), the court, by a vote of 7–1, struck down a Birmingham, Alabama, ordinance prohibiting parades and processions on city streets without first obtaining a permit. The majority opinion was written by Justice Potter Stewart. It held that the parade permit was deemed not to control traffic but to censor ideas. Justice Thurgood Marshall took no part in the decision, and Justice John Harlan wrote the sole dissenting opinion.

In *Coates v. City of Cincinnati* (402 U.S. 611, 1971), the court invalidated a city ordinance against loitering that negatively affected freedom of assembly by its use of the words "annoying conduct." In its 6–3 decision, the majority opinion, written by Justice Potter Stewart, held the local ordinance violated due process of the Fourteenth Amendment and the freedom of assembly of the First Amendment rights of Dennis Coates, a college student, because the Cincinnati ordinance that made it illegal for three or more persons to assemble on a sidewalk and "annoy" passersby was too vague and thus an infringement on the freedom of assembly and association.

The court also applied the First Amendment protections against *local* government infringement in the case of *National Socialist Party of America v. Village of Skokie* (432 U.S. 43, 1977). The Supreme Court ruled 5–4, on certiorari, by a per curiam decision (a decision issued by the court as an institution rather than issued and signed by individual justices), to reverse and remand to the Illinois Supreme Court its decision in a case involving the neo-Nazi group's right to march in Skokie, a predominantly Jewish community where many survivors of the Holocaust lived. The court lifted a lower court's injunction against the NSPA's right to march. The court held that Illinois must provide strict procedural safeguards, including appellate court review, to deny a stay for an injunction depriving the Nazi Party of protected First Amendment rights (in this case, to march down public streets. The majority in the Skokie case included Justices Brennan, Marshall, Blackmun, Powell, and Stevens. The dissenters were Justices Burger, Stewart, White, and Rehnquist.

Freedom of the Press

In the colonial period, and in the earlier years of the republic, many newspapers and political tracts were written, published, and disseminated. Nascent political parties often had particular newspapers that publicly advocated their viewpoints. Founding

Father Thomas Jefferson, in a number of letters, articulated his opinion that freedom of the press was the most essential freedom to sustain a free and democratic republican government. In a 1786 letter to John Jay, for example, Jefferson wrote, "Our liberty cannot be guarded but by the freedom of the press, nor that be limited without danger of losing it." And in an 1804 letter to John Tyler, he wrote,

> No experiment can be more interesting than that we are now trying, and which we trust will end in establishing the fact, that man may be governed by reason and truth. Our first object should therefore be to leave open to him all avenues to truth. The most effectual hitherto found, is the freedom of the press. It is, therefore, the first shut up by those who fear the investigation of their actions. (*Papers of Thomas Jefferson* 1950)

The first relevant judicial litigation on freedom of the press occurred in colonial New York. In 1735, the colony of New York tried a German American printer and journalist in New York City, John Peter Zenger, for seditious libel against the colony's governor. Zenger published the *New York Weekly Journal*. Zenger's attorney told the jury it was in their power to judge the law as well as the facts, and the jury acquitted Zenger. After the American Revolution, *Rex v. Zenger* (also known as *Crown v. Zenger*) became precedent for subsequent freedom of the press cases. It held that truthful information cannot be libelous (Kluger 2016).

After ratification of the Bill of Rights, courts ruled in ten landmark cases in which the central issue involved freedom of the press. In 1804, an important precedent for freedom of the press was set in the case of *People of the State of New York v. Harry Croswell* (3 Johns cas. 337 N.Y.). It was an important case in the evolution of defamation (libel) law. Thomas Jefferson, frustrated by the anti-administration articles being published in Federalist newspapers in 1803, encouraged the

New York Republican administration to enforce the Sedition Act of 1798. The Sedition Act, signed by Federalist president John Adams on July 14, 1798, was the fourth of a series of laws called the Alien and Sedition Acts, 1795–1798. The Sedition Act made it unlawful to combine or conspire together to oppose any measure of the government or to criticize the government in the press (LeMay and Barkan 1999, 15–16).

Harry Crosswell published anti-Jefferson stories in such Federalist papers as the *Balance and Columbian Repository*, the *Wasp*, and the *New York Evening Post*. New York attorney general Ambrose Spencer obtained an indictment on charges of criminal libel against Harry Croswell. A New York jury found Croswell guilty. Alexander Hamilton brought the case before the New York Supreme Court of Judicature on a writ of certiorari. Hamilton, a passionate advocate of freedom of the press, argued for the right of giving the truth in evidence in cases of libel (Chernow 2004). The court was deadlocked, but in 1805, the New York State Legislature enacted a law providing that truth was a defense to libel charges. In 1821, that principle was enshrined in New York State's second Constitution and has set the precedent for libel laws and freedom of the press since then.

In the case of *Near v. Minnesota* (283 U.S. 697, 1931), the U.S. Supreme Court ruled that "prior restraint" on publication violated freedom of the press guaranteed by the First Amendment. J. M. Near was avowedly anti-Catholic, anti-Semitic, antiblack, and anti-labor. In its 5–4 decision, the court ruled against Minnesota on the issue because the state used prior restraint to bar publication of Near's diatribes. Chief Justice Charles Hughes wrote the majority opinion, concurred in by Justices Oliver Wendell Holmes, Louis Brandeis, Harlan Stone, and Owen Roberts. The dissenters in the case were Justices Pierce Butler, Willis Van Devanter, James Clark McReynolds, and George Southerland.

The progressive Supreme Court under Chief Justice Earl Warren (1953–1969) decided three landmark cases on freedom of the press. In the *New York Times Co. v. Sullivan* (376

U.S. 254, 1964), the court issued a unanimous decision that restricted American public officials from suing for defamation on the basis of First Amendment freedoms. Likewise, in *Garrison v. Louisiana* (379 U.S. 64, 1964), the court issued a unanimous ruling overturning the defamation conviction of Louisiana district attorney Jim Garrison. The majority opinion written by Justice William Brennan held that the Louisiana criminal libel law used to convict him was unconstitutional. In the case of *Curtis Publishing Co. v. Butts* (388 U.S. 130, 1967), the court ruled 5–4 in favor of Georgia football coach Wally Butts against the *Saturday Evening Post*. In the *Butts* case, the majority opinion written by Justice John Harland and concurred in by Justices Thomas Clark, Potter Stewart, Abe Fortas, and Earl Warren made the distinction that whereas news organizations were protected from libel when printing allegations against public officials, they were not so protected when doing so about private individuals. The dissenters in the *Butts* case were Justices Hugo Black, William Douglas, William Brennan, and Byron White.

Under Chief Justice Warren Burger, the Supreme Court issued three landmark rulings involving freedom of the press. In the case of *New York Times Co. v. United States* (403 U.S. 713, 1971), the court ruled per curiam, 6–3, making it possible for the *New York Times* and the *Washington Post* to publish the classified Pentagon Papers without risk of government censorship or punishment. Justices Hugo Black, William Douglas, William Brennan, Potter Stewart, Byron White, and Thurgood Marshall ruled for the newspapers based on the principle of prior restraint. The dissenters in the case were Justices Warren Burger, John Harlan, and Harry Blackmun.

In *Nebraska Press Association v. Stuart* (427 U.S. 539, 1976), the Supreme Court held as unconstitutional the use of prior restraint in the case of media coverage during a criminal trial. Chief Justice Warren Burger wrote the majority opinion, concurred in by Justices Byron White, Harry Blackmun, Lewis Powell, and William Rehnquist. Justice Burger's majority opinion stressed that prior restraint on speech and publication are the most serious and the least tolerable infringement of First Amendment rights.

In *Zacchini v. Scripps-Howard Broadcasting Co.* (433 U.S. 562, 1977), the court ruled 5–4 in favor of Hugo Zacchini, the "human cannonball." Scripps-Howard had broadcast the entire act of Hugo Zacchini. The majority opinion for the court was written by Justice Byron White, concurred in by Justices Warren Burger, Potter Stewart, Harry Blackmun, and William Rehnquist. Justices William Brennan, Thurgood Marshall, Lewis Powell, and John Paul Stevens were the minority. Critical to the ruling was the fact that the majority held that broadcasting Zacchini's entire act was different from reporting on it as an event.

Two 1988 cases hinged on the nature of the persons involved in the freedom of the press cases. In *Hustler Magazine, Inc. v. Falwell* (485 U.S. 46, 1988), the case concerned a parody of the Reverend Jerry Falwell in *Hustler* magazine. The 8–0 ruling held that the First and Fourteenth Amendments prohibit "public figures" from recovering damages. The majority opinion was written by Chief Justice William Rehnquist and concurred in by Justices William Brennan, Thurgood Marshall, Harry Blackmun, John Paul Stevens, Sandra Day O'Connor, Antonin Scalia, and Byron White. Justice Anthony Kennedy took no part in the decision.

Finally, in *Hazelwood School District v. Kuhlmeier* (484 U.S. 260, 1988), the court ruled 5–3 that public school curricular student newspapers that have not been established as forums for student expression are subject to a lower level of First Amendment protection than independent student expression or newspapers (whether by policy or practice) established as forums for student expression. Justice Byron White wrote the majority opinion with Justices William Rehnquist, John Paul Stevens, Sandra Day O'Connor, and Antonin Scalia. The dissenters were Justices William Brennan, Thurgood Marshall, and Harry Blackmun.

Freedom of Speech

Sixteen U.S. Supreme Court cases serve as landmark decisions regarding freedom of speech issues. The writers of the First Amendment considered freedom of speech as important and on par with freedom of the press. However, because speech is more ephemeral than printed matter, the court had to clarify or define what exactly constitutes "speech"—direct speech or words and symbolic speech or actions. It further weighed in on how that speech is used—for example, in advertisements or political campaigns. The court also clarified what forms of speech are not protected—for example, incitement of actions that would harm others, obscene materials, or students advocating obscene speech or the use of illegal drugs.

Reflecting the times and tensions of World War I, one of the earliest freedom of speech cases was that of *Schenck v. United States* (249 U.S. 47, 1919). *Schenck* was a unanimous decision in favor of the United States, wherein the court upheld the Espionage Act of 1917 and ruled that conviction on the basis of the Espionage Act for criticizing the draft did not violate Charles Schenck's First Amendment right to freedom of speech. Schenk was arrested for distributing flyers and advocating draft-age men to resist the draft. In *Schenck*, the majority opinion was written by Justice Oliver Wendell Holmes Jr. and concurred in by Justices White, McKenna, Day, Van Devanter, Pitney, McReynolds, Brandeis, and Clarke. They ruled that the advocacy to resist the draft during wartime did constitute a "clear and present danger," and as a result, Schenck's actions were not protected speech.

Gitlow v. New York (268 U.S. 652, 1925) was the first case that the ACLU argued before the U.S. Supreme Court. In *Gitlow*, the court ruled in its 7–2 decision that the First Amendment does not prevent the government from punishing political speech that directly advocates the violent overthrow of the government. In the *Gitlow* case, the court held that the Fourteenth Amendment did extend the First Amendment to the state. The law at issue was New York's Criminal Anarchy law as well as the Espionage Act of 1917. Following the Red Scare of 1919–1920, Benjamin Gitlow, a socialist politician and journalist, published a left-wing manifesto in 1919. The majority opinion of the court was written by Justice Edward Sanford. He was joined by Justices William Taft, Willis Van Devanter, James McReynolds, George Southerland, Pierce Butler, and Harlan Stone. Justices Oliver Wendall Holmes and Louis Brandeis were in dissent.

Symbolic speech was at issue in *West Virginia State Board of Education v. Barnette* (319 U.S. 624, 1943). Several children of Jehovah's Witnesses refused to salute the flag at the beginning of the public school day. In its 6–3 decision, the court held that West Virginia's compulsory flag salute law did violate the First Amendment rights of the children who, on the basis of their religious beliefs, refused to salute the flag. The majority opinion was written by Justice Robert Jackson, joined by Chief Justice Harlan Stone and Justices Hugo Black, William Douglas, Frank Murphy, and Wiley Rutledge. The dissenters were Justices Felix Frankfurter, Owen Roberts, and Stanley Reed.

Obscene speech has been held not to be protected speech. The court had to consider what constituted obscene speech, which it did in the case of *Roth v. United States* (354 U.S. 476, 1957). The 6–3 decision in Roth was a landmark case that redefined what constitutes obscene material that was therefore not protected by the First Amendment. In *Roth*, the court held that obscenity was not within the area of constitutionally protected free speech. The majority ruled that the materials were "utterly without redeeming social importance" and that the test (thereafter known as the Roth test) to determine obscenity was "whether the average person, applying contemporary community standards, the dominant theme of the material taken as a whole appeals to prurient interests." The majority opinion was written by Justice William Brennan, joined by Chief Justice Earl Warren and Justices Felix Frankfurter, Harold Burton,

Thomas Clark, and Charles Whitaker. Justices Hugo Black, William Douglas, and John Harlan II were in dissent.

In *United States v. O'Brien* (391 U.S. 367, 1968), by a 7–1 vote, the Supreme Court ruled that a criminal prohibition against burning a draft card did not violate the First Amendment's guarantee of free speech. The majority opinion was written by Chief Justice Earl Warren, joined by Justices Hugo Black, John Harlan, William Brennan, Potter Stewart, Byron White, and Abe Fortas. The dissenting opinion was by William Douglas. Justice Thurgood Marshall did not participate in the case.

Symbolic speech was at issue in *Tinker v. Des Moines Independent Community School District* (393 U.S. 503, 1969). The 7–2 decision concerned the wearing of black armbands by students to protest the Vietnam War. Justice Abe Fortas wrote the majority opinion of the court, joined by Chief Justice Earl Warren and Justices William Douglas, William Brennan, Byron White, and Thurgood Marshall. The Fortas opinion specifically decided that the wearing of black armbands was "pure speech" and thus protected by the First Amendment. The dissenters were Justices Hugo Black and John Harlan.

In *Brandenburg v. Ohio* (395 U.S. 444, 1969), the court decided, per curiam, that a lower court cannot punish inflammatory speech unless the speech is directed at inciting, and is likely to incite, imminent lawless action. The case involved a Clarence Brandenburg, a Ku Klux Klan leader in rural Ohio, and a fiery cross-burning incident. The court struck down Ohio's Criminal Syndicalism statute finding that speech that supports lawbreaking or violence is protected by the First Amendment unless it directly encourages people to take unlawful action immediately. It thus overturned *Schenck v. United States* (1919).

In *Cohen v. California* (403 U.S. 15, 1971), the court overturned, also per curiam, the conviction of Paul Robert Cohen for the crime of disturbing the peace by wearing a jacket displaying an expletive ("F— the draft") in public corridors of a

California courthouse. The justices upheld Cohen's actions as constitutionally protected "symbolic free speech."

In yet another per curiam decision, in *Buckley v. Valeo* (424 U.S. 1, 1976), the court considered action on spending in a federal election campaign. The court ruled that although restrictions on individual campaign contributions did not violate the First Amendment, it found for Buckley that limitations on expenditures by the candidate or his family did violate their First Amendment rights and that political campaign spending was a type of free speech. The Buckley decision foreshadowed the later decision of *Citizens United* (2010).

In *Virginia State Board of Pharmacy v. Virginia Citizens Consumer Council* (425 U.S. 748, 1976), the court dealt with the competing rights of two organizations. The Supreme Court ruled 7–1 that the state could not limit a pharmacist's right to provide information about prescription drug prices. It held that the state law against advertising drug prices violated "commercial speech" under the First Amendment. The majority opinion was written by Justice Harry Blackmun, joined by Justices Burger, Brennan, Stewart, White, Marshall, and Powell. The dissenting opinion was by Chief Justice Rehnquist. Justice Stevens did not participate in the case. In a related case, *Bates v. State Bar of Arizona* (433 U.S. 350, 1977), in a 5–4 decision, the court upheld the right of lawyers to advertise their services, again as protected "commercial speech." Justice Blackmun wrote the majority opinion, joined by Justices Brennan, White, Marshall, and Stevens. Justices Burger, Stewart, Powell, and Rehnquist were in dissent.

In *Bethel School District No. 403 v. Fraser. No. 84-1667* (478 U.S. 675, 1987), the court ruled 7–1 that the First Amendment did not prevent a school district from disciplining a high school student for giving a lewd speech at a district-sanctioned high school assembly. Chief Justice Burger wrote the majority opinion, joined by Justices Brennan, White, Blackmun, Powell, Rehnquist, and O'Connor. Justice Stevens dissented, and Justice Marshall did not participate in the case.

Symbolic speech, in the form of desecrating the U.S. flag, was at issue in *Texas v. Johnson* (491 U.S. 397, 1989). In a 5–4 ruling, the majority of the court held that desecrating the flag was "protected symbolic speech" under the First Amendment. The majority opinion was written by Justice William Brennan, joined by Justices Marshall, Blackmun, Scalia, and Kennedy. The dissenters were Justices Rehnquist, White, Stevens, and O'Connor.

In *Watchtower Bible and Tract Society v. Village of Stratton, New York* (536 U.S. 150, 2002), by an 8–1 decision, the court held that a town ordinance making it a misdemeanor to engage in door-to-door advocacy without first registering with town officials and receiving a permit violated the First Amendment if it applies to religious proselytizing, anonymous political speech, and the distribution of handbills. The case was brought by Jehovah's Witnesses, and was supported by amicus briefs by the Independent Baptists of America, the Electronic Privacy Information Center, the Center for Individual Freedom, the Church of Jesus Christ of the Latter-day Saints, and Real CampaignReform.org, Inc.

The free speech rights of students were again at issue in the case of *Morse v. Frederick* (551 U.S. 393, 2007). By a 5–4 decision, the court ruled that the First Amendment does not prevent high school educators from suppressing student speech at or across the street from a school-supervised event, when that speech is reasonably viewed as promoting the illegal use of drugs. The majority opinion was by Chief Justice John Roberts, joined by Justices Antonin Scalia, Anthony Kennedy, Clarence Thomas, and Samuel Alito. Justices Breyer, Stevens, Souter, and Ginsberg dissented.

Finally, there is the case of *Citizens United v. Federal Election Commission* (558 U.S. 310, 2010). The 5–4 *Citizens United* decision is a highly controversial and complex ruling that held that the free speech clause of the First Amendment prohibits the FEC from restricting independent expenditures for political communications by corporations, including nonprofit corporations, labor unions, and other associations. The majority opinion was written by Justice Anthony Kennedy, joined by Chief Justice John Roberts and Justices Samuel Alito, Clarence Thomas, and John Stevens. In part, it was dissented by Justices Ruth Bader Ginsburg, Stephen Breyer, and Sonia Sotomayor and in parts by Justices John Stevens and Clarence Thomas. It essentially held that corporations are legal persons and therefore have the freedom of speech protection of the First Amendment.

Freedom of Religion

The First Amendment protects freedom of religion in two ways: freedom of religion by the Free Expression Clause and freedom from religion by the Establishment Clause.

Prior to independence and the adoption of a new constitution in 1789, the various colonies established along the Eastern Seaboard reflected what was common to all European nations and principalities—namely, having an established religion. At the time of the founding, church and state were not separate in the respective colonies. But the European practice of uniting church and state convulsed European nations with the wars of religion. These wars were the backdrop for the movement in North America to espouse freedom of religion, which became closely tied to the ideals of American freedom and independence and the idea that church and state should be separate, which is beneficial to both (Kornelly 2013, 189–213; Ahlstrom 1972; Baltzell 1996; Butler 2006; Miller 1986).

Colonies such as Virginia and the Carolinas, which were directly sponsored by the English Crown as royal colonies, had Anglicanism as their official religion. By the early to mid-1700s, dozens of ethnic groups, each with their own religious denominations, had settled in the North American colonies. The influx of so many immigrants holding different religious beliefs and denominational affiliations compelled the Founding Fathers, themselves often Deists, to establish a nation built on the premise of separation of church and state. The very notion of religious freedom became a foundational principle integral to American society (Holmes 2006; Mapp 2003; Walters 1992). America's religious tolerance and nearly unlimited opportunities became a pull factor drawing millions to the New World (LeMay 1987, 2). When these varying ethnic groups migrated to America, they settled in areas where they shared the ethnic and religious heritage of other members of that community, resulting in migration patterns reinforcing Old World ethnic divisions that helped develop regional cultures in the colonies (Kornelly 2013, 192–194). These migration patterns led to the development of religious pluralism and religious tolerance in North America.

These diverse groups rejected a formal establishment of religion. By the mid–seventeenth century, Pietists were challenging the tenets of mainstream Protestantism. Anabaptists (rebaptizers) and Quakers made what was at the time a radical assertion that religious practice should be separated from civil governance. In 1649, the Maryland proprietary colony granted to Cecilius Calvert, Lord Baltimore, enacted the Act of Toleration, outlining greater religious freedom than existed in the Puritan colonies of Massachusetts and Connecticut (Kornelly 2013, 200). In 1639, exiles from the Massachusetts colony founded Rhode Island as their own refuge from religious intolerance. Separatist Roger Williams and Pietist Anne Hutchinson were granted the first colonial charter to explicitly grant freedom of religious conscience (Fantel 1974; Gaustad 1999). Other colonies, such as Virginia and Maryland, continued to have an established (Anglican) government-run church that was subsidized by local taxes. In Maryland, in 1691, King William III revoked Lord Baltimore's charter, making it a royal colony. The Anglican Church became the established church in 1702, and Maryland became the most vigilant colonial supporter of the Church of England. Similarly, in 1661, Virginia passed strict regulations against Baptists and Quakers and helped create a fertile atmosphere that led to the Great

Awakening that characterized religious life in America for much of the eighteenth century (Kornelly 2013, 199). In the Carolinas, the Anglican Church was established in 1681, but South Carolina had a substantial number of Puritans and Baptists who migrated there from New England as well as French Huguenots and Quakers. North Carolina had a growing number of German-speaking Pietist communities who migrated there following the American Revolution.

Virginia had many Baptists who were successful in evangelizing settlers on the frontier. When the Virginia General Assembly passed repressive laws against nonconformists, Thomas Jefferson, then a young lawyer, witnessed their plight and advocated for their rights. That experience shaped his views and resulted in his writing of the Virginia Statute for Religious Freedom (Hening 1823, 84–86; see also Ahlstrom 1972; Butler 2006; Heimert 1966; Holmes 2006; Mapp 2003; Peterson and Vaughn 1988; and Walters 1992). In later life, Jefferson was more proud of his authorship of that statute then he was of having been elected president (Jefferson 1977; see also Holmes 2006; Levy 1994; Mapp 2003; Miller 1986; and Peterson and Vaughn 1988).

New Jersey became home to many Scotch-Irish Presbyterians who had left famine and unrest in Northern Ireland during the latter half of the eighteenth century. New Sweden's colony was established by William Penn and a small group of fellow Quakers who founded West New Jersey in 1674. Their continued persecution in England led to more Quakers settling in the Delaware Valley until Penn chartered the Commonwealth of Pennsylvania in 1681. Their religious tolerance attracted other persecuted groups, such as the Pietist community of Moravians, who arrived in 1702. Penn's colonial charter ensured freedom of religious conscience to all but Roman Catholics (Fantel 1974; see also Ahlstrom 1972; Baltzell 1996; Butler 2006; Miller 1986). Penn's sons converted to Anglicanism, and the decline in Pennsylvania's Quakerism was followed by an increase in immigrants to the colony, including the Scotch-Irish

Presbyterians, who entered through the Port of Philadelphia at a rate of 12,000 per year in 1740 and an estimated 120,000 German-speaking immigrants who landed between 1683 and 1820, which made them the largest non–English speaking population in North America by 1820 (LeMay 1987, 21–22).

By the turn of the nineteenth century, a third of Pennsylvania's population was German immigrants or of German ancestry. Most belonged to the German Lutheran or German Reform churches and small communities of German Pietists, who saw Penn's "Holy Experiment" as an opportunity to establish a home in North America. Soon they came in entire groups of hundreds, as Mennonites, Dunkers, Lutherans, Calvinists, and even a few Jews, from German states such as Palatine, Salzburg, Württemberg, and Hanover (LeMay 1987, 23; LeMay 2009, 192–200; see also Boyton 1986; Driedger and Kraybill 1994; and Nolt 1992).

Conflict between both the Old Order Amish and Old Order Mennonites and the majority culture centered on aspects of Amish and Mennonite ways of life deemed dangerous by the majority society. Their pacifism brought persecution on them during the American Civil War and even greater discrimination during World War I, when many Amish and Mennonite conscientious objectors refused to fight. They received verbal abuse and beatings and were forced to shave their beards (prescribed by their faith), occasionally even being "baptized" (urinated on) in camp latrines, mocking their Anabaptist beliefs (Nolt 1992; Wenger 1961).

Another conflict arose in 1955 when Congress extended Social Security to include self-employed farmers. The Amish had never taken part in Social Security, and when they refused to pay into the fund, the Internal Revenue Service (IRS) collected funds through their bank accounts, foreclosed and sold Amish farms, and forcibly collected Social Security payments from 130 Amish households. In 1965, after a decade of conflict, Congress finally addressed the issue by including a provision of the Medicare Act that exempted self-employed

Amish from Medicare and the Social Security system (LeMay 2009, 199).

The issue that aroused the most controversy was compulsory education. Old Order Amish and Old Order Mennonite parents refused to send their children to consolidated elementary schools or on to high school. They had repeated run-ins with school authorities in nearly every state throughout the 1950s and 1960s and were forced to pay fines and serve jail terms. Their doctrine of only educating children enough to be able to read the Bible and their separatist culture, which made them reluctant to send their children to public schools, brought the Old Order Amish and Old Order Mennonites into conflict with state mandatory public school laws, a conflict that was not settled until the 1972 case *Wisconsin v. Yoder* (406 U.S. 205), which upheld their freedom of religion rights and exempted them from the public school laws (LeMay 2009, 197–200; see also Kraybill and Olshan 1994, 162–163; Peters 2003; and Urofsky 2002).

European Unitarianism flowered in Poland and Transylvania in the sixteenth century. Unitarians promoted religious liberty, reason, and tolerance, for which they were persecuted. In Transylvania, they influenced King John Sigismund to declare the first edict of religious toleration in 1568. In England, Joseph Priestley was a Unitarian minister who espoused a number of liberal and unpopular causes. His home, laboratory (he is noted as the discoverer of oxygen), library, and Unitarian chapel were attacked and burned. In 1794, Priestley fled to the United States, at the invitation of Thomas Jefferson, and brought Unitarianism with him.

Another English Universalist, John Murray, was released from debtors' prison and allowed to emigrate. His ship was grounded off the coast of New Jersey, and he landed at a farm owned by Thomas Potter, who had built a chapel and was waiting for a preacher to appear. Murray preached at Potter's chapel and brought Universalism to that colony. Unitarianism and Universalism took root, offering relief from the Calvinist notion of damnation. Religious liberals formed their own theologies of human free will, dignity, and rationality. By the early nineteenth century, many Puritan Congregational churches began to call themselves Unitarian, and to this day, Unitarian churches are often at the forefront of the sanctuary movement.

The Constitution and the First Amendment

The Reformation served as a catalyst for challenging both civil and religious authority. It led to the development of a host of grassroots religious movements. By the mid–eighteenth century, Protestant theology in North America emphasized the conversion experience and a belief in religious freedom. The colonies became a testing ground—a Holy Experiment—and allowed for a diversity of attitudes toward religion and the cultivation of personal spirituality (Kornelly 2013, 209). Religious communities diverged from their counterparts in Europe as communication between the Old World and the New World lapsed and parishioners experienced different pressures and resolutions to their concerns.

Americans became increasingly self-sufficient. In America, the Methodist and Baptist denominations were tied to a widespread movement of evangelism as small religious communities expanded into the American frontier, which allowed for safe havens for resettlement and freedom of religious belief and practice separate from the official religious denominations of the colonial governments. The frontier was the setting for the Great Awakening, which encouraged evangelism and conversion. It coincided with the emergence of Protestant denominations such as the Baptists and Shakers and a brand of Pietism that did not need a church to cultivate spirituality. Revivalism, brought about by charismatic preachers such as George Whitefield and John Wesley, led to a "personal rebirth in Christ." People across the colonies were united through a spiritual heritage that helped forge a collective American identity during the revolutionary era (Ahlstrom 1972; Bilhartz 1986; Butler 2006; Heimert 1966; Holmes 2006).

At the same time, as nonconformist denominations began to centralize, state-sponsored churches began to disestablish. Freedom of religious choice became rallying points for uniting the American identity, and when the colonies became independent, the Bill of Rights provided for the separation of church and state in the federal government. In 1786, due largely to the efforts of Thomas Jefferson, Virginia became the first state to end state-sponsored churches. Written by Jefferson and secured in its adoption by James Madison, it became the model for other states that began to include freedom of religion provisions in their respective state constitutions, and it formed the basis of the religious freedom clauses in the Bill of Rights. By 1833, all of the states followed this model (Hening 1823; Levy 1994; Mapp 2003; Miller 1986; Peterson and Vaughn 1988; Vile 2015). The Virginia statute stated

> that no man shall be compelled to frequent or support any religious worship, place, or ministry whatsoever, nor shall be enforced, restrained, molested, or burthened in his body or goods, nor shall otherwise suffer on account of his religious opinions or belief, but that all men shall be free to profess, and by argument to maintain, their opinion in matters of religion, and that the same shall in no wise diminish, enlarge, or affect their civil capacities. (Cited in Hening 1823, 86; see also Kornelly 2013, 211; Jefferson 1977)

In 1796, the idea of the separation of civil and religious authority was recognized in one of the earliest treaties that the new American government negotiated: the Treaty of Tripoli. It ended conflict between the United States Marines and pirates who had been harassing merchant ships out of Tripoli, Lebanon, a predominantly Muslim country. It was ratified unanimously by the Senate on June 7, 1787, and signed into law by President John Adams on June 10, 1797. Through Article VI of the U.S. Constitution, it became the supreme law of the land:

> This Constitution, and the Laws of the United States which shall be made in Pursuance thereof, and all Treaties made, or which shall be made under the authority of the United States, shall be the supreme Law of the Land, and the Judges in every State shall be bound thereby, any Thing in the Constitution or Laws of any State to the Contrary notwithstanding.

An opening phrase of the Treaty of Tripoli states, "As the government of the United States is not in any sense founded on the Christian religion. . . ." It is notable that the treaty was ratified by the same Senate that passed the Bill of Rights.

Also notable was the impact of Deism. Deism was a movement that advocated natural religion, emphasizing morality and, in the eighteenth century, denying the interference of the Creator with the laws of the universe. It influenced the beliefs of several of the founders. Drawing from the philosophical works of Jean-Jacques Rousseau, Isaac Newton, and John Locke, Deism argued that human experience and rationality—rather than religious dogma and mystery—determine the validity of human beliefs. Thomas Paine, the protégé of Benjamin Franklin, was the principle proponent of Deism in America (Heimert 1966; Holmes 2006; Mapp 2003; Middlekauff 2005; Nuovo 2002).

Benjamin Franklin famously noted that "when a religion is good, I conceive it will support itself, and when it does not support itself, and God does not take care to support it so that its professors are obliged to call for help of the civil power, 'tis a sign, I apprehend, of its being a bad one" (Balmer, Grogerg and Mabry 2012). No matter their personal faith beliefs, Deism unquestionably influenced a majority of the Founding Fathers in so far as Deism opposed barriers to moral improvement and to social justice and stood for rational inquiry, skepticism about dogma and mystery, and religious tolerance. Many of its adherents favored universal education and freedom of the press as well as the separation of church and state. The Founding Fathers notably embraced political ideas that were remarkably liberal for their time. These ideas informed their insistence on enacting the First Amendment in the Bill of Rights.

Roman Catholics, mostly originally coming from Ireland or Germany, today comprise 23 percent of the U.S. population. In the early republic, however, Catholics were a minority often discriminated against by many, if not most, Protestant denominations. A sizable number of Catholics were added to the U.S. population through the Louisiana Purchase of 1803. President Thomas Jefferson sent James Monroe to France to seek to purchase New Orleans and West Florida for $10 million. A yellow fever plague decimated half of Napoleon's army in Haiti, causing him to recall the remainder of his army and ceding independence to Haiti. Napoleon decided to sell the entire Louisiana Territory to the United States for $15 million. Jefferson approved the deal, and Congress concurred, based on the principle of "implied powers" of the federal government. The purchase meant that the residents of the territory (many from Spain and a lesser but significant number from France and French-speaking Haiti) became U.S. citizens by virtue of the treaty. There were suddenly many more Catholics in the population!

In addition to the increase in Catholics within the population with the Louisiana Purchase, Catholics began arriving in large numbers in the 1840s and 1850s, fleeing religious persecution in Ireland and Northern Germany (particularly Prussia). Derided as "papists" by Protestant Americans, they experienced religious discrimination in the pre–Civil War era and set off a dramatic xenophobic reaction. They were easy scapegoats to blame for the social and economic problems generated by a rapidly urbanizing and industrializing country (LeMay 2009, 353). They were accused of importing crime and drunkenness. Protestant evangelizers seeking to preserve the nation's "purity" joined forces with radical nativists such as the secret Order the Star-Spangled Banner (which morphed into the American Party, better known as the Know-Nothing Party). A wave of xenophobia led to violent attacks on churches and convents and inflammatory anti-Catholic literature, often led by a splinter group called the Plug Uglies. They rose up "to burn Catholic convents, churches, and homes, assault nuns, and murder Irishmen, Germans, and Negroes" (Beals 1960, 9; LeMay 1987, 32–34; see also Bailey 1976 and Billington 1974). Anti-Catholic riots broke out in cities such as New York, Newark, and Baltimore. The Know Nothing movement had died out by the time of the Civil War, but conflicts with Roman Catholicism over parochial schools, prayers in public schools, and which version of the Bible to be read in schools, for example, arose again in the 1870s and 1880s, when large numbers of immigrants from Italy brought in a new wave of Catholics and a revived Ku Klux Klan espoused radical and often violent anti-Catholicism and anti-Semitism (LeMay 1987, 44).

The absorption of large numbers of Catholics by treaty rights happened again in 1848. The Treaty of Guadalupe Hidalgo, signed on February 2, 1848, was the peace treaty ending the Mexican-American War (1846–1848), which was largely fought over the annexation of Texas by the United States. The treaty added nearly a half million square miles to the U.S. territory, comprising all or parts of present-day Arizona, California, Colorado, Nevada, New Mexico, Utah, and Wyoming. Mexicans living in the newly acquired territory were made U.S. citizens unless they opted out. The treaty instantly added a large population of Roman Catholics to the national population. Acquisition of the new territory also fueled the slave state versus free state controversy that ultimately led to the Civil War.

The Rise of Homegrown Minority Religions

Not all religious groups comprising the rich and complex diversity of religion in the United States came with immigrants. There were significant homegrown minority religions in American history, each of which had a profound impact on American politics, laws, and court cases that shaped debates over First Amendment freedoms in the United States. This section discusses four such minority religions: the Mormons, who began in 1823; the Seventh-day Adventists, who appeared in 1844; the Jehovah's Witnesses, who also surfaced in 1844; and the Nation of Islam (better known as the Black Muslims), who developed in Detroit in the 1930s.

The Church of Jesus Christ of Latter-Day Saints (the Mormons)

Today, the Mormon Church is clearly mainstream, with more than seven million adherents in the United States. It is one of the fastest-growing world religions (Davies 2000, 243). Its historical significance is that it was a new religious tradition founded in nineteenth-century United States, and it exhibited a complex, embattled relationship to the society from which it emerged and to the evangelicalism that was such a dominant force in American society at the time it was founded. It has been involved in jurisprudence concerning the religious Free Exercise and Establishment Clauses and freedom of assembly.

The Mormon Church's founder, Joseph Smith Jr. (1806–1844), was born in Vermont. His family moved to Palmyra, New York, in 1816, where Smith claimed he received his first revelation from God and his first visit from an angel, Moroni, in 1823 (LeMay 2009, 173). In 1827, Smith claimed that the angel Moroni gave him tablets, which he and a few trusted associates translated over the next two years before returning the plates to Moroni. The translated text became known as *The Book of Mormon*, and in 1830, he and six of his followers established the Church of Jesus Christ of the Latter-day Saints. For Mormon believers, *The Book of Mormon* possessed the same canonical standing as the Old and New Testaments do for Protestants and Catholics. They saw Smith as a new prophet and the book as God's third and final revelation of scriptural truth. It was the "sealed" book described in the Book of Isaiah, signaling the coming of the "end-times" as predicted in the Book of Revelation. The faithful identify themselves as saints, the new Israelites called out from the Gentiles to usher in the millennium to establish the godly kingdom on earth to prepare the way for Christ's Second Coming (Abanes 2002; Arrington and Bitton 1992; Bushman and Bushman 2001; Church of Jesus Christ of the Latter-Day Saints 1989; Davies 2000, Mauss 1994; McConkie 1966).

They immediately experienced intense discrimination and moved to Kirtland, Ohio, and Independence, Missouri. In 1836, they built an elaborate temple, and like other communitarian groups (e.g., the Shakers or the Amish and Mennonites), they set up cohesive, economically self-sufficient, and largely self-governing settlements, marking themselves as a group of worshippers but also as a people set apart. Discrimination developed early and led to expulsion through the use of violence as well as applying the force of law to pressure them to change their tenets to be more acceptable to the views of the majority society. In part, this was a reaction to their dogmatism and to the "theocracy" of their communities, a dogma at odds with the democratic principles of the majority society (LeMay 2009, 173).

The tenet of their faith that caused the most trouble for them with the majority culture was polygamy, or the plural marriage principle, and "celestial marriage." It is defined in the *Mormon Doctrine* as "marriages performed in the temples for time and eternity," and it remains a central doctrine of Mormonism (McConkie 1966, 117). They stressed speaking in tongues and faith healing. Their dogmatism aroused animosity similar to anti-Catholicism, which was prevalent at the time. Every adult male adhering to the faith was considered a priest, and Mormons developed a group of Melchizedek priests (the Council of Seventies) that were considered as militant as Roman Catholic Jesuits. In the words of Stanley Hirshon (1969), "As much as a church, moreover, the Saints created a society. In specifically designed communities they gathered and became in every sense a people. Often migrating in groups, they proved a new society following the same model could even be moved physically from one part of the world to another" (18–19). Mounting tensions with their gentile neighbors escalated into armed conflict, forcing them to flee once again.

In 1821–1833, a virtual war broke out that involved some twelve hundred Mormons in pitched battles. Mormon homes were burned down, and on October 25, 1838, the Battle of Crooked River took place, known as the Mormon Rebellion. Missouri governor Lilburn Boggs issued an extermination order. Boggs had been shot and severely wounded in 1842, an act broadly held to have been ordered by Joseph Smith (LeMay 2009, 174). Boggs's extermination order stands as one of the most overt uses of state police power to discriminate against a religious minority, and it was an affront to the First Amendment and its clauses of free exercise and free assembly (LeMay 2018, 223–224).

In 1839, fifteen thousand Mormons crossed into Illinois where they bought the town of Commerce and renamed it Nauvoo. It had a charter, with Joseph Smith II as its mayor, making it an independent municipality with its own court system, militia, and political party (the Mormon People's Party). By merging the religious, military, and secular political structure, Mormonism created a virtual theocracy. Nauvoo quickly became the largest city in the state, which was then still very much a frontier state. The Mormons developed a doctrinally complex and elaborate hierarchical religious structure, embracing a Hebraic model of organization (Abanes 2002). In 1840, Mormons sent Brigham Young and several others to serve as missionaries in England. Their first year there yielded nine thousand converts, many of whom immigrated to New Zion when Young returned there in July 1841 (LeMay 2009, 174).

Mormons voted as a bloc, following directions from the pulpit. In 1844, Smith revealed a plan for organizing the Kingdom of God on earth, with himself as king, and he declared his candidacy for president of the United States (on the Mormon People's Party ticket). The plan, of course, was overtly contradictory to the Establishment Clause of the First Amendment. On June 27, 1844, Joseph Smith II and his brother, Hyrum, were arrested and then dragged from jail and murdered by a group of militia called out to protect the state from a feared Mormon uprising. Their martyrdom led to the last great migration of the Mormons, to Utah, which began in February 1846 after the State of Illinois revoked the Nauvoo Charter.

Following the Smiths' murders, the Mormons splintered. The largest group was led by Brigham Young, Smith's successor. Young led a group of about four thousand on their "great trek" westward. They first wintered in what is now Omaha, Nebraska. Then, in April 1847, Young left with a party of 148 in seventy-three wagons. On July 21, 1847, they entered Salt Lake Valley, and they stopped on July 23 at the site that became Salt Lake City. A second group of about five hundred joined them. They settled in the Utah Territory, where they established a virtual Mormon kingdom, centered in Salt Lake City, which they called the State of Deseret.

In Utah, Brigham Young commenced a long period of leadership (1847–1877). Mormon leadership elaborated on the precepts of plural marriage and patriarchal governance promulgated by founder Joseph Smith II. The Utah Mormons, with an influx of converts from England and elsewhere in Europe, soon numbered close to 150,000, and the Great Basin Kingdom remained largely intact into the 1880s, despite military occupation of the territory by the Union Army from 1858 to 1860 (Arrington and Bitton 1992, 169).

Brigham Young died in 1877, and the practice of polygamy began to wither. Congress declared the practice of polygamy illegal in 1882, using a bigamy law, and under great pressure (a number of Mormon leaders were arrested), the president of the church, Wilford Woodruff, in exchange for granting statehood to the Utah Territory, agreed to halt the *practice* of plural marriage (though maintaining the *doctrine* of celestial marriage) and to dissolve the separate Mormon political party (LeMay 2009, 175–176; Abanes 2002; Launius and Thatcher 1994).

Two U.S. Supreme Court rulings upheld the acts of Congress against polygamy. The first, *Reynolds v. United States* (98 U.S. 145, 1878), written for a unanimous court by Chief Justice Morrison Waite, expounded the "wall of separation" doctrine with regard to church and state relations. The case ruled that religious *beliefs* do not justify polygamy as a *practice*. The final case, *The Late Corporation of the Church of Jesus Christ of Latter-Day Saints v. United States* (136 U.S. 1, 1890), upheld the validity of an 1887 act of Congress that annulled the charter of the Mormons and declared all church property forfeit save for a small portion used exclusively for worship. That case was necessitated by the fact that the Mormons ignored the earlier ruling and continued to practice polygamy despite the law. The ruling led to the1890 Manifesto promulgated by Mormon president Woodruff (LeMay 2009, 177; LeMay 2018, 302, 315).

The manifesto led to schisms as splinter groups broke away from the main body to continue the practice of plural marriage. Even in the main body, polygamous marriages continued after the 1890 Manifesto with the consent of general authorities (Abanes 2002). Within the main body, however, the practice increasingly withered under the pressures of the dominant society and adverse testimony of Mormon "apostates" (Young 1972).

Since that split, the main Mormon church has become increasingly incorporated into American politics and society, perhaps best exemplified by the candidacy for president of the United States by Republican nominee Mitt Romney in the 2008 and 2012 elections (LeMay 2009, 181–182). Mormons have become mainstream in American politics, typically supporting Republican candidates. The church still dominates Utah politics, as exemplified by Romney's election to the U.S. Senate in 2018.

The Seventh-Day Adventist Church

Seventh-day Adventists emerged from the religious revival in the Northeastern United States known as the Second Great Awakening, specifically from a millennial movement led by Baptist preacher William Miller (Bilhartz 1986).

Millennial movements can be religious, political, social, or a combination of those types. It typically refers to a long period of time (hence, millennial, or a thousand years) and involves belief in a prophecy of a major event, in religious terms, associated with the end of times (Ahlstrom 1972; Casey 1918; Fenn 1997; Kaplan 1997; Landes 2000; Landes 2011; Wessinger 2000; Wojcik 1997). Its members typically feel they are under attack by a "they" group bent on destroying their way of life. In the Christian tradition, they identify themselves with the oppression and deliverance of the Israelites of the Old Testament. Given their vision of the future, they are often referred to as *revitalization movements*.

Millennial ethnoreligious movements are often perceived as cults or sects. *Cults* are often small groups who hold a system of religious worship or ritual. They often live in a colony led by charismatic leaders. *Sects* are typically religious bodies that form in small to medium-sized groups that break away from an established orthodoxy or church. They share common leadership; hold a strong set of opinions, philosophical doctrines, and religious principles and practices; and often have associated political principles. A member of a sect—a sectarian—is a person who is rather blindly and narrow-mindedly devoted to the sect. Examples of groups considered sects by the orthodox and mainline denominations include Mormons, Jehovah's Witnesses, the Unification Church (more commonly known as Moonies, after their founder, Sun Myung Moon), New Age, the Christian Science Church, the Church of Scientology, the Worldwide Church of God, Unitarian/Universalists, and Socinianism. Historically, other Christian cults, considered heresies, were Gnosticism, Neo-Gnosticism, and Agnosticism (LeMay 2009, 243–244).

Seventh-day Adventists (who takes their name from holding Saturday as the Sabbath day) believe that other Christian denominations moving the celebration of the Sabbath to Sunday, the day of Christ's resurrection, is unbiblical. Adventists believed the end of the millennium would begin the thousand-year reign of Christ and his saints, when Christ and the Holy City would descend from heaven to earth, and the redeemed would live eternally on the New Earth; God would dwell with his people and the condemned would be consumed by fire and be annihilated. The Second Great Awakening, 1798–1820s, was a revival movement in the United States that stimulated many Bible societies and a reform movement that sought to remedy the evils of society before the anticipated Second Coming of Jesus Christ.

The Seventh-day Adventist Church formed out of one of the Second Great Awakening movements, known as the Millerites. Based on the Old Testament scripture of Daniel 8:14, Miller had calculated that the Second Coming would occur between March 1843 and March 1844, and he gathered a following that included Baptist, Methodist, Presbyterian, and Christian Connection church members. When it did not come to pass, Samuel Snow recalculated it would occur in 1844. They linked the cleansing of the sanctuary in Daniel with the Jewish Day of Atonement, believed to be October 22, 1844. Some one hundred thousand people awaited the Second Coming, and when it passed without their expectations being fulfilled, the event became known as the Great Disappointment.

After the Great Disappointment, many left the church, and Miller withdrew from its leadership and died in 1849. Ellen and James White, Joseph Bates, J. N. Andrews, Hiram Edson, and other Adventists formed a group of several hundreds in Washington, New Hampshire, on the farm of Hiram Edson, which became the Seventh-day Adventist Church in 1863. The church is best known for its Saturday Sabbath. Ellen White (1827–1915) is considered by the faithful to be a prophet as well as one of the church founders. Adventists see themselves as heirs of earlier outcast believers and Protestant Reformers, such as the Anabaptists and English and Scottish Puritans; eighteenth-century evangelicals, such as the Methodists and Seventh Day Baptists; and other sects or denominations that rejected the established church traditions. In 1874, J. N. Andrews became the first official missionary, traveling to Switzerland, and the church became worldwide from then on.

The church was heavily involved in the temperance movement of the late 1800s, and it promoted religious liberty. Given their doctrine that the Sabbath day should be Saturday, the Adventists were opposed to Sunday "blue" laws, common in many states, and fought establishment of a National Day of Worship. Many of its members were arrested for working on Sunday. As Sabbatarians, they had to fight for their liberty to worship on that day, and soon they were fighting for religious liberty on a far broader basis.

Jehovah's Witnesses

The Jehovah's Witnesses began in 1872, started by Charles Taze Russell (Bowman 1992; Penton 1997). Russell struggled with the doctrine of heaven and hell, and his studies led him to reject not only eternal punishment but also the Trinity, the deity of Christ, and the Holy Spirit.

In 1879, Russell copublished the *Herald of the Morning* magazine with its founder, N. H. Barbour. By 1884, Russell controlled the publication, and he renamed it *The Watchtower*. That year, he founded Zion's Watch Tower Tract Society, known today as the Watch Tower Bible and Tract Society. The *Watchtower* magazine began with a circulation of six thousand copies a month. Today, the church publishes eight hundred thousand copies of its two magazines monthly.

Russell claimed the Bible could only be understood according to his interpretation, an assertion typical among cult leaders (Bowman 1992; Penton 1997). Russell died in 1916. He was succeeded in the presidency of the Watch Tower Society, which was then known as the International Bible Students Association, by Joseph Rutherford. In 1931, Rutherford changed the organization's name to the Jehovah's Witnesses, and they began to aggressively proselytize, recruiting some two hundred thousand new members annually. Members attend several book studies each week. They learn chapter and verse of the Bible by rote and can easily outargue the average Christian when it comes to defending their beliefs (Bowman 1992; Penton 1997).

Jehovah's Witnesses have been strident defenders of the First Amendment's freedom of religion and freedom of assembly to protect their ability to proselytize, which is central to their faith. They have helped to define civil liberties case law in both the United States and Canada. Their legal struggles involved seventy-two cases and many important judicial decisions regarding freedom of religion, press, speech, and assembly. A number of such cases are now considered landmark decisions of First Amendment law. Of the seventy-two cases, forty-seven were won by the Jehovah's Witnesses, and even in cases in which they lost, they helped the Supreme Court to more clearly delineate First Amendment rights.

Between 1935 and up to 2002, there were a number of Supreme Court decisions involving the Jehovah's Witnesses versus various state, local, and even federal governments over issues of First Amendment freedoms in which the court ruling clarified the practical implications of freedom of religion, freedom of assembly, and freedom of speech.

In 1938, in *Lovell v. City of Griffin* (303 U.S. 444), the Jehovah's Witnesses contested a local law requiring them to seek government sanction to distribute religious materials. In 1940, in *Cantwell v. Connecticut* (310 U.S. 296), the issue was over whether the Jehovah's Witnesses could utilize streets and parks to proselytize. The court's "public forum" doctrine established that access to public streets and parks was protected by the First Amendment because they are government property; therefore, restricting a religious group from using them violates the Establishment Clause. Also in 1940, in *Minersville School District v. Gobitis* (310 U.S. 586), the conflict was over a school district policy requiring forced recital of the Pledge of Allegiance. In 1942, the Supreme Court issued the "fighting words" doctrine in *Chaplinsky v. New Hampshire* (315 U.S. 568). In *West Virginia State Board of Education v. Barnette* (319 U.S. 624, 1943), the court overturned the earlier *Gobitis* ruling and ruled a West Virginia law requiring mandatory flag salute unconstitutional.

Also in 1943, in *Murdock v. Pennsylvania* (319 U.S. 105, 1943), the court ruled that a state law requiring religious solicitors to obtain a license was an unconstitutional tax on a religious group. In 1946, in *Estep v. United States* (327 U.S. 114), the court ruled against a draft board that had refused to classify Jehovah's Witnesses members as ministers of a faith and thereby qualified for a draft deferral or exemption. In *Niemotko v. Maryland* (340 U.S. 268, 1951), the court reversed a lower court decision convicting two Jehovah's Witnesses lecturers from conducting public speeches in a city park without a county-issued permit. In 1953, in *Fowler v. Rhode Island* (345 U.S. 67), the court remanded the Supreme Court of Rhode Island's upholding the conviction of an ordained minister of Jehovah's Witnesses for violation of holding a religious meeting in a city park of Pawtucket, ruling that a religious service of the Jehovah's Witnesses was treated differently from religious services of other denominations (Catholic and mainline Protestant) and therefore amounted to the state preferring one religious group over this one.

Finally, in 2002, in *Watchtower Bible and Tract Society of New York v. Village of Stratton* (536 U.S. 150), the court ruled that the state could not require by penalty of a misdemeanor that the Jehovah's Witnesses refrain from door-to-door advocacy without first registering with town officials and applying for and receiving a permit; the law violated the First Amendment as it applies to religious proselytizing, anonymous political speech, and the distribution of handbills.

The Nation of Islam

The Nation of Islam (NOI), also known as the Black Muslims, is an example of another millennial movement.

The Black Muslims began in the 1930s, during the Great Depression, arising out of various mystic black nationalist sectarian cults located in the nation's urban ghettos, such as the Moorish-American Science Temple, founded by Timothy Drew in North Carolina (1886–1929), who proclaimed himself Prophet Noble Drew Ali in Newark, New Jersey, in 1913, and that he had been commissioned to preach Islam to black Americans (Lincoln 1994). The movement soon established temples in Chicago, Detroit, and Pittsburgh. Another millennial group was the Peace Mission movement of Father Divine, which was established on Long Island in 1919. It blended social and religious black nationalism, which peaked between 1931 and 1936, and claimed a following of one million. Another was the Ethiopian Pacific movement begun in Chicago in 1932 (LeMay 2009, 213–214).

The Black Muslims, first known as the Lost-Found Nation of Islam and then simply the Nation of Islam, began in Detroit's black ghetto and was led by Wali D. Fard, or Mr. W. Fard Muhammad, or simply Wallace. His most trusted follower and successor was Elijah Muhammad, who was born Elijah Poole (1897–1975). Fard led a following of about eight thousand faithful before he disappeared in June 1934. Elijah Muhammad, declaring himself Allah's Prophet, then led the movement, which at its height became the United States' foremost black nationalist movement, with sixty-nine temples in twenty-seven states and claiming a membership in excess of one million, roughly one-third of all American Muslims at the time (Brooks 1996, 143–155). They established temples in Chicago, Milwaukee, and Washington, DC, appealing to the black underclass.

Black Muslims desired to free blacks from white oppression by securing land for themselves within the continental United States. Preaching an assertive, militant separatism, they formed economic self-independent groups and promoted black pride. They rejected both white society and the Judeo-Christian heritage underpinning the dominant culture and its value system (LeMay 2009, 214–215).

In 1934, the Chicago Temple Number 2 served as the headquarters of the NOI and the "Mecca" of the movement.

Showing remarkable growth, it started with about 10,000 members and had more than 250,000 members by 1960. Its most famous speaker, Malcolm X (born Malcolm Little), referred to American blacks as the Lost Nation of Islam in North America. Its members immersed themselves in a new Muslim culture, with temples, schools for children, and numerous daily and weekly publications filled with Black Muslim ideology, the most famous of which was *Muhammad Speaks*, with a circulation of six hundred thousand. They set up Muslim community centers, offered employment training, and ran a variety of retail and service businesses and the University of Islam (which is more like a high school).

The NOI promoted a collective identity through such symbols as a flag, the reference to God as Allah, use of the star and crescent, its own version of the Koran, and Islamic names and terms. Like the Old Order Amish and Mennonites, NOI has elaborate prohibitions and prescribed behaviors as well as clothing styles for men and women. Collectively, these practices work to promote self-identification and black pride.

NOI clashed with majority society over a number of policies—refusing to accept or pay into Social Security and opposing the draft. Its members have been arrested and jailed for tax evasion.

In the early 1960s, Malcolm X wrote many newspaper and magazine articles, including ones in *Muhammad Speaks*, which rose in circulation to nine hundred thousand. He was a frequent speaker on college campuses and began to rival Elijah Muhammad for leadership. He eventually split with the Black Muslims and founded his own group, the Organization of Afro-American Unity (OAAU). He was assassinated in 1965 by three NOI followers at a rally in New York City's Harlem (LeMay 2009, 220–222).

When Elijah Muhammad died in 1975, NOI was then led by his son, Wallace Deen Muhammad, who soon rejected much of his father's teachings and returned Black Muslim followers to conventional Sunni Islam, forming and leading the

American Society of Muslims. He formally dissolved the sect. NOI was revived and soon led by Minister Louis Farrakhan, who attempted to return Black Muslims to their origins under Elijah Muhammad. Today, many black American Muslims attend mainstream Islam temples of Sunni and Shi'a affiliation.

Non-Christian Minority Religions and First Amendment Freedoms

There are any number of non-Christian minority religions in the United States, several of which experience discrimination and outright hostility and some of which have occasional issues or conflicts with the majority society over their religious beliefs and practices involving issues of First Amendment freedoms. And there are the religious "nones"—atheists and agnostics—who also on occasion raise issues with freedom *from* religion.

Jewish Americans

According to a 2017 worldwide survey, there are 14.5 million persons who self-identify as Jewish. In the United States, they comprise 5.7 million Jews, who make up 1.76 percent of the total population and 39 percent of worldwide Jewry. Judaism is traditionally divided into three groups: Orthodox, Reform, and Conservative. According to research by the Public Religion Research Institute (PRRI), as of 2017, about 28 percent of American Jews identify as Reform, 14 percent as Conservative, and 10 percent as Orthodox (LeMay 2018, 36–38, 119–122). There are more than 3,700 synagogues in the United States. Among them, the total Orthodox synagogues number just over 1,500, or about 40 percent of all U.S. synagogues. Total Reform synagogues number just under 1,000, or 26 percent, and total Conservative synagogues number 865, or slightly more than 23 percent. Among the Orthodox are the Hasidic synagogues; the Lubavitch/Chabad (346), or mixed synagogues; the Orthodox Union/Lubavitch; and the Young Israel and Lubavitch (Singer and Grossman 2003, 128–129).

A 2007 study put the Jewish population at six million, and it found that there are 180,000 ultra-Orthodox Jews, the Hasidic (also spelled Chasidic, from the Hebrew word meaning "pious") (LeMay 2018, 36). Hasidic Jews do not seek converts, so their growth is almost entirely due to births; nonetheless, they are a fairly rapidly growing population—doubling every twenty years or so—because they tend to have many children. The average Hasidic family has four to six children, while non-Orthodox Jewish groups have flat or falling rates.

Hasidic Jews believe in living close together, within walking distance of their synagogues. Their neighborhoods are islands of traditional Judaism. Signs on stores are in Yiddish and Hebrew, the men wear long beards and black garb, and the women wear scarves or wigs and dress in modest clothing. Their distinctiveness from the majority culture is palpable, from their apparent community tightness to the ever-present consciousness of the group. There is an emphasis on custom and religious law and the high degree of ritual instructions found in the Torah. Ritual observance permeates every corner and includes giving to charity, not mixing wool and linen, following strict kosher dietary laws, refraining from work on the Sabbath, regulating sexual behavior, studying the Torah, and loving and fearing God.

Hasidic Jews live in a traditional patriarchal system. Hasidism is a mystic and enthusiastic sect, emphasizing the importance of inner intent and carrying out ritual obligations. In Hasidism, the community leader is the rebbe, a social and spiritual teacher. The word *rebbe* means "rabbi" in Yiddish and is distinctly Hasidic; it means one trained as a teacher. Historically, each rebbe came from the town in which their court was located in Eastern Europe: the Lubavitch from Lubavitch, Russia; the Satmar from Satu Mare, Hungary; the Bobover from the Polish town of Bobova; and so on (LeMay 2009, 231–232).

Their comparative growth rate means that in fifty years they will constitute a majority of American Jews, marking profound cultural and political change in Judaism. Ultra-Orthodox Jews tend to be politically conservative and send their children to religious schools, making them more sympathetic to faith-based initiatives promoted by the Republican Party. Although they live apart culturally, they are politically active and vote in majority society elections. They oppose contraception, abortion, and divorce. They aim not to change beliefs but the believer.

Hasidic Jews immigrated to the United States in the 1870s and 1880s and especially after World War I and again in 1940 as they fled strong and open anti-Semitism, mostly from what is today Poland, Belorussia, and Ukraine. In Europe, they lived in *shtetls* (villages). In the United States, the world headquarters of the Lubavitch Hasidic sect is in Crown Heights, Brooklyn. Rebbe Menachem Schneersohn organized three Chabad (Hasidic movement) divisions: publishing, educational outreach missions, and social services. Their children attend special schools (called a *yeshiva*) (Schaefer 1998). Like the Amish and Mennonites, they maintain a high degree of cultural identity despite living within the heart of the majority culture (LeMay 2009, 237).

Hasidic Jews have been involved in First Amendment issues, particularly concerning the Free Exercise and Establishment Clauses, for example, in the case of *Board of Education of Kiryas Joel Village School District v. Grumet* (512 U.S. 687, 1994). In *Kiryas Joel*, the court held, 5–3, that creating a school district just to serve one religious group—a Hasidic Jewish community—violated the Establishment Clause. The majority opinion was written by Justice David Souter, joined by Justices Harry Blackmun, John Stevens, Sandra Day O'Connor, and Ruth Bader Ginsburg. The dissenters were Justices Antonin Scalia, William Rehnquist, and Clarence Thomas, who argued that the Hasidic group was a cultural group as well as a religious one; therefore, the Establishment Clause did not apply.

Muslim Americans

A 2017 Pew Research survey put the adult Muslim population in the United States at 3.45 million, or 1.1 percent of the total U.S. population. By 2040, they are projected to replace Jewish

Americans as the nation's second-largest religious group after Christians. By 2050, they are projected to reach 8.1 million, or 2.1 percent of the nation's total population, nearly twice the share of today (Mohamed 2018).

Swelled by higher immigration and conversion rates, Islam has surpassed Judaism as a minority religion, and worldwide it has more than 1.2 billion adherents, making it one of the largest religions in the world. It is now the second-largest religion in Europe and Russia. Despite their being stereotyped as Arabs, only about 18 percent of all Muslims come from the Middle East.

The two main branches of Islam are Sunni (at about 90 percent worldwide) and the Shi'a (about 10 percent). The Shi'a are predominately found in Iraq, Iran, Lebanon, Yemen, and Bahrain, a fact that figures prominently in the growing anti-Islamic attitude and now policy in the United States (LeMay 2009, 228; see also Hourani 1991).

Muslims came to the United States during the Great Migration in the late 1800s and early 1900s, the majority from Syria. They spoke Arabic. Their first permanent mosque was built in 1923 in Cedar Rapids, Iowa, and it is still often referred to as the Mother Mosque of America.

A post-1965 immigration flow came from Palestine and Lebanon but also from other parts of the Arabic-speaking world. Many were refugees seeking to escape violence in their homelands, such as the 1975–1990 Lebanese Civil War, Palestinians from the West Bank and Gaza Strip, displaced Kurds and Shi'a from Iraq, war-weary Afghanis, and survivors of the 1992–1995 war in Bosnia.

Since the terrorist attacks of September 11, 2001, however, immigration from "high-risk" countries—defined by the U.S. Department of Homeland Security (DHS) as Muslim-majority countries—has slowed significantly, and Muslim immigrants are subject to special registration and more stringent vetting. They are specifically targeted by the Trump administration's travel ban policy. The current unfavorable social climate and the threat of violence has kept the American Muslim community in a state of flux. Muslim organizations, such as the Council on American-Islamic Relations (CAIR), the Muslim Pacific Affairs Committee, the Institute of Islamic Information and Education, and the Islamic Society of North America, use political protest to counter discrimination (LeMay 2009, 228–230). In particular, they advocate for religious free exercise, antiestablishment, and freedom of assembly. They have joined with other civil rights groups (both secular- and religious-based) to lobby against hate crimes, of which they are a frequent target (LeMay 2018, 38–39).

Buddhism, Hinduism, and Sikhism

A 2014 Pew Forum Religious Landscape Study put the Buddhist and Hindi populations at 0.7 percent of the total population (Pew Research Center 2015). Another study (Barrett 2001) put their numbers at 2.4 million Buddhists and 1 million Hindi. Immigrant adherents to these religions mostly arrived in the post-1970 immigration wave. Because Buddhism and Hinduism do not proselytize and are viewed as mostly passive, even quaint, cultures and religions, they have experienced little overt discrimination and evidence few conflicts with majority society and its laws.

Sikhs number approximately 140,000 to 200,000 in the United States, and there are 246 Sikh congregations (known as *gurdwaras*). Sikhism is equally a nonthreatening (to the majority culture) minority religion, but the fact that they wear distinctive garb (chiefly the use of turbans) has resulted in misinformed discrimination against Sikhs with anti-Arab animus and violence, especially in the immediate aftermath of the 9/11 attacks, when they were targets of hate crimes. An August 5, 2012, attack on a Sikh temple in Oak Creek, Wisconsin, for example, left six dead. Their freedom to practice their faith, and the protection of their right to assemble in their places of worship unimpeded by threats of violence against them are guaranteed by the First Amendment (LeMay 2018, 39–40).

Native American Religions

Native American religions are quite diverse, reflecting many tribal traditions and practices. Beyond question, however, they were subjected to the most suppression of religious beliefs and practices by the U.S. government. For many decades, the federal government had a policy of "forced assimilation" that targeted the eradication of Native American languages, cultures, customs, and religious practices. Many tribes used herbal hallucinogens in their ceremonies to gain greater insight, experience visions, or communicate with the gods. Most such ceremonies included feasts, music, dances, and other performances and employed symbolism, especially with animals, as part of Native American religion. Animals were used to represent certain ideas, characteristics, and spirits and to tell the story of creation—for example, the Tlingit Indian creation story centered on a raven. Some tribes had shaman, or medicine men, instead of preachers or clergymen, as found in Christianity. The shaman was believed to be able to communicate with their god or Great Spirit. They considered the shaman a wise and experienced man and accorded him high status among the tribal groups. A shaman played an important role in decisions, ceremonies, and traditions (LeMay 2018, 40–41).

In recent years, Native American religions have politically mobilized and have succeeded in winning some policy concessions from the national government to reform past repression. For instance, they have won the right to use peyote (an otherwise controlled substance) in their religious ceremonies, mostly conducted on reservation lands. The various Indian residential schools, such as the Carlisle Indian Industrial School in Pennsylvania, that conducted forced assimilation, suppressing Native American language, religious practices, and culture and espousing a philosophy to "kill the Indian to save the man," have all been closed (LeMay 2009, 187–188).

In 1946, perhaps in recognition of the special contributions that the code talkers played in World War II, Congress created the Indian Claims Commission to settle grievances. The schools were ended with passage of the Indian Education Act (1972), the Indian Financing Act (1974), and the Indian Self-Determination and Education Assistance Act (1975). In 1978, Congress passed three laws: the American Indian Religious Freedom Act (AIRFA, Pub. L. 96-341, 92 Stat. 469), designed to protect sacred sites and allow certain religious practices, such as the use of eagle feathers and peyote; the Tribally Controlled Community College Assistance Act; and the Indian Child Welfare Act.

In 1979, Congress enacted the Indian Archaeological Resources Protection Act. In 1988, it passed the Indian Gaming Regulatory Act, which resulted in ninety-seven tribes in twenty-two states operating more than two hundred casinos (LeMay 2009, 190–191, 314). In 1988, the U.S. Supreme Court decided a case involving eminent domain versus the free exercise of religion of Native Americans in *Lyng v. Northwest Indian Cemetery Protective Association* (485 U.S. 439).

Atheists and Agnostics

Avowed atheists do not believe in the existence of God. Agnostics profess that the existence of God cannot be known or proved, and so they simply do not know whether or not to believe in any deity. In both cases, they reject joining any religion or religious organization. The 2004 ARIS survey found that just over 1.5 million people self-identified as agnostics (0.5 percent of the 2000 population) and 1.3 million as atheists (0.4 percent of the 2000 population). The 2014 Pew Research Center Religious Landscape Study found that 22.8 percent of Americans were religiously unaffiliated. Self-identified atheists were at 3.1 percent, agnostics at 4.0 percent, and the "nothing in particular" group at 15.8 percent (Pew Research Center n.d.).

The religiously unaffiliated comprise 24 percent of the American population. Among the unaffiliated, 31 percent are atheists, and 24 percent are agnostics. Among these secularists, political party identification is as follows: 47 percent independents, 33 percent Democrats, and 11 percent Republicans.

They are politically active and especially support antiestablishment laws and court cases.

The American Atheists (AA) organization was formed in 1963, largely to fight for the civil liberties of atheists and to support the total, absolute separation of government and religion. In many respects, they arose out of a lower court case, *Murray v. Curlett* (228 MD 239, 1959), that challenged prayer recitation in public schools. In that case, Murray stated the following characterization of her atheist beliefs:

> Your petitioners are atheists, and they define their lifestyle as follows. An atheist loves himself and his fellow man instead of a god. An atheist accepts that heaven is something for which we should work now—here on earth—for all men together to enjoy. An atheist accepts that he can get no help through prayer, but that he must find in himself the inner conviction and strength to meet life, to grapple with, to subdue it and to enjoy it. An atheist accepts that only in a knowledge of himself and a knowledge of his fellow man can he find the understanding that will help lead to a life of fulfillment.

Murray v. Curlett led to the Supreme Court decision in *Abington School District v. Schempp* (374 U.S. 203, 1963), the Supreme Court, in an 8–1 decision, found for Edward Schempp, a Unitarian Universalist, against the Abington Township school district in Pennsylvania and declared school-sponsored Bible reading in public schools to be unconstitutional. The majority opinion by Justice Tom Clark was joined in by Chief Justice Earl Warren and Justices Hugo Black, Byron White, William Douglas, Arthur Goldberg, John Harlan, and William Brennan. Only Justice Potter Stewart dissented.

Since its formation, AA has consistently fought to defend the separation of church and state, to appear in all forms of the media to defend atheism from criticisms of religion and religious entities, and to support atheist public gatherings, such as

Atheist Pride marches in state capitals. AA members have pick-
eted on behalf of atheist rights and church-state separation. The
organization publishes hundreds of books about atheism as well
as newsletters, magazines, and member alerts. It has promoted
a network of activists throughout the United States to moni-
tor First Amendment issues. AA has preserved atheist literature
and history in the nation's largest archive of its kind. It provides
speakers for colleges, universities, clubs, and the news media
and has granted college scholarships to young atheist activists

The Fourteenth Amendment's Due Process Clause

The U.S. Supreme Court, through its decisions in more than
forty cases, gradually interpreted the First Amendment freedoms of assembly, press, religion, and speech. With the adoption of the Fourteenth Amendment, the court incorporated
First Amendment freedoms to state and local governments via
its Due Process Clause in some forty cases. The U.S. Senate
enacted the Fourteenth Amendment on June 13, 1866, by a
vote of 33 to 11. The House of Representatives passed it on
June 16, 1866, by a vote of 120 to 32. It was adopted (ratified) on July 9, 1868. As one of the Reconstruction's civil rights
amendments, its Section 1 states the following:

> All persons born or naturalized in the United States,
> and subject to the jurisdiction thereof, are citizens of the
> United States and of each state wherein they reside. No
> State shall make or enforce any law which abridges the
> privileges and immunities of citizens of the United States,
> nor shall any State deprive any person of life, liberty, or
> property, without due process of law, nor deny any person
> within its jurisdiction the equal protection of the law.

Conclusion

Since its inception and the adoption of the United States
Constitution in 1789, the nation has struggled with how to

live up to the lofty principles of the First Amendment: that government shall make no law establishing a religion; prohibiting the rights of the free exercise of religion; abridging freedom of speech or the press or the rights to peaceably assemble and to petition the government for a redress of grievances. Through the Fourteenth Amendment's Due Process Clause and by various court decisions, those principles were applied to state and local governments as well.

The great diversity of religious denominations whose members immigrated to the United States or that developed within the American polity led to a perennial struggle in American politics of more than two hundred years to understand, protect, and extend religious tolerance, free assembly, free speech, and free press. Minority religions were often persecuted or discriminated against by the general society; by the state, local, and federal governments; and by other more dominant religious denominations. Gradually, minority religious groups used public law and especially the courts to protect themselves from such discrimination and to extend First Amendment rights.

The Establishment Clause of the First Amendment likewise took the enactment of many laws, and the interpretation through many landmark Supreme Court cases, to define what precisely the clause means in public policy, law, or in the practices of government that intrude on American culture and on the norms and customs of society in ways that enhance or breach the "wall of separation" between church and state. These battles, and the struggles of a host of religious and avowedly nonreligious groups, are not confined to the distant or even near past. They are constant and ongoing, infusing American politics in a fundamental way. Freedom of religion and freedom from religion are principles requiring constant vigilance to maintain and ongoing conflict, literally a perennial struggle, to refine the practical meaning thereof. Likewise, freedom of assembly, free press, and free speech are fundamental rights protected by the First Amendment. They require constant vigilance, and often court action, against all levels of government and all manner of officials. Absent that vigilance, government might otherwise infringe on those rights and privileges, and groups might use law and policy against minority persons or unpopular ethnic, social, or religious groups whose rights, without the application by the courts of those First Amendment freedoms, would be subject to attack or restriction.

Further Reading

Abanes, Richard. 2002. *One Nation under Gods: A History of the Mormon Church*. New York: Four Walls Eight Windows.

Ahlstrom, Sydney. 1972. *A Religious History of the American People*. New Haven, CT: Yale University Press.

Arrington, Leonard J., and Davis Bitton. 1992. *The Mormon Experience: A History of the Latter-Day Saints*. 2nd ed. Urbana: University of Illinois Press.

Bailey, Thomas. 1976. *Voices of America*. New York: The Free Press.

Balmer, Randall, Lee Grogerg, and Mark Mabry. 2012. *First Freedom: The Fight for Religious Liberty*. American Fork, UT: Covenant Communications. Ind.

Baltzell, E. Digby. 1996. *Puritan Boston and Quaker Philadelphia*. New Brunswick, NJ: Transaction Publishers.

Barrett, David. 2001. *World Christian Encyclopedia*. New York: Oxford University.

Beals, Carleton. 1960. *Brass Knuckle Crusade*. New York: Hasting House.

Bilhartz, Terry D. 1986. *Urban Religion and the Second Great Awakening*. Madison, NJ: Fairleigh Dickenson University Press.

Billington, Ray. 1974. *The Origins of Nativism in the United States, 1800–1844*. New York: Arno Press.

Bowman, Robert M., Jr. 1992. *Understanding Jehovah's Witnesses*. Grand Rapids, MI: Baker Book House.

Boyd, Julian P. et al., eds. 1950–2017. *The Papers of Thomas Jefferson*. Princeton: Princeton University Press.

Boyton, Linda L. 1986. *The Plain People: An Ethnography of the Holdeman Mennonites*. Salem, WI: Sheffield.

Brooks, Roy. 1996. *Integration or Separation? A Strategy for Racial Equality*. Cambridge, MA: Harvard University Press.

Bushman, Claudia L., and Richard Bushman. 2001. *Building the Kingdom: A History of Mormons in America*. New York: Oxford University Press.

Butler, Jon. 2006. *Religion in Colonial America*. New York: Oxford University Press.

Casey, Shirley. 1918. *The Millennial Hope*. Chicago: University of Chicago Press.

Chernow, Ron. 2004. *Alexander Hamilton*. New York: Penguin Press.

Church of Jesus Christ of the Latter-Day Saints. 1989. *Church History in the Fullness of Time*. Salt Lake City, UT: Church of the Latter-Day Saints.

Davies, Douglas T. 2000. *The Mormon Culture of Salvation*. New York: Ashgate.

Driedger, Leo, and Donald B. Kraybill. 1994. *Mennonite Peacemaking*. Scottsdale, PA: Herald Press.

Fantel, Hans. 1974. *William Penn: Apostle of Dissent*. New York: William Morrow.

Fenn, Richard K. 1997. *The End of Time: Religion, and the Forging of the Soul*. New York: Pilgrim Press.

Gaustad, Edwin S. 1999. *Liberty of Conscience: Roger Williams in America*. Valley Forge, PA: Judson Press.

Heimert, Alan. 1966. *Religion and the American Mind: From the Great Awakening to the Revolution*. Cambridge, UK: Cambridge University Press.

Hening, W. W., ed. 1823. *Statutes at Large of Virginia*. Vol. 12. Richmond, VA: George Cochran, 84–86.

Hirshon, Stanley. 1969. *The Lion and the Land.* New York: Knopf.

Holmes, David R. 2006. *The Faith of the Founding Fathers.* New York: Oxford University Press.

Hourani, Albert. 1991. *A History of the Arab Peoples.* New York: Warner Books.

Jefferson, Thomas. 1977. *The Portable Thomas Jefferson.* Edited by Merrill Peterson. New York: Penguin Books.

Kaplan, Jeffrey. 1997. *Radical Religion in America: Millenarian Movements from the Far Right to the Children of Noah.* Syracuse, NY: Syracuse University Press.

Kluger, Richard. 2016. *Indelible Ink: The Trials of John Peter Zenger and the Birth of America's Free Press.* New York: W. W. Norton.

Kornelly, Sharon. 2013. "A Holy Experiment: Religion and Immigration to the New World." In *Transforming America: Perspectives on U.S. Immigration,* edited by Michael LeMay, vol. 1, 189–213. Santa Barbara, CA: Praeger.

Kraybill, Donald B., and Marc O. Olshan, eds. 1994. *The Amish Struggle with Modernity.* Hanover, NH: University Press of New England.

Landes, Richard, ed. 2000. *Encyclopedia of Millennialism and Millennial Movements.* New York: Routledge.

Landes, Richard. 2011. *Heaven on Earth: Varieties of the Millennial Experience.* New York: Oxford University Press.

Launius, Roger D., and Linda Thatcher, eds. 1994. *Differing Visions: Dissenters in Mormon History.* Urbana: University Press of Illinois.

LeMay, Michael. 1987. *From Open Door to Dutch Door: An Analysis of Immigration Policy since 1820.* New York: Praeger.

LeMay, Michael. 2009. *The Perennial Struggle.* 3rd ed. Upper Saddle River, NJ: Prentice-Hall.

LeMay, Michael, ed. 2013. *Transforming America: Perspectives on Immigration.* 3 vols. Santa Barbara, CA: ABC-CLIO.

LeMay, Michael. 2018. *Religious Freedom in America: A Reference Handbook.* Santa Barbara, CA: ABC-CLIO.

LeMay, Michael C., and Elliott Robert Barkan, eds. 1999. *U.S. Immigration and Naturalization Laws and Issues: A Documentary History.* Westport, CT: Greenwood Press.

Levy, Leonard W. 1994. *The Establishment Clause and the First Amendment.* Chapel Hill: University of North Carolina Press.

Lincoln, C. Eric. 1994. *The Black Muslims in America, 3ed.* Trenton, NJ: African World Press.

Mapp, Alf. 2003. *The Faith of Our Fathers: What America's Founders Really Believed.* Lanham, MD: Rowman & Littlefield.

Mauss, Armand. 1994. *The Angel and the Beehive: The Mormon Struggle with Assimilation.* Urbana: University of Illinois Press.

McConkie, Bruce R. 1966. *Mormon Doctrine.* Salt Lake City, UT: Bookcraft.

Middlekauff, Robert. 2005. *The Glorious Cause: The American Revolution, 1763–1789.* New York: Oxford University Press.

Miller, William Lee. 1986. *The First Liberty: Religion and the American Republic.* Washington, DC: Georgetown University Press.

Mohamed, Besheer. 2018. "New Estimates Show U.S. Muslim Population Continues to Grow." Pew Research Center, January 3. Accessed January 8, 2019. https://www.pewresearch.org/fact-tank/2018/01/03/new-estimates.

Nolt, Steven M. 1992. *A History of the Amish.* Intercourse, PA: Good Books.

Nuovo, Victor. 2002. *John Locke: Writings on Religion.* New York: Oxford University.

Penton, M. James. 1997. *Apocalypse Delayed: The Story of the Jehovah's Witnesses.* Toronto: Toronto University Press.

Peters, Shawn Francis. 2003. *The Yoder Case: Religious Freedom, Education, and Parental Rights.* Lawrence: University Press of Kansas.

Peterson, Merrill D., and Robert C. Vaughn, eds. 1988. *The Virginia Statute for Religious Freedom: Its Evolution and Consequences in American History.* Cambridge, MA: Cambridge University Press.

Pew Research Center. 2015. "America's Changing Religious Landscape." Pew Forum.org. Accessed January 28, 2017. https://www.pewforum.org/2015/05/12 /americas-changing-religious-landscape.

Pew Research Center. n.d. "Religious Landscape Study." Accessed January 26, 2017. https://www.pewforum.org /religious-landscape-study.

Schaefer, Richard. 1998. *Racial and Ethnic Groups, 7ed.* New York: Harper Collins.

Singer, David, and Lawrence Grossman, eds. 2003. *American Jewish Yearbook, 2002.* New York: American Jewish Committee.

Urofsky, Melvin I. 2002. *Religious Freedom: Rights and Liberties under the Law.* Santa Barbara, CA: ABC-CLIO.

Vile, John. 2015. *The United States Constitution: One Document, Many Choices.* New York: Palgrave Macmillan.

Walters, Kerry S. 1992. *The American Deists: Voices of Reason and Dissent in the Early Republic.* Lawrence: University Press of Kansas.

Wenger, John. 1961. *The Mennonites in Indiana and Michigan.* Scottsdale, PA: Herald Press.

Wessinger, Catherine. 2000. *Millennialism, Persecution, and Violence: Historical Cases.* Syracuse, NY: Syracuse University Press.

Wojcik, Daniel. 1997. *The End of the World as We Know It: Faith, Fatalism, and Apocalypse in American.* New York: New York University Press.

Young, Ann Eliza. 1972. *Wife No. 19: The Story of a Life in Bondage.* New York: Arno Press.

2 Problems, Controversies, and Solutions

Introduction

This chapter focuses on some of the more prominent problems and controversies arising from the stipulations of freedoms guaranteed by the First Amendment to the U.S. Constitution. In December 1791, when the state of Virginia became the tenth of the then fourteen states to approve ten of the twelve proposed amendments, the Bill of Rights amendments were ratified, making them legal (Levy 1994). At that time, the United States was a small nation of states huddled along the East Coast, and the population of less than four million was overwhelmingly made up of rural residents involved in agriculture. As the nation changed, problems and controversies unforeseen by the founders developed, and it became necessary to refine and change our ideas of exactly what behavior is protected by the First Amendment.

This chapter also discusses some solutions to those problems and controversies. These solutions have primarily involved key U.S. Supreme Court decisions handed down in landmark cases in which local, state, or federal laws or other actions by those

Citizens with a sign demonstrating against what they saw to be controversial textbooks, Washington, D.C., 1975. Parents have tried on numerous occasions to ban fiction, poetry, plays, and textbooks from classrooms and school libraries. The Supreme Court's ruling in *Island Trees Union Free School District v. Pico* (1982) determined that local school boards should have broad discretion in managing schools, but that, at the same time, local school officials must adhere to the First Amendment by ensuring that a school library is a place where students can be exposed to new ideas. (Library of Congress) governments were challenged on First Amendment constitutional grounds. The order of the problems and controversies discussed herein follows the order of the First Amendment clauses that guarantee those freedoms: establishment of religion, free exercise of religion, freedom of speech, freedom of press, freedom of assembly, and the right to petition the government for a redress of grievances.

Problems and controversies arose over exactly what is meant by each of those clauses. First Amendment jurisprudence is the process by which the meaning of the language in the amendment is clarified and defined. Solutions—or at least resolutions that prevail for some time—often involve the Supreme Court developing and handing down specific "tests" to use in reaching decisions regarding the constitutionality or unconstitutionality of government actions and laws. The Supreme Court and the U.S. Congress have also distinguished categories of groups of persons afforded these protections and expanded on those "protected classes" over time as societal conditions required.

As American society evolved, problems and controversies arose, often in ways that the Founding Fathers simply could not have anticipated. Political parties developed, and political campaigns began to publish newspapers and political pamphlets that some governments and politicians wanted to suppress. Minority parties advocating radical laws and policy as solutions to problems they considered to be critical challenged local, state, and the national government in ways that required rethinking basic values of democracy itself (Zentner and LeMay 2020). These developments required new definitions of what exactly is freedom of the press that is protected by the First Amendment. When the United States expanded and developed over time, immigration brought in new groups of people, many of whom came to be considered ethnic and religious minorities, and, as such, they were for some time particularly vulnerable to laws and government actions detrimental to their First Amendment freedoms. In times of war, freedom of speech and assembly were particularly challenged as public sentiment and government actions and laws sought to regulate citizens and noncitizens alike in response to perceived wartime needs and a desire for conformity.

As the United States urbanized and industrialized, "assembly" had to be redefined to include, for example, groups of workers who formed labor unions to petition to redress grievances. Technological developments, such as the development of motion picture films and the internet, required laws and the courts to reconsider what is and is not protected speech, what constitutes symbolic speech, and what constitutes "protected commercial speech." Courts had to define precisely what constitutes libel and, in times of war or extensive social unrest, what is meant by "seditious libel." Developments in international law and the adherence by the United States to international protocols on human rights further impacted U.S. law in regard to various civil rights and liberties, including those guaranteed by the First Amendment. Indeed, First Amendment jurisprudence, the theory of law, involves an ongoing struggle to more precisely define what is meant by the very general language that is used in the various clauses of the First Amendment.

The story of the American experiment in democracy, in self-governance, is a story involving an ongoing political and legal struggle to define and refine what is meant by the lofty goals set in the First Amendment freedoms and the limitations it imposes on government. What is meant by the aspirational goals and values of the First Amendment requires a perennial struggle to achieve them in practice, to grapple with issues arising when those very values clash and to seek a balance between clashing rights, and to innovate new solutions to those problems and controversies through the enactment of new laws and through the complex jurisprudence by federal courts and, in particular, by landmark rulings of the U.S. Supreme Court. The decisions rendered by courts, especially by "tests" articulated by landmark Supreme Court rulings, draw lines between permissible and impermissible behavior by governments and by citizens or groups of citizens (Alley 1999; Urofsky and Finkelman 1987).

Freedom of Religion and the Establishment Clause

The first problem to be discussed herein arose from the First Amendment's freedom of religion and its Establishment Clause and the gradual acceptance of the idea and value of the separation of church and state principle and its extension to state governments. As discussed in chapter 1, having an established or official church (i.e., one that is legal and supported by taxes) was the norm during colonial times. All thirteen colonies had established churches or required officeholders to profess a certain faith (Butler 2005). In 1781, the Articles of Confederation were ratified without a bill of rights, and the general norm was that established religion was necessary to protect morality and to uphold social order. Excesses of the French Revolution, however, precipitated heated debates in the United States, and questions were raised about the future of religion in the country. Particularly within the frontier states, religious denominations other than the predominant Anglican and Congregational Churches arose, and support for disestablishment developed along with the Second Great Awakening movement (1798–1820) (Butler 2005; Dreisbach 2002; Green 2010; Witte 2012).

Thomas Jefferson led the movement to disestablish the Anglican Church that culminated in 1786 with the enactment of the Virginia Statute for Religious Freedom within the Virginia Constitution, and he played a leading role among the Founding Fathers in including the freedom of religion clauses in the U.S. Constitution. Jefferson famously described it as the need to erect a "wall of separation" between church and state (Dreisbach 2002; Holmes 2006; Lambert 2003; Levy 1994; Mapp 2003; Peterson, Vaughan, and Lovin 1988; Rogasta 2013). At the Constitutional Convention of 1787, the Founding Fathers rather easily agreed that the national government should not have an official religion, and the consensus was upheld in 1791 when the First Amendment, with its guarantee of religious liberty, was ratified.

The First Amendment was viewed by all the founding leaders as applying only to the federal government, along with the other amendments in the Bill of Rights. And even with regard to the national government, it took some decades of discussion to clarify the limits of federal disestablishment (Green 2010). Congress had chaplains, and the national government supported missionaries to Native Americans well into the nineteenth century. Americans continued to struggle to understand what it meant for Congress not to establish a religion. Debate over whether the U.S. Postal Service should operate on Sundays or whether non-Christians could act as witnesses in federal courts if they did not swear on the Christian Bible occurred until the Civil War (Feldman 2005; Green 2010; Levy 1994; McGarvie 2004).

With respect to the actions of state and local governments, the process to define and clarify the meaning of "establishment of religion" took even longer. It took a gradual process of "disestablishment," as it is called by historians, that took place over fifty years (between 1778 and 1833) to change that then spread to all the state governments. Some states took action even before adoption of the U.S. Constitution and its Bill of Rights. South Carolina, for example, dropped the adherence to the Anglican Church as its official church in its 1778 constitution. Any church could become "incorporated" as a state-supported church. It only needed to agree to a set of basic Christian theological tenets that were vague enough that most denominations could support them. As Christian denominations proliferated between 1780 and 1840, often spurred by the Great Awakening, new denominations challenged the assumption that all Americans were Christian. In 1790, South Carolina removed the Establishment Clause and any religious restrictions on officeholders. The remaining states gradually disestablished official churches. In 1833, following a state supreme court decision, Massachusetts became the last state to disestablish, in that case, state support for the Congregational Church (Flowers, Green, and Rogers 2008).

After the Civil War, the enactment of the Fourteenth Amendment raised issues regarding the Establishment Clause that increasingly came before the U.S. Supreme Court, which dealt with a number of problems raised by thorny issues in a host of cases wherein the court resolved an establishment question. In what form was aid permissible to church-related schools? What role, if any, could religion have in (secular) public education? Could local or state governments sponsor religious displays such as the Ten Commandments or Christmas nativity scenes? Under what conditions or auspices was it possible to say prayers in public schools? Could local government ordinances restrict business activity on Sundays (known as blue laws)? Under what circumstances, if any, could religious institutions function as government agencies? Under what conditions was it permissible to extend tax exemptions to religious institutions? Was it permissible for the federal government to support chaplains in the armed forces or to daily open and lead the U.S. Congress or the state legislature in prayer? Was it permissible to insert the phrase "Under God" in the Pledge of Allegiance or to print it on U.S. currency? Under what conditions did religious institutions have standing to sue in federal courts?

Aid to Church-Related Schools

Between 1925 and 2011, the U.S. Supreme Court handed down eighteen major decisions concerning *aid to church-related schools* and exactly what was or was not permissible aid under the Establishment Clause. During the 1890s to 1920s, when Roman Catholic immigrants came in great numbers and established parochial schools, debate raged over the reading of the Bible in public schools and which translation of the Bible would be used. Mainline Protestant denominations went so far as to seek to legally abolish parochial schools altogether. In *Pierce v. Society of Sisters* (268 U.S. 510, 1925), the Supreme Court ruled that it was constitutional for religious institutions to operate schools and that parents could send their children to them instead of public schools and still be in compliance with state compulsory education laws (Abrams 2009). In *Cochran v. Louisiana State Board of Education* (281 U.S. 370, 1930), the Supreme Court adopted a "child benefit theory" to uphold a Louisiana law allowing the state to purchase and lend secular subject textbooks to students attending parochial schools as well as public schools.

In a similar ruling, in *Everson v. Board of Education of the Township of Ewing* (330 U.S. 1, 1947), the Supreme Court applied the Establishment Clause, through the Due Process Clause of the Fourteenth Amendment, to a New Jersey township school board, finding 5–4 that the New Jersey law providing for public reimbursement funding for the costs of transportation of children to and from parochial Catholic schools did not violate the Establishment Clause. In his majority opinion, Justice Hugo Black cited the writings of James Madison and Thomas Jefferson. The majority ruled that the law was constitutional because the reimbursements were offered to the parents of all students regardless of religion and not directly to any religious institution.

In *Abington School District v. Schempp* (374 U.S. 203, 1963), the court decided 8–1 for the respondent, Edward Schempp, by declaring that the school-sponsored Bible reading in public schools was unconstitutional. In *Board of Education v. Allen* (392 U.S. 236, 1968), the court used similar reasoning when upholding a New York state law allowing for the loan of secular textbooks to schoolchildren, including those in parochial schools, as having passed the two-part "purpose and effect" test established by the court in *Abington v. Schempp*. The court established another three-part test for determining whether a law meets the requirements of the establishment clause in *Lemon v. Kurtzman* (403 U.S. 602, 1971). In *Lemon*, the court held two Rhode Island laws were unconstitutional. The Lemon test required the law (1) to have a legitimate secular purpose, (2) to not have the primary effect of either advancing or inhibiting religion, and (3) to not result in the excessive entanglement of government and religion (Smith 2016; Urofsky 2002; Witte 2012).

On the same day as the *Lemon* decision, the Supreme Court decided *Tilton v. Richardson* (403 U.S. 672, 1971). In its 5–4 decision, the court decided to largely uphold provisions of the Higher Education Facilities Act of 1963 that permitted federal aid for the construction of secular buildings at church-sponsored colleges and universities, holding that the act did not violate the religious clauses of the First Amendment. Yet, in the case of *Committee for Public Education and Religious Liberty v. Nyquist* (413 U.S. 756, 1973), the court invalidated a New York state law providing money grants to parochial schools for maintenance and repair of school facilities. The court ruled that the programs of the New York plan violated the Establishment Clause by impermissibly advancing religion. The court held similarly in *Meek v. Pittenger* (421 U.S. 349, 1975) in regard to a Pennsylvania law that authorized providing aid directly to children attending nonpublic elementary and secondary schools for auxiliary services, loans for textbooks, and instructional materials and equipment. In *Meek*, the court upheld the constitutionality of the textbook loan program but held that the loans to schools for instructional materials and auxiliary services violated the First Amendment because such loans could be diverted to religious purposes.

The court applied the Lemon test in *Roemer v. Board of Public Works of Maryland* (426 U.S. 736, 1976). In the *Roemer* case, the question was whether a 1971 state law that allocated Maryland taxpayer money to private and religious-affiliated schools for "nonsectarian purposes" violated the First Amendment. In its 5–4 decision, the court held that the Maryland law passed the Lemon test and therefore did not violate the First Amendment. The Supreme Court also used the Lemon test in *Wolman v. Walter* (433 U.S. 229, 1977). In *Wolman*, the court upheld the State of Ohio by ruling that it could provide nonpublic schools with secular textbooks, standardized testing, and scoring diagnostic services, but it rejected aid from Ohio to such schools in the form of instructional materials and equipment and for field trip services as violations of the Establishment Clause. In a related issue, the court decision in *Committee for Public Education and Religious Liberty v. Regan* (444 U.S. 646, 1980) hinged on the secular purpose for such aid. By a 5–4 vote, the court ruled that a New York law allocating funds to reimburse religious as well as secular private schools for testing and other services mandated by state law did not violate the Establishment Clause. The majority opinion stressed that the New York statute had a clear secular purpose. That was also the reasoning in *Mueller v. Allen* (463 U.S. 388, 1983), which addressed the question of whether taxpayers should be allowed to deduct expenses in providing tuition, textbooks, and transportation for their children attending elementary and secondary schools even if they are parochial schools. In a 6–3 decision, the court upheld the Minnesota statute allowing for such tax deductions, ruling that the statute passed all three elements of the Lemon test.

The Lemon test was also applied in *Aguilar v. Felton* (473 U.S. 402, 1985). At issue in this case was New York City's use of federal funds under Title I of the Elementary and Secondary Education Act of 1965 to pay the salaries of public school employees who teach in parochial schools in the city. By a 6–3 decision, the court held that the program was unconstitutional in that it resulted in excessive entanglement of church and state and thereby violated the Establishment Clause. In *Grand Rapids School District v. Ball* (473 U.S. 373, 1985), the court used the Lemon test in regard to a Grand Rapids community education program that offered a variety of after-school classes, such as chess, home economics, and nature appreciation. The program employed parochial school teachers and used both public and religious school facilities. By a 7–2 vote, the court struck down the program, holding that although it had a secular purpose, it had an "impermissible effect of religious indoctrination."

In response to the *Aguilar* and *Ball* rulings, New York City revised its program by using mobile instructional units (vans) which they parked on public areas near religious schools, spending about $100 million to run the van program between 1986 and 1993. The Supreme Court reversed course in regard to "shared-time programs" in *Agostini v. Felton* (521 U.S. 203, 1997), in effect overturning *Ball* and *Aguilar* (Parker, Davison, and Finkelman 2003).

In *Zobrest v. Catalina Foothills School District* (509 U.S. 1, 1993), the court held, in a 5–4 decision, that under the Individuals with Disabilities Education Act (IDEA, 104 Stat. 1142, 1997), a public school was required to provide on-site services of a sign language interpreter to a hearing-impaired student attending a private religious school. Using the Lemon test, the court rejected the argument that it violated the Establishment Clause.

The use of school vouchers was the issue in *Zelman v. Simmons-Harris* (536 U.S. 639, 2002). In the *Zelman* case, by a 5–4 decision, the court upheld an Ohio program that used school vouchers, ruling that it did not violate the Establishment Clause even if the parents used the vouchers to send their child to parochial schools. Similar to the rationale of voucher programs, the use of tax credits for school expenses was at issue in *Arizona Christian School Tuition Organization v. Winn* (563 U.S. 125, 2011). An Arizona tax law gave credits for contributions to school tuition organizations to then be used to provide scholarships to students attending private and religious schools. The court rejected the respondents challenge to a tax credit as opposed to a governmental expenditure on the grounds that they lacked legal standing to sue.

Religion in Public Education

The U.S. Supreme Court handed down nine major or landmark decisions that addressed resolution to issues involving the use or introduction of religion into public education. In the case of *McCollum v. Board of Education* (333 U.S. 203, 1948), at issue was the use by religious groups of public school facilities in Champaign County, Illinois. The Champaign Board of Education allowed the use of public school buildings to representatives of Catholic, Protestant, and Jewish faiths to give religious instructions in public schools once per week. A resident and taxpayer sued in a state court for a writ of mandamus requiring the Board of Education to terminate this practice. The Supreme Court reversed the state supreme court's decisions to deny a writ of mandamus. The court held that public schools cannot allow religious groups to use their facilities to provide religious instruction to children.

In *Zorach v. Clauson* (343 U.S. 306, 1952), at issue was a New York state law that allowed New York City to permit its public schools to release students during school hours, on written request of the parents, to leave school buildings and grounds to go to religious centers for religious instruction and devotional exercises. The court decided that the New York City program did not violate the First Amendment's Establishment Clause in that it involved neither religious instruction in public schools nor the expenditure of public funds and that there was no evidence that the school system involved the use of coercion to get public school students into religious classrooms.

What about prayers in public schools? They were specifically at issue in *Engel v. Vitale* (370 U.S. 421, 1962). This was a landmark Supreme Court decision that, by a 6–1 ruling with two justices not taking part, held it is unconstitutional for state officials to compose an official school prayer and encourage its recitation in public schools. Likewise, in *Abington School District v. Schempp* (374 U.S. 203, 1963), in its 8–1 decision, the Supreme Court ruled that school-sponsored Bible reading in public schools was unconstitutional.

Epperson v. Arkansas (393 U.S. 97, 1968) was another landmark Supreme Court decision in which the unanimous court invalidated an Arkansas statute that prohibited the teaching of evolution in public schools as opposed to teaching creationism. The court overturned the Arkansas law on the grounds that it did not manifest religious neutrality.

In *Stone v. Graham* (449 U.S. 39, 1980), the Supreme Court ruled 5–4 that a Kentucky statute was an unconstitutional violation of the Establishment Clause because it lacked a nonreligious legislative purpose. The Kentucky law mandated the posting of a framed copy of the Ten Commandments in each public classroom in the state. Using the Lemon test, the court overturned the Kentucky statute.

In *Rosenberger v. University of Virginia* (515 U.S. 819, 1995), the court ruled 5–4 that the University of Virginia's denial of funding to a Christian student magazine due to the content of its message imposed a financial burden on the student, thus violating his free speech, and it amounted to *viewpoint discrimination*, contrary to the Establishment Clause.

In *Agostini v. Felton* (521 U.S. 203, 1997), the Supreme Court held that New York State did not violate the Establishment Clause by administering a federally funded program in which public school teachers provided remedial instruction in private and religious schools. In doing so, the court overturned its prior decisions in *Aguilar v. Felton* (473 U.S. 402, 1985) and *Grand Rapids School District v. Ball* (473 U.S. 373, 1985). In its 5–4 decision, Justice Sandra Day O'Connor's majority opinion held that the state's Title I program served a secular purpose in serving disadvantaged children.

Finally, *Mitchell v. Helms* (530 U.S. 793, 2000) was another case in which the court applied the Lemon test. In its 6–3 decision, the court used the test to assess a Louisiana program using the Educational Consolidation and Improvement Act of 1981 that gave federal funds to state educational agencies that in turn provided local educational agencies educational materials and equipment on loan to both public and private elementary and secondary schools to implement "secular, neutral, and non-ideological programs." The court found the program constitutional. It ruled that the loans were acceptable because they did not represent governmental indoctrination or advancement of religion and the loans were used in a nondiscriminatory and constitutional fashion to both secular and nonsecular private schools.

Government-Sponsored Religious Displays

Another establishment-based controversy involved questions of whether or not and under what conditions government-sponsored religious displays were permissible. The U.S. Supreme Court handed down five noteworthy decisions to provide some resolution of that question. In *Lynch v. Donnelly* (465 U.S. 668, 1984), the court rendered a 6–4 decision in regard to the use of a crèche (nativity) scene in a public display. The city of Pawtucket, Rhode Island, had for more than forty years annually erected a Christmas display in a park owned by a nonprofit organization located in the heart of the city's shopping district. The display included such objects as a Santa Claus house, a decorated Christmas tree, a banner reading "Season's Greetings," and a crèche. Respondents brought a suit in federal court challenging the inclusion of the crèche on the grounds that it violated the Establishment Clause. The court overturned a court of appeals injunction permanently banning the crèche in the display. It held that, notwithstanding the religious significance of the crèche, Pawtucket did not violate the Establishment Clause. Based on the city's record of having a secular purpose for the display and for including the crèche, it had not impermissibly advanced religion nor created an excessive entanglement between religion and government. In a similar case, in *Board of Trustees of Scarsdale v. McCreary* (471 U.S. 83, 1985), in an evenly split ruling, the court upheld per curiam a lower court's decision that a display of a privately sponsored nativity scene on public property does not violate the Establishment Clause.

The nativity scene display was at issue again in *County of Allegheny v. ACLU Greater Pittsburgh Chapter* (492 U.S. 573, 1989). This case concerned two recurring holiday displays located on public property in downtown Pittsburgh: a crèche in the county courthouse and an eighteen-foot Chanukah menorah or candelabrum placed just outside the City-County Building next to the city's forty-five-foot decorated Christmas tree. Justice Blackmun delivered the majority opinion of the splintered court that, under the Lemon test, the crèche display inside the courthouse violated the Establishment Clause but that another display, with the menorah and a Christmas tree and other decorations outside the City-County building, a block away from the courthouse, did not. Blackmun's majority opinion stressed whether the challenged governmental practice had the purpose or effect of "endorsing" religion. Using this "endorsement" test, the court held that the singular display of the nativity scene endorsed Christian religion. In his dissent, Justice Brennan argued that both displays violated the First Amendment. Justice Kennedy wrote a separate opinion arguing that the proper test should be whether the government used its "coercive powers to aid religion."

Coercive power was at issue in *McCreary County v. ACLU of Kentucky* (545 U.S. 844, 2005). The ACLU sued three Kentucky counties in federal district court for displaying framed copies of the Ten Commandments in courthouses and public schools, arguing that the displays violated the Establishment Clause. The case posed two questions: (1) were the displays in public schools and courthouses a violation of the Establishment Clause, and (2) was a determination that the display's purpose was to advance religion sufficient for the display's invalidation? The Supreme Court, in Justice David Souter's majority opinion, answered both questions in the affirmative, concluding that an observer would conclude that the government was endorsing religion and that an exhibit by the county "reached for any way to keep a religious document on the walls of courthouses."

Finally, in *Van Orden v. Perry* (545 U.S. 677, 2005), the court reached a different solution. Van Orden sued in a federal court, arguing that a Ten Commandments monument on the grounds of the Texas State Capitol violated the Establishment Clause. The federal district court and the Fifth Court of Appeals ruled against Van Orden, stating that the monument served a valid secular purpose and would not appear to a reasonable observer to represent a government endorsement of religion. In a 5–4 decision, delivered by Chief Justice William Rehnquist, the court agreed and held that the monument was part of the nation's tradition of recognizing the historical meaning of the Ten Commandments and that although the commandments are religious, the plurality argued, "simply having religious content or promoting a message consistent with religious doctrine does not run afoul of the establishment clause."

Prayers in Public Schools

Four U.S. Supreme Court decisions dealt directly with the question of the constitutionality of prayers in public schools, drawing some lines between permissibility and unconstitutionality. In *Wallace v. Jaffree* (472 U.S. 38, 1985), the constitutionality of the use of "silent" prayer was at issue, in this case challenging an Alabama law that authorized teachers to conduct regular religious prayer and silent meditation services in school classrooms during the school day. The court considered the question of whether the Alabama law violated the Establishment Clause. In a 6–3 decision, the majority opinion, written by Justice John Paul Stevens, determined that it did violate the Establishment Clause. The court applied the secular purpose test and held that Alabama's passage of the prayer and meditation statute was not only a deviation from the state's duty to maintain absolute neutrality toward religion but was also an affirmative endorsement of religion and lacked any secular purpose.

The principals of public middle and high schools in Providence, Rhode Island, were permitted to invite members of the clergy to give invocations and benedictions at their graduation ceremonies. A challenge to that statute was filed in *Lee v. Weisman* (505 U.S. 577, 1992). Lee, a middle school principal, invited a rabbi to offer prayers at the graduation ceremony. On behalf of his daughter, Deborah, Weisman sought a permanent injunction barring Lee and other Providence public school officials from inviting clergy to deliver invocations and benedictions at future graduations. The district court enjoined petitioners from continuing the practice, and a court of appeals affirmed that decision. The Supreme Court affirmed the decision as well, concluding that inviting clergy to offer prayers as part of an official school graduation ceremony is forbidden by the Establishment Clause.

Is a policy allowing student-led and student-initiated prayer at high school football games permissible? Prior to 1995, a student elected by the Santa Fe High School student council as its "chaplain" delivered a prayer over the public address system at each home varsity football game. Respondents, Mormon and Catholic students, alumni, and some mothers, filed a suit challenging the practice as a violation of the Establishment Clause. A district court ordered a modifying policy to permit only nonsectarian prayer. The Fifth Circuit Court, on appeal, held that even the modified prayer violated the Establishment Clause. In *Santa Fe Independent School District v. Doe* (530 U.S. 290, 2000) the Supreme Court, in a 7–2 decision, held that the school district's policy permitting student-led, student-initiated prayer at football games did violate the Establishment Clause.

Finally, there was the issue of public schools and the recitation of the Pledge of Allegiance with its words "under God." Elk Grove, California, teachers began school days by leading students in the Pledge of Allegiance, including the words "under God," which were added to the pledge by a 1954 act of Congress. The practice was challenged as unconstitutional on First Amendment establishment grounds in *Elk Grove Unified School District v. Newdow* (542 U.S. 1, 2004). Newdow sued in federal court, arguing that making students listen, even if they did not participate, to the words "under God" violates the Establishment Clause. The district court dismissed the suit on the basis that Newdow did not have standing to sue because he did not have custody of his daughter. Hearing the case on appeal, the Ninth Circuit Court ruled that the 1954 act adding the words "under God" to the pledge violated the Establishment Clause. The Supreme Court, in a unanimous opinion written by Justice John Paul Stevens, also found that Newdow did not have standing to sue because he did not have custody over his daughter. The court did not specifically address the constitutional question with regard to the pledge, but three of the justices wrote separate concurring opinions arguing that having teachers lead the recitation of the pledge is constitutional.

Sabbatarian Laws (Blue Laws)

The U.S. Supreme Court heard four cases challenging the constitutionality of Sabbatarian laws on the grounds of the Establishment Clause. In *McGowan v. Maryland* (366 U.S. 420, 1961), the court ruled 8–1 that laws with religious origins are not unconstitutional if they have a secular purpose. In this case, a large discount store in Anne Arundel County, Maryland, was fined for selling goods on Sunday in violation of a local and state blue law. (Laws prohibiting certain activities on Sundays are known as "blue laws," likely after Samuel A. Peters' 1781 work *General History of Connecticut*, which was printed on blue paper.) The court held that the U.S. Constitution does not ban federal, state, or local regulations of conduct if the reason or effect merely happens to coincide with tenets of some or all religions. It held that most Sunday laws are secular rather than of a religious character, promoting a "uniform day of rest" for all citizens. The majority opinion held that to ban such laws because they may have had their genesis in religion would be constitutional hostility toward public welfare rather than one of separation of church and state.

Braunfeld v. Brown (366 U.S. 599, 1961) was a similar Supreme Court decision in which the court held, 6–3, that a Pennsylvania law forbidding the sale of various retail products on Sunday was constitutional. Abraham Braunfeld owned a retail clothing and home furnishing store in Philadelphia. His Orthodox Judaism forbade him from working on Saturday, their Sabbath. Pennsylvania's blue law only allowed certain stores to remain open on Sundays, and his was not one of them. He challenged the blue law as a violation of the religious liberty law. The court held the Pennsylvania blue law did not violate the Free Exercise Clause and that the Sunday Closing Law had a secular basis and did not make any religious practice unlawful. The state had a secular purpose in providing for a uniform day of rest, and any indirect burden, such as an economic sacrifice that may be a result of the statute, did not make the blue law unconstitutional.

In *Gallagher v. Crown Kosher Super Market of Massachusetts* (366 U.S. 617, 1961), a Massachusetts statute was at issue. The owner and a majority of the patrons at Crown Kosher Super Market are members of the Orthodox Jewish faith, which forbids shopping on the Sabbath, in Judaism defined as from sundown on Friday to sundown on Saturday. Crown Kosher had previously been open on Sundays, when it did about one-third of its total weekly business. Massachusetts had enacted a statute forbidding shops to be open on Sunday. Crown Kosher brought suit, arguing that provision violated the Equal Protection Clause of the Fourteenth Amendment because it does not respect their religious practices.

The district court held that the statute was unconstitutional. The First Circuit Court of Appeals reversed the district court decision. The case was appealed to the U.S. Supreme Court. In a 6–3 decision, in a majority opinion written by Chief Justice Earl Warren, the court held that the law requiring stores to stay closed on Sunday did not violate the Fourteenth Amendment and that the Massachusetts statute does not prohibit the free exercise of religion simply because it might result in some inequality. The court concluded that the statute was not for religious purposes but had the secular purpose of providing a uniform day of rest. In dissenting opinions, Justices William Brennan and Potter Stewart argued that making a citizen choose between his faith and economic survival is a cruel choice as well as unconstitutional.

In *Thornton v. Caldor* (472 U.S. 703, 1985), the Supreme Court ruled 8–1 that government could not single out religious observers for special treatment when it found that a Connecticut law giving employees an absolute right not to work on their chosen Sabbath was in violation of the Establishment Clause of the First Amendment. Thornton, a Presbyterian, asserted he had a right not to work on Sundays because of his religious beliefs. Chief Justice Burger, writing for the majority, found that the Sabbath law had the primary effect of advancing a particular religious practice by promoting religious interests over all secular interests in the workplace.

Religious Institutions Functioning as Government Agencies

Three U.S. Supreme Court cases addressed and resolved controversies arising from policy enabling a religious institution to function, in effect, as a government agency. Can a church effectively act as a liquor licensing commission with respect to granting such a license? In *Larkin v. Grendel's Den* (459 U.S. 116, 1982), the Supreme Court struck down a Massachusetts law permitting churches to veto applications for liquor licenses. Grendel's Den is a popular Cambridge, Massachusetts, restaurant. It was denied a liquor license following an objection by its next-door neighbor, the Holy Cross Armenian Catholic Church. The Massachusetts statute permitted churches and schools to veto liquor license applications if the applying business was located within five hundred feet of the church or school. In its 8–1 decision, with the majority opinion written by Chief Justice Warren Burger, the court applied the Lemon test and held that the church's unregulated veto meant that there was no way to prevent it from advancing "explicitly religious goals," and, moreover, the law excessively entangled the church in the government process and therefore was unconstitutional on First Amendment Establishment Clause grounds.

In *Bowen v. Kendrick* (487 U.S. 589, 1988), the Supreme Court ruled that the 1981 Adolescent Family Life Act (AFLA), which channels federal funds to religious organizations via nonprofit organizations that offer adolescent pregnancy prevention and care services, does not violate the Establishment Clause. In the court's 5–4 majority opinion, Chief Justice William Rehnquist applied the Lemon test and held that the AFLA had a legitimate secular purpose—the prevention of teen pregnancy and the resulting social and economic costs. The court found that the AFLA's purpose and effect were neutral with respect to religion because religious affiliation was not a criterion in allocating funds and that the government's monitoring of applications was not enough to violate the "excessive government entanglement with religion" part of the Lemon test.

The *Board of Education of Kiryas Joel Village School District v. Grumet* (512 U.S. 687, 1994) was a case that centered on a 1989 New York statute that created a special school district that followed the village lines of Kiryas Joel, a village whose residents were all of the Salmar Hasidic sect. The district was created to accommodate the needs of disabled children and those with special education needs of the Salmar Hasidic sect. The Hasidic children with mental, physical, and emotional disabilities could not attend the religious sect's private schools because they were unable to bear the high costs of accommodating them, and the Hasidic Jewish leaders did not want them to attend nearby public schools located outside the village. The Supreme Court ruled 6–3 that the school district created by the special statute violated the Establishment Clause because it failed the test of neutrality in that it favored one religion over another. In essence, the New York state statute created a school district in which the Hasidic sect members functioned as the school board, and general taxpayer funding bore the cost of providing for the special needs children.

Tax Exemption to Religious Institutions

Three U.S. Supreme Court decisions provided resolution to the issue of the constitutionality of granting tax exemptions to religious institutions and whether such exemptions violated the Establishment Clause. In *Walz v. Tax Commission of the City of New York* (397 U.S. 664, 1970), the court confronted the question directly. Frederick Walz, a real estate owner in New York, sued the New York City Tax Commission, challenging the granting of tax exemptions for churches and alleging that such exemptions forced him, as a taxpayer, to indirectly contribute to those churches. The Supreme Court had to decide whether property tax exemptions to churches violate the Establishment

Clause of the First Amendment. In a 7–1 decision, with the majority opinion for the court written by Chief Justice Warren Burger, the court held that tax exemptions did not violate the Establishment Clause. The court found that the purpose of the exemptions was to neither advance nor inhibit religion, that no one particular church or religious group had been singled out to receive tax-exempt status, and that tax exemptions, unlike direct subsidies, did not unduly entangle the state with religion, creating only "minimal and remote" involvement between church and state and far less such entanglement than would taxation of churches. The court noted "benevolent neutrality" toward churches and religion was "deeply imbedded in the fabric of our national life."

Can tax-exempt status be given to a religious educational institution that racially discriminates in its admission policy? In *Bob Jones University v. the United States* (461 U.S. 574, 1983), the Supreme Court held that the racially discriminatory policies and practices of institutions such as Bob Jones University did not serve a legitimate public purpose and therefore concluded that in denying them tax-exempt status the IRS did not exceed its authority. The court further held that the government's interest in eliminating racial discrimination outweighed the private institution's exercise of religious beliefs. The Supreme Court's opinion held that because nonprofit private universities that enforce discriminatory admission policies based on religious doctrine do not qualify for tax exemptions, and contributions to such institutions are not deductible as charitable donations within the meaning of the Internal Revenue Code. In 2000, Bob Jones University acknowledged it had been wrong in not admitting African American students and lifted its ban on interracial dating as well.

Texas Monthly, Inc. v. Bullock (489 U.S. 1, 1989) was a case that tested the legality of a Texas statute that exempted religious publications from paying state sales tax. Texas Monthly, a nonreligious publisher, claimed this promoted religion in violation of the First Amendment's Establishment Clause. A state court agreed, ruling that the exemption violated the Establishment Clause by advancing religion and violated the Free Press Clause by discriminating on the basis of the content of the publication. It invalidated taxes levied on nonreligious publications and ordered the state to refund Texas Monthly's tax payments. A state appeals court reversed the lower court, and the case was appealed to the U.S. Supreme Court.

In a 6–3 decision, the Supreme Court held that the state did violate the Establishment Clause and the Free Press Clause by exempting religious publications from paying state taxes that all nonreligious publications had to pay. Applying the Lemon test, Justice William Brennan's majority opinion held that the Texas government "directs a subsidy exclusive to religious organizations" by providing the exemption and that the exemption did not have a secular purpose and used state mechanisms to give religious publishers an advantage over nonreligious publishers in violation of the Establishment Clause.

Legislative Chaplains and Prayers

Two U.S. Supreme Court decisions resolved questions about the use of legislative chaplains and prayers to open legislative sessions. In 1983, Ernest Chambers, a member of the Nebraska Legislature, challenged the state's chaplaincy practice in federal court. The practice involved offering a prayer at the opening of each legislative session by a chaplain chosen by the state and paid with public funds. The district court found for Chambers as to the use of public funds, and an appeals court held for Chambers on the prayer practice. Both parties appealed to the U.S. Supreme Court.

In *Marsh v. Chambers* (463 U.S. 783, 1983), the Supreme Court resolved the issue. In a 6–3 majority opinion by Chief Justice Warren Burger, the court upheld the chaplaincy practice. Chief Justice Burger did not apply the Lemon test. Instead, he rested the court's opinion on historical custom, ruling that the chaplaincy practice had become "part of the fabric of our society." Burger wrote that the invocation of divine guidance is "simply a tolerable acknowledgment of beliefs widely held among the people of this country."

Standing to Sue in Establishment Challenges

Two U.S. Supreme Court decisions addressed the issue of standing to sue in cases that raised challenges to law based on First Amendment Establishment Clause grounds. In *Flast v. Cohen* (392 U.S. 83, 1968), the court allowed taxpayers standing to sue within limited parameters. The *Flast* ruling stated that there needed to be a logical link between the status of the taxpayers and the type of enactment being challenged. The taxpayers had to show a link between the expenditure of funds and a specific challenge to congressional actions based on the Establishment Clause. The *Flast* ruling does not apply to general regulatory legislation.

Florence Flast alleged that the enforcement of the Elementary and Secondary Education Act of 1965 and its spending of funds for textbooks, instructional tools, and transportation extended to religious schools violated the Establishment Clause. A ruling at the district court level held that the plaintiffs lacked standing to sue. The Supreme Court ruled that Flast had standing based on a specific challenge to congressional action under the First Amendment's freedom of religion. The court's majority opinion held that the power to raise and spend money can be challenged by taxpayers if they allege that money spent will favor one specific religion or religion in general over nonreligion.

The court, however, has refused to extend the precedent set by the *Flast* ruling in several subsequent cases. In *Valley Forge Christian College v. Americans United for Separation of Church and State* (454 U.S. 464, 1982), the court refused to extend the *Flast* ruling. The Valley Forge Christian College (VFCC) case concerned the conveyance of surplus property from the U.S. Department of Health, Education, and Welfare (HEW) to the college. Congress enacted the Federal Property and Administrative Service Act of 1949 to allow for an economical and efficient system to dispose of surplus federal government property. The act authorizes the secretary of HEW to dispose of such property to nonprofit, tax-exempt educational institutions. The Americans United for Separation of Church and State brought suit in federal district court challenging the conveyance of the property to the Christian College on the grounds that it violated the Establishment Clause. The district court dismissed the complaint on the grounds that the respondents lacked standing to sue under the *Flast v. Cohen* ruling and failed to show any actual injury beyond a generalized grievance common to all taxpayers. A court of appeals reversed the district court's decision.

Respondents appealed to the Supreme Court, which held that the respondents do not have standing, either in their capacity as taxpayers or as citizens, to challenge the conveyance in question. Judicial power, the majority opinion held, is restricted to litigants who can show "injury in fact." The ruling also found that the respondents lacked standing to sue as taxpayers because the source of their complaint is not a congressional action but a decision by HEW to transfer a parcel of federal property. The court again refused to extend the *Flast* precedent in *Hein v. Freedom from Religion Foundation* (551 U.S. 587, 2007).

Teaching Creationism in Public Schools

In *Edwards v. Aguillard* (482 U.S. 578, 1987), the U.S. Supreme Court resolved a question of whether it was permissible to mandate the teaching of creationism in public schools. The U.S. Supreme Court considered the constitutionality of a Louisiana state law requiring that where evolutionary science was taught (in public high school biology or natural science classes), that "creation science" must also be taught. The court applied the three-pronged Lemon test. Creationism is a biblical belief that advanced forms of life abruptly appeared. In schools that taught evolution, teachers were required to discuss creationism as well.

In a 7–2 decision, the court held that the Louisiana law violated the Establishment Clause. The majority opinion of Justice William Brennan found that (1) the Louisiana law lacked a clear secular purpose, (2) the law's primary effect was to advance the viewpoint that a "supernatural being created humankind," and (3) the law significantly entangled the interests of church in state by seeking "the symbolic and financial support of government to achieve a religious purpose."

Unequal Government Treatment of Religious Groups

In *Larson v. Valente* (456 U.S. 228, 1982), the U.S. Supreme Court considered a constitutional challenge to a 1961 statute enacted by the Minnesota State Legislature. The Charitable Solicitation Act established a system of registering charitable organizations that solicit money, requiring them to file annual reports with the Minnesota Department of Commerce (MDC). In 1978, the state legislature amended the act to include a provision that religious organizations that receive more than 50 percent of their funds from solicitation of nonmembers must so register and report annually. The MDC so notified the Holy Spirit Association for the Unification of World Christianity (or the Unification Church). Pamela Valente and other church members sued, alleging that the act violated the First and Fourteenth Amendments.

A district court granted summary judgement in favor of the plaintiff. The U.S. Court of Appeals for the Eighth Circuit affirmed in part and reversed in part. The court of appeals affirmed that the 50 percent rule violated the Establishment Clause, but it held proof of status as a religious organization was required to be exempt from the act. In a 5–4 decision, the majority opinion by Justice William Brennan found that the Minnesota law failed the three-part test established in *Lemon v. Kurtzman* (Lemon test) by fostering the government entanglement in religion and by its 50 percent provision.

Free Exercise Clause

Despite the simplicity of the language of the First Amendment's Free Exercise Clause—indeed, it is better said *because* of that simplicity—religious freedom has been embroiled in controversy. Controversies over the precise meaning of the Free Exercise

Clause and the limits it imposes on governments—especially state and local governments—have typically involved minority religions. U.S. Supreme Court decisions have discerned a difference between members of a minority religion being free to exercise their belief versus their freedom to put that belief into practice when the resulting behavior was viewed by society as in some manner threatening to the health, safety, or similar "public interest," for example, bigamy laws being used against the Mormon practice of polygamy. Minority religions involved in adjudication over religious free exercise include, for example, the Old Order Amish and Mennonites and society's compulsory education laws, the Jehovah's Witnesses and their aggressive proselytism versus city nuisance ordinances or their objection to saluting the flag, the aforementioned Church of Jesus Christ of the Latter-day Saints (more commonly known as the Mormons), and the Unification Church and city ordinances regarding solicitation of donations (LeMay 2018). Such problems and the need of the courts, and especially the U.S. Supreme Court, to resolve them more often arise when the religious minority group or sect is one that actively, some might say aggressively, proselytizes; that is, members go door-to-door seeking to convert new members or actively solicit donations from the general public.

Solicitations by Religious Groups

This section discusses seven important U.S. Supreme Court decisions wherein the case involved problems with the rights of members of a religious group to solicit the public for donations that were mostly decided in the 1940s but even up to 1981. Six of the seven cases involved the Jehovah's Witnesses and one the Krishna sect. In *Cantwell v. Connecticut* (310 U.S. 296, 1940), a unanimous Supreme Court held that the government has no role in determining religious truth and that the peaceful expression of beliefs, even religious views that may be offensive to some, is protected by the First Amendment. The court ruled that the Connecticut government could not require special permits for religious solicitation.

Requiring Jehovah's Witnesses to obtain a license was at issue in several cases. In *Jones v. City of Opelika-I* (316 U.S. 584, 1942), the court ruled on an Alabama city ordinance that required licenses be procured and fees be paid for conducting business within the municipality, including selling books and pamphlets on the streets and from house-to-house. The case was brought by Jehovah's Witnesses members who challenged the ordinance on free exercise grounds. In a 5–4 decision, the court held that the statute was constitutional because it only covered individuals who engaged in a commercial activity, not a religious ritual. Jehovah's Witnesses were also a party to a suit on freedom of religion in *Marsh v. State of Alabama* (326 U.S. 501, 1946). In the *Marsh* case, at issue was whether a company-owned town (Chickasaw, Alabama), a suburb of Mobile with a business block, as opposed to a public municipality, could require a license for the distribution of religious literature without receiving prior permission from the town's management, which was appointed by the company. The Supreme Court held, 5–3, against the town because its shopping district was freely accessible to and freely used by the public in general and that their use of the power of the state to criminally punish those who attempted to distribute religious literature violated the First and Fourteenth Amendments.

In *Murdock v. Pennsylvania* (319 U.S. 105, 1943), the court held, 5–4, that a Jeannette, Pennsylvania, ordinance requiring solicitors to purchase a license from the borough was an unconstitutional tax on religious exercise and that the state may not impose a charge for the enjoyment of a right protected by the U.S. Constitution. It ruled similarly in *Jones v. City of Opelika-II* (319 U.S. 103, 1943), which overturned the *Opelika I* decision of 1942. A change in one member of the Supreme Court made the difference in the new 1943 case reversing the 1942 decision.

What if the local ordinance concerned a child labor law? In *Prince v. Massachusetts* (321 U.S. 158, 1944), the court decided another case involving the Jehovah's Witnesses. Sarah Prince was a Witness member who was the guardian of a nine-year-old girl. She took the girl with her to sell pamphlets on the public streets. Prince was convicted for violating a child labor law by having her dependent involved in selling Jehovah's Witnesses literature on public streets. The state law provided that no minor (defined as a boy under twelve or a girl under eighteen) shall sell or offer to sell on the streets or other public places any newspaper, magazine, periodical, or other article of merchandise. In its 5–4 decision in *Prince,* the court upheld the Massachusetts law, ruling that the government had broad authority to regulate the actions and treatment of children (LeMay 2018, 86–87).

The Hare Krishna cult was involved in the case *Heffron v. International Society for Krishna Consciousness* (452 U.S. 640, 1981). The case involved a Minnesota statute that allowed the Minnesota Agricultural Society to devise rules to regulate the state fair in St. Paul. One rule required organizations wishing to sell or distribute goods and written materials to do so from an assigned location (a booth) on the fairgrounds. Walking vendors or solicitors were not allowed. The Krishna Society challenged the rule, arguing it restricted their free exercise of religious beliefs at the state fair.

In its 5–4 decision, the court upheld the rule. Using the Cox test, a valid time, manner, and place criteria that the court employs to assess government restrictions on First Amendment cases, the court held that the rule did not violate the Constitution in that it was applied equally to all groups wanting to solicit on the fairgrounds. The majority opinion stated that allowing all religious, nonreligious, and commercial groups to move about the grounds distributing literature and soliciting funds would potentially be dangerous to the fair's visitors.

Religious Tests for Public Benefits or Services

Can an atheist be required to swear an oath to be appointed to a public office? That was the issue in *Torcaso v. Watkins* (376 U.S. 488, 1961). The U.S. Supreme Court reaffirmed that the

U.S. Constitution prohibits state and federal governments from requiring any kind of a religious test for public office. Torcaso, a notary public and avowed atheist, was denied a commission as notary for refusing to swear an oath declaring a belief in God, as required by the Maryland Constitution. A court of appeals affirmed the state constitution, but the Supreme Court reversed that decision. Justice Hugo Black delivered the unanimous opinion of the court.

Conflict between the Establishment Clause and the Free Exercise Clause, and between religious belief versus religious action, and the right to religious belief versus the right to run for public office were at issue in *McDaniel v. Paty* (435 U.S. 618, 1978). Paty, a candidate for a Tennessee constitutional convention, sued in the state chancery court for a judgment that appellant McDaniel, an opponent who was a Baptist minister, was disqualified from serving as a delegate by a Tennessee law on the qualifications for constitutional convention delegates to be the same as for membership in the State House of Representatives, which barred ministers or priests of any denomination. The Tennessee Supreme Court upheld the statute. The U.S. Supreme Court, in a unanimous decision written by Chief Justice Warren Burger, reversed the decision of the Tennessee Supreme Court, holding that the challenged provision violated the appellant's right to the free exercise of religion, applied to the states by the Fourteenth Amendment, because it conditions his right to the free exercise of his religion on his surrendering the right to seek public office.

The case of *Thomas v. Review Board of the Indiana Employment Division* (450 U.S. 707, 1981) resolved a conflict between free exercise and establishment. Petitioner Thomas, a Jehovah's Witness, was hired to work at a roll foundry fabricating sheet steel for industrial use. When the foundry closed, he was transferred to a department of the company that fabricated turrets for military tanks. He asked to be laid off, asserting his religious beliefs prevented him from participating in the production of weapons of war. Thomas applied for unemployment benefits and was denied. The Indiana Court of Appeals reversed the review board's decision. The Indiana Supreme Court vacated the court of appeals' decision and denied benefits, holding Thomas had quit voluntarily for personal reasons, a "personal philosophical choice." The U.S. Supreme Court, in the majority opinion written by Chief Justice Warren Burger, held that a person may not be compelled to choose between First Amendment right and participation in an otherwise available public program and that the payment of unemployment benefits would not involve the state in fostering a religious faith in violation of the First Amendment's freedom of religion clauses.

Free exercise of religion versus the need for military uniformity was the conflict at issue in *Goldman v. Weinberger* (475 U.S. 503, 1986). Petitioner Goldman was an air force officer and a practicing Jew. He was denied the right to wear a yarmulke when in uniform on the grounds that the Free Exercise Clause applies less strictly to the military than to ordinary citizens. He was ordered not to wear a yarmulke while on duty and in uniform indoors as a commissioned officer at the March Air Force Base pursuant to air force regulations; authorized headgear could be worn outside, but such headgear was not to be worn indoors except by armed security police in the performance of their duties. The Supreme Court upheld the air force regulations, drawing the line essentially between religious apparel that is visible and that which is not and observing that the challenged air force regulation reasonably and evenhandedly regularized dress in the interest of the military's perceived need for uniformity.

The Supreme Court established limits on the freedom of religion in its 8–1 decision in *Bowen v. Roy* (476 U.S. 693, 1986). The plaintiffs were Native American parents who applied for financial aid under an Aid to Families with Dependent Children (AFDC) welfare program. Roy and his family were receiving benefits—AFDC and food stamps. When they refused to provide a Social Security number for their daughter, Little Bird, on the grounds that it violated their Native American religious beliefs, the Pennsylvania Department of Welfare terminated their benefits. The Roys argued that the Free Exercise Clause provided an exemption to the Social Security number requirement. In the lower court, Roy disclosed that Little Bird had a Social Security number but that the widespread use of the number would "rob the spirit" of Little Bird, violating their religious beliefs. The Supreme Court restrained the government from denying benefits for Little Bird until she was sixteen, but denied Roy's request for damages.

Free Exercise and Public Education

Five U.S. Supreme Court decisions drew lines and distinctions on limits on the free exercise and public policy and law regarding public education, particularly mandatory public education attendance laws. In *Wisconsin v. Yoder* (406 U.S. 205, 1972), the Supreme Court ruled that Amish adolescents could be exempt from a state law requiring school attendance for all fourteen- and fifteen-year-olds because their religion required living apart from the world and worldly influence. The court recognized that the Old Order Amish and the Conservative Amish Mennonites had demonstrated three centuries of being religious sects and that they had a long history of being a successful and self-sufficient segment of society. The court held that the state's interest in universal education is not totally free from a balancing process when it infringes on other fundamental rights, such as those protected by the Free Exercise Clause.

In *Widmar v. Vincent* (454 U.S. 263, 1981), the U.S. Supreme Court ruled against the University of Missouri at Kansas City, a state university, making its facilities available for activities of registered student groups. One such group was denied access to university buildings for holding worship or religious teaching. In a 7–2 decision, the Supreme Court held that the university's exclusionary policy violated the fundamental principle that a state regulation should be content neutral and affirmed the court of appeals decision that the regulations were content-based discrimination against religious speech.

The court found no compelling justification to bar equal access to facilities that were open to groups and speakers of all kinds.

Equal access for religious groups in public schools was also at issue in the *Board of Education of Westside Community Schools v. Mergens* (496 U.S. 226, 1990). In 1984, Congress passed the Equal Access Act, which requires public schools to give religious groups the same access to facilities as other extracurricular groups. The Equal Access Act forbids public schools from receiving federal funds if they deny students the First Amendment right to conduct meetings because of "religious, political, or other content of the speech at such meetings.

The Equal Access Act was motivated by *Widmar v. Vincent* (1981), which guaranteed those protections on public university campuses. It was the part of an ongoing effort by religious conservatives to secure a presence for religion in public schools at the middle and secondary levels following the decisions in *Engle v. Vitale* (370 U.S. 421, 1962) and *Abington School District v. Schempp* (374 U.S. 203, 1963). In *Mergens*, the court ruled that allowing religious clubs to meet is not a violation of the Establishment Clause, distinguishing between "curriculum" and "noncurriculum" student groups. Because Westside permitted other noncurricular clubs, it was prohibited by the Equal Access Act from denying equal access to any other after-school club based on the content of its speech.

In *Lambs Chapel v. Center Moriches Union Free School District* (508 U.S. 384, 1993) the court dealt with the question of whether a public school could prohibit the use of its property to any religious group. The Center Moriches School District prohibited the use of its property for any religious group, refusing repeated requests for an after-hours religious-oriented film series on family values and child-rearing. In *Lambs Chapel*, the Supreme Court, by unanimous vote, held that the school district violated the First Amendment on two grounds: (1) it had denied the requests solely on the basis that such movies were religious oriented, and (2) the district's granting of permission would not have amounted to an establishment of religion because the showing of the films would be neither school-sponsored during school hours nor closed to the public.

Finally, the problem of religion in education was at issued in *Rosenberger v. Rector and Visitors of the University of Virginia* (515 U.S. 819, 1995), which had religious free expression as well as establishment considerations. Rosenberger, a University of Virginia student, requested $5,800 from a student activities fund to subsidize the cost to publish "Wide Awake: A Christian Perspective at the University of Virginia." The University refused funding solely because the publication "primarily promotes or manifests a particular belief in or about a deity or an ultimate reality," thereby prohibited by university guidelines. In its 5–4 opinion, the court held that the university's denial of funding due to the content of the message imposed a financial burden on Rosenberger's speech and amounted to viewpoint discrimination. The court ruled that if the university chooses to promote free speech at all, it must do so equally and be "content neutral." The court held that the University of Virginia must provide financial subsidy to a student religious publication on the same basis as other student publications (LeMay 2018, 94–95).

Religion and the Right to Work

Some religious beliefs affect when and on what their adherents can work. Over the course of three decades, five U.S. Supreme Court decisions have addressed problems arising from religious beliefs and the right to work, clarifying limits and the rights accorded to persons with such religious beliefs protected by the First Amendment's Free Exercise Clause. The court devised guidelines to determine those limits (LeMay 2018, 95–99).

In *Sherbert v. Verner* (374 U.S. 398, 1963), the court distinguished what became known as the Sherbert test. Sherbert, the appellant, was a member of the Seventh-day Adventist Church. She was fired by her employer, a textile mill in South Carolina, because she would not work on Saturday, her Sabbath day. She filed for unemployment benefits and was denied under the South Carolina Unemployment Compensation Act. The Supreme Court, in a 7–2 decision, held that the law abridged her right to the free exercise of her religion, violating the First Amendment. The majority of the court held that the state showed no compelling state interest enforced under the eligibility provisions of the state law. The Sherbert test stipulated that there must be a compelling state interest shown and that provisions for denying benefits must be narrowly tailored.

Work-shift scheduling can involve complex issues in agreements with employer, employee, unions, and state laws. Such complexities were at issue in *Transworld Airlines, Inc. v. Hardison* (432 U.S. 63, 1977). Hardison worked for TWA at an airplane maintenance and overhaul base at which work scheduling was strictly based on a seniority system in which the most senior employee had first choice in job shift assignment per a collective bargaining agreement between TWA and the International Association of Machinists & Aerospace Workers. When he was transferred to a job at which he had less seniority, he was assigned to work on Saturdays, his Sabbath day. The union and TWA refused to violate the seniority system, and Hardison sued. A court of appeals affirmed judgment for the union but held that TWA had not satisfied its duty to accommodate respondent's religious needs under the Equal Employment Opportunity Commission guidelines. The Supreme Court reversed the court of appeals' decision, holding that (1) the seniority system itself was a significant accommodation to the needs—both religious and secular—of all of TWA's employees; (2) TWA could not be faulted for failing to work out a shift or job swap for the respondent; (3) absent a discriminatory purpose, the seniority system cannot be an unlawful employment practice; and (4) requiring TWA to bear substantial costs to give respondent Saturdays off would be an undue hardship.

Likewise, work cases can sometimes raise complex issues involving state and federal jurisdiction as well as Free Exercise, Establishment, and Equal Protection Clauses. In *Ohio Civil Rights Commission v. Dayton Christian Schools* (477 U.S. 619,

1986), the appellee was the Dayton Christian School, a non-profit elementary and secondary private Christian school that requires its teachers to subscribe to a particular set of religious beliefs, including internal resolution of disputes through the "biblical chain of command." After a pregnant teacher was told her contract would not be renewed because their doctrine said that mothers should stay at home with preschool-aged children, she contacted an attorney. The school then fired her for violation of the internal dispute resolution requirement. She filed suit with the Ohio Civil Rights Commission, alleging sex discrimination. The commission began proceedings against the school, which answered the complaint by asserting that the First Amendment prevented the commission from exercising jurisdiction over the complaint. A district court refused to issue an injunction, ruling the commission's actions did not violate the First Amendment. A court of appeals then heard the case and ruled that the commission's actions would not violate the First and Fourteenth Amendments.

The Supreme Court held that the district court should have abstained from adjudicating the case, and it reversed and remanded the case. The court held that it is sufficient under Ohio law that constitutional claims may be raised in state court judicial review of administrative proceedings (i.e., by the Civil Rights Commission). Chief Justice Rehnquist delivered the 5–4 decision finding that the court of appeals erred in ruling that the commission's jurisdiction violated both the Free Exercise and Establishment Clauses and the Equal Protection Clause of the Fourteenth Amendment. Instead, it should have invoked the federal abstention doctrine.

The Mormon Church was involved in a similarly highly complex issue in *Corporation of the Presiding Bishop of the Church of Jesus Christ of Latter-Day Saints v. Amos* (483 U.S. 327, 1987). In this case, Arthur Mayson had worked for sixteen years as an engineer at the Deseret Gymnasium, a nonprofit facility in Salt Lake City. The Corporation of the Presiding Bishop (CPB) fired him when he failed to obtain a certificate authorizing him to attend the church's religious temple. He filed a class action suit in district court, alleging the CPB violated the Civil Rights Act of 1964 by dismissing him for failing to satisfy certain religious conditions. The CPB claimed that Section 702 exempted them from claims of religious discrimination. Mayson claimed Section 702 violated the Establishment Clause by allowing religious organizations to practice discriminatory hiring for nonreligious jobs. The district court agreed that his job was nonreligious and that Section 702 violated the Establishment Clause because it allowed religious adherents exclusive participation in nonreligious jobs. The Supreme Court, in a unanimous decision, held that Section 702 did not violate the Establishment Clause because it passed the three-part Lemon test of *Lemon v. Kurtzman*. In this case, the government allowed for a church to advance in religion but did not directly intervene, and by allowing religious organizations to employ whomever they pleased, the state became less entangled in religion.

The Native American Church was involved in a case involving religious freedom versus the government's right to enact drug laws. In *Employment Division v. Smith* (494 U.S. 872, 1990), two Native American workers, who served as counselors in an Oregon-located private drug rehabilitation organization, were fired because they used peyote—a powerful hallucinogen— as part of their religious ceremonies as members of the Native American Church. They filed for unemployment compensation benefits, which were denied because the government ruled they were fired for work-related misconduct. The U.S. Supreme Court vacated the Oregon Supreme Court's judgment against the employees and remanded the case for determination whether or not sacramental use of illegal drugs violated Oregon's drug law. On remand, the Oregon Supreme Court ruled that although Oregon drug laws prohibited use of illegal drugs for sacramental religious uses, this prohibition violated the Free Exercise Clause. The case was then returned to the U.S. Supreme Court to determine whether a state can deny unemployment benefits to a worker fired for using illegal drugs for religious purposes.

In a 6–3 decision, the court ruled that the state could deny benefits. In his majority opinion, Justice Antonin Scalia held that an individual's religious beliefs did not excuse him from compliance with an otherwise valid law prohibiting conduct that the government is free to regulate. Scalia wrote, "Allowing exceptions to every state law or regulation affecting religion would open the prospect of constitutionality required exemptions from civic obligations of almost every conceivable kind." His opinion cited compulsory military service, payment of taxes, vaccination requirements, and child-neglect laws.

Government Intrusion into Church Internal Affairs

Several U.S. Supreme Court cases involved judicial resolution concerning problems in which the parties were churches asking the government to intervene in a church controversy or to judge whether the defendants truly believed their claimed religious belief (LeMay 2018, 100–103). Five such cases that occurred between 1944 and 2012 will be briefly discussed here.

The case of *United States v. Ballard* (322 U.S. 78, 1944) was an appeal of a fraud conviction of two leaders of a new religious movement, *I Am Activity*, for fraudulently seeking and collecting donations totaling $3 million on the basis of religious claims that they themselves did not believe. In the *Ballard* ruling, the Supreme Court held that the question of whether their claims about their religious beliefs and experiences were actually true should not have been submitted to a jury. In his majority opinion for the 5–4 decision of the court overturning the fraud conviction, Justice William Douglas opined, "Freedom of religious belief embraces the right to maintain theories of life and death and of the hereafter which are rank heresy to followers of orthodox faiths. . . . The First Amendment does not select any one group or any one type of religion for preferred treatment. It puts them all in that position."

Does the fear of potential subversive activity by a church leader justify the intrusion of the government into internal church disputes? That was at the heart of a 1952 case that occurred during the Korean War involving a dispute with the Russian Orthodox Church in New York City. *Kedroff v. St. Nicholas Cathedral* (344 U.S. 94, 1952) concerned a dispute over a New York corporation holding title to a property for the court to determine which prelate was entitled to occupancy and use of a cathedral. The court of appeals held for the plaintiff on the grounds that the Religious Corporation Law of New York had the purpose of affecting the transfer of administrative control of the Russian Orthodox Church in North America from the Supreme Church Authority in Russia to authorities selected by a convention of the North American churches. In *Kedroff*, the Supreme Court held that the New York state statute interferes with the free exercise of religion and that the New York law had acted inappropriately in determining for the Russian Orthodox Church, a hierarchical church in its ecclesiastical administration, appointment of clergy, and the transfer of a church property from one group to another within the broader church. The court found that doing so interferes with the free exercise of religion and is contrary to the U.S. Constitution.

Court involvement in settling internal property disputes was also at the heart of the decision in *Presbyterian Church v. Hull Church* (393 U.S. 440, 1969). The U.S. Supreme Court heard the case involving two local churches in Georgia. The local churches had voted to withdraw from the national church, with which they had a doctrinal dispute, and wanted to reconstitute themselves as autonomous religious organizations. A tribunal of the general church took over the respondent's property on behalf of the general church. The Georgia Supreme Court enjoined the general church from trespassing on the disputed property. The general church moved to dismiss the case and cross-claimed for injunctive relief on the grounds that civil courts had no power to determine whether the general church had departed from its tenets of faith and practices. The motion to dismiss was denied, and the case went to jury on the theory that Georgia's statute implied a trust of local church property for the benefit of the general church adheres to doctrinal tenets existing at the time of the affiliation with the local churches. The jury, having been instructed to determine whether the general church had substantially abandoned its original doctrines, found for the respondents, and the trial judge issued an injunction against the general church, which was affirmed by the state supreme court.

The U.S. Supreme Court reversed, holding that civil courts cannot, consistent with the First Amendment, determine ecclesiastical questions in resolving property disputes. The court held that Georgia's "implied trust" theory requires civil courts to weigh the significance and meaning of religious doctrine. The court held the meaning of religious doctrine can play no role in judicial proceedings.

Another dispute within the Georgia Presbyterian Church was at issue in *Jones v. Wolf* (443 U.S. 595, 1979). Again, the case involved a dispute in a local church that was an affiliate of a hierarchical church organization over the ownership of church property following a schism. The property of the Vineville Presbyterian Church in Macon, Georgia, (the local church) was held in trust by the local church. The church was established affiliated with the Presbyterian Church of the United States (PCUS), a hierarchical form of government. At a congregational meeting of the local church, 164 members voted to separate from the national church, and 94 opposed the resolution. The minority faction brought class action in state court seeking declaratory and injunctive orders giving them exclusive right to the property as members of the PCUS. The trial court, applying Georgia's "neutral principles of law," granted judgment to the majority, which was affirmed by the Georgia Supreme Court.

On appeal, the U.S. Supreme Court held that the process of identifying the factions is to be determined by the laws and regulations of the PCUS. The court held that the First Amendment requires that Georgia courts give deference to the Presbyterian commission's determination that the minority faction represents the true congregation. The Georgia Supreme Court's decision was vacated and remanded.

Finally, the U.S. Supreme Court grappled with internal church disputes in *Hosanna-Tabor Evangelical Lutheran Church and School v. Equal Employment Opportunity Commission* (EEOC) (565 U.S. 171, 2012). Chief Justice John Roberts delivered the unanimous decision of the court. The petitioner, Hosanna-Tabor Evangelical Church and School, is an affiliated and congregational member of the Missouri Synod of the Lutheran Church. They have two types of teachers at the school: *called* and *lay*. Lay are not required to be trained by the synod. Respondent Perich completed her synod training and became a called teacher and a commissioned minister. She later developed narcolepsy and began the 2004–2005 year on disability leave. When she reported that she could return to work in February, the principal responded that the school had contracted a lay teacher to fill her position for the year. The congregation offered to pay a portion of her health insurance premiums in exchange for her resignation as a called teacher. She refused to resign and reported to work but was not allowed to teach. The school and congregational board voted to rescind her call, and Hosanna-Tabor sent her a termination letter. She filed a charge with the EEOC claiming the termination violated the Americans with Disabilities Act (ADA), but Hosanna-Tabor invoked the "ministerial exception" to the act. The district court granted summary judgment to Hosanna-Tabor. The Sixth Circuit Court of Appeals vacated and remanded, concluding that Perich did not qualify as a "minister" under the exception rule.

The U.S. Supreme Court held that (1) the Establishment and Free Exercises Clauses bar suits on behalf of ministers against their church; (2) because Perich was a minister within the meaning of the exception, the First Amendment requires dismissal of the employment discrimination suit against her employer; and (3) the ministerial exception only bars an unemployment suit brought on behalf of a minister challenging her church's decision to fire her. The court's decision expresses no views on whether the exception bars other types of suits.

Free Exercise versus Eminent Domain

The U.S. Supreme Court issued decisions in two important cases that dealt with the government's eminent domain authority versus claims of freedom of religion. In *Lyng v. Northwest Indian Cemetery Protective Association* (485 U.S. 439, 1988), the conflict was between the U.S. Forest Service's eminent domain authority and claims by Native Americans about sacred lands that were seized to build a road for timber harvesting. The land in question was the Chimney Rock area of the Six Rivers National Forest, located in California. Opposed to the plan's effect on nearby sacred sites used for religious ceremonies, an Indian organization, several individual Indians, and nature organizations sued in federal court challenging the use of eminent domain for both road building and timber harvesting on the grounds that the plans violated the American Indian Religious Freedom Act (92 Stat. 469, 1978). The 1978 act was expressly created to protect and preserve the traditional religious rights and cultural practices of American Indians, Eskimos, Aleuts, and Native Hawaiians. The Supreme Court affirmed that the Free Exercise Clause does not prohibit the government from permitting timber harvesting in the Chimney Rock area, nor the construction of the proposed road.

In *City of Boerne v. Flores* (521 U.S. 507, 1997), the court ruled on a conflict between a local zoning ordinance board and a church. The archbishop of San Antonio filed suit claiming that the local zoning authority violated his rights under the Religious Freedom Restoration Act of 1993 (RFRA; 42 U.S.C. 2000) that was enacted to "ensure that interests in religious freedom are protected." The bishop alleged the act was violated by the local zoning authority's denying him a permit to expand his church in Boerne. The zoning authority argued it had refused the permit because the church was located in an historic preservation district that forbids new construction and that the RFRA was unconstitutional.

The court, in a 6–3 decision, ruled for the city of Boerne, holding that the U.S. Congress had exceeded its Fourteenth Amendment enforcement powers by enacting the RFRA in that it subjected local ordinances to federal regulation. The opinion held that there was no evidence that the historic preservation ordinance favored one religion over another or that it was passed on animus or hostility for free religious exercise or expression.

Free Exercise of Religion versus Freedom of Speech

The U.S. Supreme Court heard two cases in which the conflict was between two sacred First Amendment rights: the free exercise of religion and freedom of speech. In *R. A. V. v. City of St. Paul* (505 U.S. 377, 1992), the question was whether a hate crime or speech was protected free speech. The Supreme Court unanimously struck down a St. Paul, Minnesota, ordinance that proscribed cross burning and other actions that "one knows or has reasonable grounds to know" will cause "anger, alarm or resentment in others on the basis of race, color, creed, religion, or gender." The local ordinance was an attempt to join a "hate crime" to the "fighting words" exemption of free speech. The Supreme Court found the St. Paul ordinance was unconstitutional, but the justices differed on the grounds for doing so. Justices White, Blackmun, Stevens, and O'Connor did so solely on the grounds that the ordinance was overly broad. Five justices concurred in the majority opinion of Justice Antonin Scalia that found the ordinance "an unconstitutional content-based regulation of speech."

Conflict between the RFRA of 1993 and the Controlled Substance Act was what the court had to decide in *Gonzales v. O Centro Espirita Beneficente Uniao do Vegetal* (UDV) (546 U.S. 418, 2006). UDV is a small religious sect from the Amazon region of Brazil. It sued Attorney General Gonzales to prevent the U.S. Department of Justice (DOJ) from interfering with its use of *hoasca*, a hallucinogenic herbal tea that they used during religious ceremonies. They alleged that the RFRA of 1993 established their right to use *hoasca*. The district court ruled in favor of UDV, which was affirmed by the Tenth Circuit Court of Appeals. Attorney General Gonzales argued prohibiting the drug was required by international treaty.

The Supreme Court had to decide whether the RFRA required the government to permit the importation, distribution, possession, and use of an otherwise illegal drug by a religious organization when Congress found the drug had high potential for abuse, was unsafe, and violated an international treaty against its importation and distribution. In an 8–0 decision, the court answered yes. Chief Justice John Roberts wrote the majority opinion, finding the government had failed to prove a compelling interest in regulating UDV's use of the drug for religious purposes. The court held that it was required by the RFRA to examine individual religious freedom claims and grant exceptions to generally applicable laws absent showing a compelling government interest.

Polygamy and Religious Freedom Rights

The Church of Jesus Christ of Latter-day Saints (more commonly known as Mormons) practiced polygamy based on a "religious doctrine of celestial marriage." That practice directly conflicted with bigamy laws. The U.S. Supreme Court had to resolve that conflict in two cases. In *Reynolds v. United States* (98 U.S. 145, 1878) the court upheld a federal law banning polygamy. The court ruled that although the Free Exercise Clause forbids the government to regulate *belief*, it does allow the government to regulate *actions*, such as marriage. George Reynolds was convicted and sentenced to two years' hard labor and a fine by the Territory of Utah for bigamy in violation of the Morrill Anti-Bigamy Act of 1862.

In *Reynolds*, Chief Justice Morrison Waite wrote the unanimous opinion holding that religious duty is not a sustainable defense to a criminal indictment. In a follow-up decision, *Davis v. Beason* (133 U.S. 333, 1890), the court was blunt and direct in deciding on the question of free exercise of religion. In a 9–0 decision, the court ruled that the federal law against polygamy did not conflict with the Free Exercise Clause, stating, "Bigamy and polygamy are crimes by the laws of the United States, by the laws of Idaho, and by the laws of all civilized and Christian countries, and to call their advocacy a tenet in religion is to offend the common sense of mankind. A crime is nonetheless so, nor less odious, because sanctioned by what any particular sect may designate as religious."

Ritual Sacrifice of Animals and Religious Freedom

What is the solution when there is a conflict between religious belief and practice that involves the ritual sacrifice of animals (in this case, chickens), local ordinances protecting animal cruelty, and the applicability of the Free Exercise Clause? That problem was addressed in *Church of Lukumi Babalu Aye v. City of Hialeah* (508 U.S. 520, 1993). The Yoruba people were brought to Cuba as slaves by the hundreds of thousands. They brought with them the practices of the Santeria religion, of which the Church of Lukumi Babalu Aye was a small sect located in the city of Hialeah, Florida. The City of Hialeah enacted ordinances against the sacrifice of animals, forbidding the "unnecessarily killing of an animal in a public or private ritual or ceremony not for the primary purpose of food consumption."

The U.S. Supreme Court found that the city did not understand and failed to perceive or chose to ignore the fact that its official actions violated religious freedom. In his majority opinion, Justice Kennedy wrote, "The challenged laws had an impermissible object; and in all events the principle of general applicability was violated because the secular ends asserted in the laws were pursued only with respect to conduct motivated by religious belief. We invalidate the challenged enactments and reverse the judgment of the Court of Appeals." The court ruled that the ordinance was unconstitutional.

Freedom of Speech

In dealing with problems and controversies regarding freedom of speech, and in order for the Supreme Court to decide resolutions, society had to further define what exactly "speech" is and what type of speech is or is not protected. To decide, courts had to distinguish answers to such questions as, what is pornography; what is symbolic speech, and is it protected; and what is commercial speech? Freedom of speech problems develop or are exacerbated during times of war or extensive social unrest when unpopular political and social minorities seek to exercise their freedom of speech and the laws, social customs, and norms tend to limit speech that is naturally upsetting to members of the majority. Majority members of society seek to limit free speech by unpopular minority group members through laws, customs, and at times outright violence or intimidation (an implied threat of violence). Ideological political minorities, such as anarchists, communists, and socialists, raise their concerns and often seek protection and redress through the courts. With respect to freedom of speech issues, from World War I until the current time, many U.S. Supreme Court decisions grappled with freedom of speech issues and sought to hand down solutions by their decisions. This section will briefly highlight nineteen of those cases and how the Supreme Court resolved the issues before them.

During World War I, the desire for conformity was heightened. Political minority groups considered radicals (anarchists, communists, and socialists) were targeted, and federal law was enacted to restrict their freedom of speech—such as the Espionage Act of 1917 and the Sedition Act of 1918. In a landmark case concerning the enforcement of the Espionage Act of 1917, the Supreme Court ruled that the government could restrict spoken or written words if they posed a "clear and present danger." The first such case was *Schenck v. United States* (249 U.S. 47, 1919).

Schenck was general secretary of the U.S. Socialist Party, which printed and distributed fifteen thousand leaflets opposing the draft and urging men to resist military service. In a unanimous decision, with the majority opinion written by Justice Oliver Wendell Holmes Jr., Holmes wrote, "Freedom of speech may become subject to prohibition when of such a nature and used in such circumstances as to create a clear and present danger that they will bring about the substantive evils which Congress has a right to prevent." The court used much the same reasoning in *Abrams v. United States* (250 U.S. 616, 1919), wherein "revolutionists" printed pamphlets that denounced sending troops to Russia and urged curtailment of production of essential war materiel. And in *Debs v. United States* (249 U.S. 211, 1919), the court upheld the Espionage Act of 1917 and the Sedition Act of 1918. Debs was the leader of the Socialist Party, a pacifist, a candidate for president on the Socialist Party ticket, and a sharp critic of the ongoing war. He was convicted for obstructing military recruitment and enlistment. In his opinion, Justice Holmes stated, "Even though Debs did not expressly advocate draft resistance, his intent and the general tendency of his words were together sufficient for a jury to convict him fairly."

In *Gitlow v. New York* (268 U.S. 652, 1925), Gitlow, a socialist, was arrested in 1919 for distributing a "Left Wing Manifesto" calling for the establishment of socialism through strikes and class action. He was convicted under New York's Criminal Anarchy Law. The Supreme Court held, in a 7–2 decision in which the majority opinion was written by Justice Edward Sanford, that New York State could prohibit the advocating of violent efforts to overthrow the government. Justice Holmes, in dissent, argued that Gitlow had not violated the clear and present danger test because his call to action was abstract and would not resonate with a large number of people.

Social tensions were again high during World War II. Mandatory saluting of the American flag was common, but members of the Jehovah's Witnesses refused to salute the flag. In *West Virginia v. Barnette* (319 U.S. 624, 1943), the Supreme Court held, 6–3, in a majority opinion written by Justice Robert Jackson—and overturning *Minersville School District v. Gobitis* (310 U.S.

586,1940)—that compulsory flag salute for public schoolchildren violated the First Amendment's freedom of speech.

During the Vietnam War, again pressures to conform were heightened, and antiwar protests and protestors were often the targets for suppression of their speech and demonstrations. In *Tinker v. Des Moines Independent Community School District* (393 U.S. 503, 1969), the court dealt with the issue of the rights of three high school students to protest the war by wearing black armbands. The court held, 6–3, that school authorities could not "censor" their speech (in this case, symbolic speech) without showing the speech would significantly interfere with the discipline needed for the school to function. The majority opinion of Justice Abe Fortas found that the student's protest was "passive, silent, and peaceful" and therefore could not be censored.

The court distinguished a different test than the clear and present danger test in *Brandenburg v. Ohio* (395 U.S. 444, 1969). Brandenburg was a member of the Ku Klux Klan who was arrested and convicted for violation of the Ohio Criminal Syndicalism Law. Justice William Brennan wrote the majority per curiam opinion in which he substituted an "imminent lawless action" test for the clear and present danger test. *Brandenburg* held that speech that supports lawbreaking or violence in general is protected unless it directly encourages people to take an unlawful action immediately.

The court overturned Cohen's conviction for "disturbing the peace" by wearing a jacket in the corridors of the local courthouse displaying the phrase "Fuck the Draft." In *Cohen v. California* (403 U.S. 15, 1971), the court overturned Cohen's conviction in a 5–4 decision. The majority opinion by Justice John Harlan noted that Cohen's conviction was based solely on "speech" and not any "separately identifiable conduct." The court ruled that, although his jacket was vulgar and offensive, it was protected "symbolic" free speech.

The right of free speech is conditioned to a degree on characteristics of the speaker. Students of minority age have less right to free speech than adult citizens. In *Bethel School District v. Fraser* (478 U.S. 675, 1986), the court ruled, 7–2, that public schools have a right to discipline a student for giving a speech at a school assembly that is indecent, although not obscene. The majority opinion was written by Chief Justice Warren Berger. It upheld a Washington State law. *Fraser* limits the scope of the *Tinker* decision by prohibiting certain styles of expression that are sexually vulgar.

The more limited right of a student to free speech was also at issue in *Hazelwood School District v. Kuhlmeier* (484 U.S. 260, 1988). In a 5–3 decision, Justice Byron White wrote the majority opinion that found that educators did not infringe on the First Amendment when exercising control over student speech in school-sponsored activities so long as the actions of the school administrators are reasonably related to legitimate pedagogical concerns. In stipulating the reduced right of student speech, the *Hazelwood* decision overrode the precedent set in *Tinker*.

The protection of "symbolic speech" was at issue in *Texas v. Johnson* (491 U.S. 397, 1989). A Texas law outlawed the desecration of the U.S. flag under a law prohibiting the "desecration of a venerated object." Greg Johnson was a member of the Revolutionary Communist Youth Brigade, a group protesting at the 1984 Republican National Convention. Johnson set a U.S. flag on fire. The court overturned his conviction for "breach of peace." The Court majority held that burning the flag was protected symbolic speech. The majority opinion of the court was written by Justice William Brennan and concurred in by Justices Thurgood Marshall, Harry Blackmun, Antonin Scalia, and Anthony Kennedy—thus representing both the liberal and conservative ideological tendencies on the Supreme Court. Justice Brennan wrote, "The expressive, overtly political nature of the conduct was both intentional and overwhelmingly apparent." Using the "imminent lawless action" test established in *Brandenburg*, the court found that there was no breach of peace and no imminent lawless action.

Cross burning as speech was at issue in *R. A. V. v. St. Paul* (505 U.S. 377, 1992). R. A. V. was a teenager and a member of the Ku Klux Klan. In this decision, the court struck down St. Paul's "Bias-Motivated Crime Ordinance." The majority opinion was written by Justice Antonin Scalia. It found that cross burning was symbolic speech. It held the St. Paul ordinance was "facially unconstitutional" and that cross burning did not amount to "fighting words" that would render the speech unprotected. In Justice Scalia's words, "The First Amendment does not permit the city of St. Paul to impose special prohibitions on those speakers who express views on disfavored subjects."

The development of new technology can raise new problems and issues regarding free speech. To what extent can the national government regulate online material that may be considered by some as pornographic? In *Reno v. ACLU* (521 U.S. 844, 1997), the Supreme Court unanimously ruled that the anti-indecency provisions of the 1996 Communications Decency Act violated the First Amendment's freedom of speech. Justice John Paul Stevens wrote the majority opinion in the case. It was the first major Supreme Court ruling on regulation of materials distributed via the internet.

The Jehovah's Witnesses and their aggressive proselytizing were often the targets of local ordinances that sought to limit their door-to-door style of recruiting converts to the faith. In *Watchtower Bible and Track Society of New York, Inc. v. Village of Stratton* (536 U.S. 150, 2002), the court, in an 8–1 decision, held that the Village of Stratton, Ohio, ordinance prohibiting "canvassers" engaging in door-to-door advocacy without first registering with town officials and receiving a permit violated the First Amendment as it applies to religious proselytizing, anonymous political speech, and the distribution of handbills. The Jehovah's Witnesses were supported in their case by amicus briefs filed by the Independent Baptist Church of America, the Election Privacy Information Center, the Center for Individual Freedom, and the Church of Jesus Christ of Latter-day Saints.

Access to the internet and the possibility of pornographic matter being viewed by children at public library computer sites was at issue in *United States v. American Library Association* (539 U.S. 194, 2003). The Supreme Court ruled that the U.S. Congress had the authority to require public schools and libraries receiving E-Rate discounts to install web-filtering software as a condition of receiving federal funds. The decision did not find the Children's Internet Protection Act unconstitutional, and the school and library use of web-filtering software does not violate the free speech of patrons of the library.

Can a redevelopment and housing authority bar nonresidents from access? Did such barring infringe on the free speech of persons wanting to access the property? The court applied its "speech overbreadth doctrine" to resolve the issue in *Virginia v. Hicks* (539 U.S. 113, 2003). The case concerned the policy of the Richmond Redevelopment and Housing Authority that barred nonresidents from a public community room unless they could demonstrate a legitimate business or social purpose to be on the premises. In a unanimous decision, the Supreme Court held that the policy was not facially invalid under the First Amendment's freedom of speech.

The Ku Klux Klan's use of cross burning was again at issue in *Virginia v. Black* (538 U.S. 343, 2003). Virginia enacted a law that made cross burning illegal. The statute stipulated any cross burning shall be prima facie evidence of intent to intimidate a person or group. In its 5–4 decision, the court overturned the Virginia state law. In the majority opinion for the court, Justice Sandra Day O'Connor wrote, "A State may choose to prohibit only those forms of intimidation that are most likely to inspire fear of bodily harm." The cross burning took place on the private property of a Klan member and was not part of a Klan rally or event on public property or on the property of another individual (although it was across the street from a African American homeowner).

In an attempt to control use of the internet to protect children from pornography the U.S. Congress enacted the Child

Online Protection Act (COPA). In the case of *Ashcroft v. ACLU* (535 U.S. 564, 2004), the Supreme Court held that the act is unconstitutional. Congress attempted to criminalize the internet distribution of what is considered pornography, simulated pornography, and artwork. The Supreme Court found the act too restrictive of adult's access to the internet and that Congress could use a less restrictive alternative to COPA. It noted that blocking and filtering technologies and software are far less restrictive. The Supreme Court effectively struck COPA from the U.S. Code before it ever took effect.

Finally, the right of student speech versus the authority of school officials was again at issue in *Morse v. Frederick* (551 U.S. 393, 2007). In this case, Frederick, a high school student, unfurled a banner promoting drug use across the street from a school at a school-sponsored event (watching the arrival to the community of the Olympic torch). The Supreme Court decided, 5–4, against Frederick, upholding the right of public school officials to censor student speech that can reasonably be understood to promote illegal drug use (in this case, marijuana). The court held the right of free speech by students (in this case, high school students) had to be considered in light of "special characteristics" of the school environment and that it was an important responsibility of schools and school officials to deter drug use among young people.

Freedom of the Press

Freedom of the press is among the most important of First Amendment freedoms, considered by the Founding Fathers to be among the very most important rights to preserve and protect democracy. But limits on freedom of the press could also be stipulated, and issues such as *prior restraint* and *libel* (and the definition of *seditious libel* and to what extent public figures are less protected by libel laws) had to be considered. This section discusses about a half dozen cases that addressed the issue and distinguished some "tests" to guide the court in determining the acts of federal and state governments as to whether their actions were limited or constrained by freedom of the press (Parker, Davison, and Finkelman 2003).

Two court decisions, one by a colonial court and one by a New York State court, were early jurisprudence on freedom of the press and libel. *Defamation* is the oral or written communication of a false statement about another that unjustly harms the person's reputation or livelihood. Defamation usually constitutes a tort. Tort is a wrongful act or an infringement of a right (other than under contract) leading to civil liability. Libel is a written or published defamatory statement, and slander is defamation that is spoken by the defendant.

Crown v. John Peter Zenger (1735) was a precedent-setting free speech case described in chapter 1. It took place in New York Colony and set the important doctrine that the truth of a statement may be a defense against libel. Although it did not establish precedent in seditious libel cases nor guarantee freedom of the press, it was an inspiration to subsequent jurisprudence on freedom of the press. In the words of colonial Gouverneur Morris, the *Zenger* case was "the germ of American freedom, the morning star of that liberty which subsequently revolutionized America" (cited in Finkelman 1994). The concept that truth cannot be libelous and that the press should be free of government censorship was thereafter embodied in the U.S. Constitution and the Bill of Rights.

In *People of New York v. Croswell* (3 Johns. Cas. 337, N.Y., 1804), an evenly divided New York Supreme Court upheld the libel conviction of the Rev. Dr. Harry Croswell, the rector of the Trinity Episcopal Church in New Haven, Connecticut. He was convicted for publishing an article alleging that President Thomas Jefferson had paid James Callender to assert derogatory statements about George Washington and John Adams. By the time of the ruling, however, the state had enacted a law that effectively incorporated Judge James Kent's opinion that defendants should be able to assert the truth of the libel as a defense and that, in the trial of Rev. Croswell, the jury should have been granted the right to decide whether the words published were criminal.

In *Near v. Minnesota* (283 U.S. 697, 1931), the U.S. Supreme Court held that prior restraint of publication, in this case a Minnesota law, violated the freedom of the press protection of the First Amendment. The Minnesota statute was the Public Nuisance Law. It provided that any publishing business circulating an obscene, lewd, and lascivious or a malicious, scandalous, and defamatory newspaper or periodical could be enjoined from further committing or maintaining the nuisance—in essence, a "gag law." In its 5–4 decision, written by Chief Justice Charles Hughes, the court held that the Minnesota law was facially unconstitutional. The *Near* decision established the doctrine that, with some narrow exceptions, the government cannot censor or otherwise prohibit a publication in advance.

New York Times v. Sullivan (376 U.S. 254, 1964) was a landmark freedom of the press case that held that the First Amendment protects newspapers even when they print false statements as long as the newspaper did not act with actual malice. Sullivan, a Montgomery, Alabama, police official, won his case in the Alabama court, which ordered the *New York Times* to pay $500,000 in damages. The *Times* appealed to the U.S. Supreme Court. The court ruled unanimously that, to prove libel, a public official must show that the newspaper acted with actual malice—that it knew the statement was false or published it with reckless disregard for the truth. The court asserted that the country's national commitment to the principle that debate in public issues should be uninhibited, robust, and wide open and that debate is more important than occasional honest factual errors that may hurt or damage public officials' reputations.

In *Curtis Publishing v. Butts* (388 U.S. 130, 1967), the Supreme Court upheld a libel judgment on behalf of Wally Butts, the athletic director at the University of Georgia. A *Saturday Evening Post* article alleged that Butts had fixed a game.

He challenged the veracity of the article and accused the magazine of a serious departure from investigative standards. The jury in the trial court awarded Butts $60,000 in compensatory damages and $400,000 in punitive damages. The award was upheld by the Court of Appeals. In a 7–2 decision, the Supreme Court considered Butts a public figure but noted that public figures may win a libel case under finding of highly unreasonable conduct. Justice Harlan, in the majority opinion, held that a "public figure" who is not a public official may recover damages for defamatory falsehoods that substantially endanger his reputation.

New York Times v. United States (403 U.S. 713, 1971) was a landmark decision that enabled the *New York Times* and the *Washington Post* to print illegally leaked classified documents about U.S. involvement in the Vietnam War—the so-called Pentagon Papers. Daniel Ellsberg copied more than seven thousand pages of documents that revealed the history of the government's actions in the Vietnam War and gave them to the *New York Times*. As the *Times* began to publish them, the government obtained a court order preventing the newspaper from publishing more of the documents (i.e., prior restraint). In response, Ellsberg released the papers to the *Washington Post*, and it began to publish them. The government sought another injunction, but the *Washington Post* case, combined with the *New York Times*, was heard by the Supreme Court on appeal. The Supreme Court ruled 6–3 that prior restraint was unconstitutional.

Finally, *Nebraska Press Association v. Stuart* (427 U.S. 539, 1976) was another landmark freedom of the press case in which the court unanimously held that it was unconstitutional to use prior restraint on media coverage during criminal trials. The court held that the trial judge (Stuart) did not have authority to place gag orders on reporting about a specific criminal case prior to the jury being impaneled. Writing for the majority, Chief Justice Warren Burger stated that prior restraint must be presumed to violate the First Amendment even while trying to balance two rights: the First Amendment's freedom of the press and the Sixth Amendment's right to a fair trial. The opinion held that reporting on criminal proceedings takes priority, reasoning that pretrial publicity does not inevitably lead to an unfair trial. The court recognized that the trial judge had acted responsibly and out of a legitimate concern that adverse publicity could affect the trial in an effort to protect the defendant's right to a fair trial but that other alternatives to the gag order could have been used, such as a change of venue, postponement of the trial to allow public attention to subside, searching questions of prospective jurors to screen out those with fixed opinions of guilt or innocence, or the use of emphatic and clear jury instructions.

Freedom to Assemble and Petition the Government for Redress of Grievances

Between 1937 and 2011, the U.S. Supreme Court heard and decided on ten cases important to clarifying the right to freedom of assembly and to petition the government for redress of grievances. These cases dealt with defendants who belonged to politically unpopular minority groups who at the time were using the courts to press their claims of discrimination and challenging the laws and actions of state and local officials on First Amendment constitutional grounds.

De Jonge v. Oregon (299 U.S. 353, 1937) applied the Fourteenth Amendment's Due Process Clause to a freedom of assembly challenge to an Oregon state law. In its 8–0 decision, the Supreme Court held that Dirk De Jonge had the right to speak at a peaceful public meeting held by the Communist Party. De Jonge challenged Oregon's Criminal Syndicalism statute that made it a crime to assist in conducting any assemblage of persons that teaches or advocates crime, physical violence, sabotage, or any unlawful acts or methods as a means of accomplishing or effecting industrial or political change or revolution. Justice Charles Hughes wrote the majority opinion that reversed De Jonge's conviction. Hughes stated, "Freedom of assembly cannot be denied without violating those fundamental principles of liberty and justice which lie at the base of all civil and political institutions" and that "consistent with the Federal Constitution, peaceable assembly for lawful discussion cannot be made a crime" (Chafee 1941).

NAACP v. Alabama (357 U.S. 449, 1958) was a landmark and unanimous ruling by the Supreme Court on the right of freedom of association of the NAACP and its rank-and-file members. As the civil rights movement began, Alabama probed organizations like the NAACP that were not officially registered with the state. The NAACP handed over financial business records to the state but refused to hand over the names of rank-and-file members. The Supreme Court ruled that the First Amendment's freedom of association applied to state governments and held that the membership lists had to remain confidential to protect its members from unlawful attacks. The case allowed only the NAACP and a few other active civil rights organizations to exist in the South with a minimum level of protection from intimidation.

In *Edwards v. South Carolina* (372 U.S. 229, 1963), the court ruled that South Carolina had violated students' First Amendment rights to peaceably assemble, speak, and petition when police dispersed a peaceful protest against segregation. In this incident, a group of high school and college students had marched on the South Carolina State House in Columbia to protest segregation. A total of 187 students were arrested, convicted, and fined from $10 to $100 and given jail sentences of ten to thirty days. In the majority opinion for the court, Justice Potter Stewart stated, "Students actions reflect an exercise of these basic constitutional rights to speech, assembly, and petition in their most pristine and classic form."

In *Lloyd Corporation v. Tanner* (407 U.S. 551, 1972), the court ruled 5–4 that passing out anti-war leaflets at the Lloyd Center in Portland, Oregon, was an infringement on the property rights of the corporation. The majority opinion by Justice

Powell recognized that the defendants' actions were a Vietnam War protest, but it held that shopping centers can forbid the dissemination of handbills unrelated to their operations despite the First Amendment. As private corporations, the shopping center business has no obligation to entitle groups to exercise First Amendment rights that are unrelated to the center's operations.

The highly unpopular Nazi party—the Nationalist Socialist Party—was the group challenging a local ordinance on First Amendment grounds in *Nationalist Socialist Party v. Village of Skokie* (432 U.S. 43, 1977). The Supreme Court upheld the right of the Nationalist Party to display swastikas, holding that doing so did not constitute "fighting words," and thus enjoining of the right to speech and assembly was unconstitutional prior restraint. The *Skokie* case was one of the first "hate speech" decisions.

The Village of Skokie had a population of 70,000, among whom 40,500 were Jews and some 5,000 to 7,000 were survivors of Nazi concentration camps. The village sought to enjoin a demonstration by the National Socialist Party. The majority decision of the court, however, held that public expression of ideas cannot be prohibited merely because the ideas themselves are offensive to some hearers. It ruled that the government had the heavy burden of justifying the imposition of prior restraint of the defendant's right to freedom of speech and assembly.

Can an international organization ban a local chapter from accepting female members into what was a male-only organization? In *Rotary International v. Rotary Club of Duarte* (481 U.S. 537, 1987), the Supreme Court ruled that the local club must be allowed to accept or allow women members and that Rotary International did not have the right to exclude women. The court affirmed the judgment of the Court of Appeals of California, respecting a state statute requiring that business establishments admit women members. California's Unruh Civil Rights Act entitles "all persons, regardless of sex, to full and equal advantages, facilities, and services of all business establishments in the State."

In *Madsen v. Women's Health Center* (512 U.S. 753, 1994), in a 6–3 vote, the court partially upheld and partially overturned a Florida Supreme Court decision regarding the assembly rights of abortion protestors and the rights of an abortion clinic to legally operate. The case concerned abortion protestors against the Women's Health Center and other abortion clinics in Melbourne, Florida. A restraining order against the protestors was upheld by the Florida Supreme Court. The protestors appealed to the U.S. Supreme Court.

The issues before the U.S. Supreme Court to consider were the following: Did the state have a significant interest in restricting the petitioners First Amendment rights? Was a thirty-six-foot buffer zone around the clinic a constitutional restriction? Did the thirty-six-foot provision apply to private property around the clinic? Was a noise prohibition within the injunction constitutional? Was the "images observable prohibition" within the injunction constitutional? Was a three hundred–foot no-approach zone around the clinic permissible?

Chief Justice William Rehnquist's majority opinion upheld the constitutionality of the thirty-six-foot buffer zone and the noise level prohibitions but struck down the thirty-six-foot provision applying to private property, the "images observable provision," and the three hundred–foot buffer zone. It held that those latter provisions were more broad than necessary to protect the state's interest.

In *Hurley v. Irish-American Gay, Lesbian and Bisexual Group of Boston* (515 U.S. 557, 1995), the Supreme Court, in a unanimous decision written by Justice Souter, held that the private group sponsoring a St. Patrick's Day parade in Boston (the South Boston Allied Veteran's Council) had the right to determine which groups were allowed to participate in the parade. The court held that the council and the parade's sponsor, the Ancient Order of Hibernians, could exclude a homosexual group that wanted to be able (by marching with a banner) to identify themselves as such. In 2017, the group was again banned. After a few days of negative media attention, however, they were allowed to march in the parade.

In *Boy Scouts of America v. Dale* (530 U.S. 640, 2000), the court ruled 5–4 that the right to freedom of association allowed the Boy Scouts of America (BSA) to exclude a person from membership despite a state law requiring equal treatment of homosexuals in public accommodations. The Supreme Court decision reversed a ruling by the New Jersey Supreme Court that had held that New Jersey's public accommodation law required the BSA to readmit scoutmaster James Dale, who had come out as a homosexual and was expelled from the BSA for that reason. The majority opinion of the court, written by Chief Justice William Rehnquist, stated, "We are not, and we must not be, guided by our views of whether the Boy Scout's teaching with respect to homosexual conduct are right or wrong. Judicial approval of a tenet of an organization's expression does not justify the state's effort to compel the organization to accept members when such acceptance would derogate from the organization's expressive message" (Koppelman and Barrington 2009).

Finally, in *Christian Legal Society v. Martinez* (561 U.S. 661, 2010), the court upheld, in a 5–4 decision, the policy of the University of California–Hastings that requires student groups to accept all students regardless of their beliefs to obtain official recognition as a reasonable, viewpoint-neutral condition on access to the forum and does not transgress their constitutional First Amendment rights. The Christian Legal Society (CLS) had asked Hastings for an exception to the policy on the basis of its freedom of religion, but CLS would not admit students whose beliefs differed from those set forth in its Statement of Faith. The majority opinion was written by Justice Ruth Bader Ginsburg, joined by liberal justices John Stevens, Stephen Breyer, and Sonia Sotomayor and the swing vote of moderately conservative justice Anthony Kennedy. The dissenters were the court's conservative justices: Samuel Alito, John Roberts, Antonin Scalia, and Clarence Thomas.

Conclusion

As this chapter makes clear, the precise meaning of the clauses of the First Amendment—the Establishment Clause and Free Exercise Clause of religion, freedom of speech, freedom of the press, and the freedom of association to assemble and petition redress of grievances—have changed over time as conditions in American society have changed. As the nation grew and industrialized and urbanized, and as an ever-growing number of ethnic and religious groups immigrated to the United States or arose within the population, problems maintaining and understanding those constitutional guarantees of First Amendment rights arose as well.

Conflicts between members of the majority society and minority group members frequently resulted in the majority seeking to limit the minority's constitutional rights. Those problems and controversies particularly arose during times of war, when the desire for conformity heightened, and during times of social unrest and agitation by unpopular ethnic, ideological, racial, religious, or social minority groups pressed to assert their constitutional rights. The majority sought to impose their viewpoints through law, social customs, and norms and at times through violent confrontations with minority group members. Minority members responded by challenging in the courts, on constitutional grounds, those laws and policies.

Over the long history of the United States, the U.S. Supreme Court has played a special role, through a series of landmark decisions, to resolve, for a time at least, those issues and conflicts. On occasion, the court has overturned its own prior rulings. In a number of critically important landmark cases, it developed tests to discern the constitutionality, or lack of constitutionality, of federal, state, and local laws and ordinances. It is the special role of the U.S. Supreme Court to lead the ongoing struggle to better understand and to live up to the fundamental rights guaranteed by the First Amendment and to define the practical limits those rights place on governmental authority at all three levels of government. The Supreme Court remains the final arbiter in resolving conflicts between those fundamental rights, and it seeks to strike a balance when those rights clash with respect to majority society's needs and understanding of the U.S. Constitution and the needs and understanding of individuals and minority groups who challenge the majority society on constitutional grounds.

Further Reading

Abrams, Paula. 2009. *Cross Purposes: Pierce v. Society of Sisters and the Struggle Over Compulsory Education*. Ann Arbor: University of Michigan Press.

Alley, Robert. 1999. *The Constitution and Religion: Leading Supreme Court Cases on Church and State*. Amherst, NY: Prometheus Books.

Butler, Jon. 2005. *Religion in Colonial America*. New York: Oxford University Press.

Chafee, Zachariah. 1941. *Free Speech in the United States*. Cambridge, MA: Harvard University Press.

Dreisbach, Daniel. 2002. *Thomas Jefferson and the Wall of Separation of Church and State*. New York: New York University Press.

Feldman, Noah. 2005. *Divided by God*. New York: Farrar, Straus, and Giroux.

Finkelman, Paul. 1994. "The Trial of John Peter Zenger." In *American Political Trials*, edited by Michael Belknap. Westport, CT: Greenwood Press.

Flowers, Ronal, Stephen Green, and Melissa Rogers. 2008. *Religious Freedom and the Supreme Court*. 8th ed. Waco, TX: Baylor University Press.

Green, Stephen. 2010. *The Second Disestablishment: Church and State in Nineteenth-Century America*. New York: Oxford University Press.

Holmes, David. 2006. *The Faith of the Founding Fathers*. New York: Oxford University Press.

Koppelman, Andrew, and Tobias Barrington. 2009. *A Right to Discriminate: How the Case of* Boy Scouts of America v. James Dale *Warped the Law of Free Association*. New Haven, CT: Yale University Press.

Lambert, Frank. 2003. *The Founding Fathers and the Place of Religion in America*. Princeton, NJ: Princeton University Press.

LeMay, Michael. 2018. *Religious Freedom in America*. Santa Barbara, CA: ABC-CLIO.

Levy, Leonard. 1994. *Establishment Clause and the First Amendment*. Chapel Hill: University of North Carolina Press.

Mapp, Alf. 2003. *The Faith of Our Fathers: What America's Founders Really Believed*. Lanham, MD: Rowman & Littlefield.

McGarvie, Mark. 2004. *One Nation under Law: America's Early National Struggle to Separate Church and State*. DeKalb: Northern Illinois University Press.

Parker, J. Wilson, Douglas Davison, and Paul Finkelman. 2003. *Constitutional Law in Context*. Vol. 1. Durham, NC: Carolina Academic Press.

Peterson, Merrill, Robert Vaughan, and Robin Lovin, eds. 1988. *The Virginia Statute for Religious Freedom: Its Evolution and Consequences in American History*. Cambridge, UK: Cambridge University Press.

Rogasta, John. 2013. *Religious Freedom: Jefferson's Legacy, America's Creed*. Charlottesville: University of Virginia Press.

Smith, Frank, ed. 2016. *Religion and Politics in America: An Encyclopedia of Church and State in American Life*. 2 vols. Santa Barbara, CA: ABC-CLIO.

Urofsky, Melvin. 2002. *Religious Freedom: Rights and Liberties under the Law*. Santa Barbara, CA: ABC-CLIO.

Urofsky, Melvin, and Paul Finkelman. 1987. *The March of Liberty: A Constitutional History of the United States*. 3rd ed. Vol. 1, *From Founding to 1900*. New York: Oxford University Press.

Witte, John. 2012. *No Establishment of Religion: America's Original Contribution to Religious Liberty*. New York: Oxford University Press.

Zentner, Scot, and Michael C. LeMay. 2020. *Party and Nation: Immigration and Regime Politics in American History*. Lanham, MD: Lexington Books.

3 Perspectives

Introduction

This chapter presents nine original essays on the topic of First Amendment freedoms contributed by various scholars from assorted disciplines who study the subject. The essays collectively provide further insights and a perspective beyond or different from the expertise of the author. The essays are presented in alphabetical order by the contributors' surnames.

The First Amendment and the Struggle for Civil Rights
Kenneth Bedell

The First Amendment covers freedoms related to both religion and politics. U.S. Supreme Court rulings related to political freedoms protected activists during the civil rights movement in the 1950s and 1960s. The National Association for the Advancement of Colored People (NAACP) successfully convinced the Supreme Court that organizations and individuals have First Amendment protections to protest, assemble, and associate in the struggle for civil rights. In possibly the most important ruling for the movement, the Supreme Court decided to protect journalists from libel suits for reporting on civil rights abuses. These and other First Amendment rulings by the Supreme Court were important, but the First Amendment

Dr. Martin Luther King, Jr. founded the Southern Christian Leadership Conference in 1957, which led the civil rights movement of the 1960s. (Library of Congress)

protection of freedom of religion did not need Supreme Court intervention at that time.

In the 1950s and 1960s, African Americans were accustomed to being harassed. When white people felt threatened by preachers and churches, they responded violently, particularly in the South. Church burnings, lynchings, and other intimidations were the extralegal methods used by white people who supported segregation and white superiority. The bombing of the 16th Street Baptist Church in Birmingham, Alabama, in 1964, brought the attention of the nation to attempts by white citizens to deny freedom of religion and to silence the voices demanding civil rights for all.

When the Reverend Dr. Martin Luther King Jr. explained the religious foundation for civil rights, he was standing on the shoulders of generations of mostly black preachers and religious leaders, including his father, who had proclaimed a philosophy that for those same generations was largely hidden from the consciousness of white Americans. King's preaching was severely criticized by some. He was called a Communist, un-American, a troublemaker, the Antichrist, a heretic, and much worse. Yet, the long tradition of freedom of religion, starting with the First Amendment, was essential for the 1950s and 1960s civil rights movement.

The founders were not all of the same mind about the importance of separating church and state. The Massachusetts Constitution of 1780 required taxation to support religious teachers. Until the constitution was amended in 1833, legislators had argued that having religion taught to all citizens is essential for the preservation of civil society. When ten states submitted their approval of the Bill of Rights, it was added to the U.S. Constitution on December 15, 1791. Massachusetts was not one of the states that approved.

When Dr. King used religious imagery and made theological arguments, he was exercising his constitutional right of freedom of religion. King's vision for the United States was quite different from the American founders' vision of a nation governed by a wealthy, educated, elite group of white men. But they shared a vision of each person being free to choose and practice his or her own religion.

Racism that is the foundation for denying full participation by people of color in American society extends far beyond the South. Racism was hidden in the religious perspectives and conserving nature of religious practices. White people were not willing or able to hear King's philosophical and theological rationale for a just society.

The vision of the civil rights movement was a society where each person experiences no greater barriers than any other person in pursuing his or her personal goals or aspirations and where all identity, ethnic, and racial groups have full participation in the social, cultural, and governmental institutions of the nation. This was ignored by whites, as if King's only dream was for his little children to play happily with white children.

King was a Christian, but his message was universal. Everything that he taught was based on the value of nonviolence. He was inspired by the example of Mahatma Gandhi, a Hindu. For King and others, nonviolence is not just a strategy to bring social change. Nonviolence starts with recognizing the humanity of those who oppress and works for a solution where there are no winners or losers.

King's message also called for justice for the poor. This is a theme from Hebrew scriptures. A centerpiece of Jewish teaching is condemnation of those who oppress. But it is more than that; justice for the poor is justice for all.

Finally, King challenged Americans to join a "beloved community." He took this idea from Christian scripture, where love is the basis of human relationships. This love is not a sentimental love or a romantic love, but agape love. *Agape* is a Greek word that means the selfless, nonjudgmental love of others. A beloved community is a community without racism.

After King's assassination, civil rights leaders such as John Lewis, Jesse Jackson, and Andrew Young turned their attention to achieving political goals. Some of the preachers who worked with King, such as Gardner Taylor, Kelly Miller Smith, and Wyatt Tee Walker, continued to hone the theological message.

Those who committed themselves to politics continued to make slow progress toward building a race-free country. However, the African American preachers were quickly ignored by the white community and mostly returned to preaching to African American congregations.

Looking back, we should not be surprised. Since colonial times, white people in America have accepted without question an ideology that what is white and European is superior to any other perspective. We see this clearly in their early engagement with Native Americans. The colonists were committed to the superiority of their religions and culture. This commitment to superiority by European Christianity has made it difficult for white people to hear and understand a philosophy that rejects the superiority of white people and white culture.

Since the 1960s and 1970s, progress has been very slow toward the goal of ending racism. I propose that the reason is because First Amendment political rights can only take us so far. Laws such as the Voting Rights Act and the Civil Rights Act are important in protecting people of color from specific abuses. But the failure to achieve full civil rights for all is a result of white Americans holding on to the idea of their superiority. They successfully isolated the African American preachers and ignored the philosophical and religious rationale for civil rights.

Kenneth Bedell is the author of Realizing the Civil Rights Dream *(Praeger, 2017).*

Creationism and Religious Freedom
Michelle D. Deardorff

In 2004, the Dover, Pennsylvania, Area School Board announced that teachers of ninth-grade biology classes at Dover High School would read the following to their students before teaching evolution:

The Pennsylvania Academic Standards require student to learn about Darwin's Theory of Evolution and eventually to take a standardized text of which evolution is a part. Because Darwin's Theory is a theory, it continues to be tested as new evidence is discovered. The Theory is not a fact. Gaps in the Theory exist for which there is no evidence. A theory is defined as a well-tested explanation that unifies a broad range of observations. Intelligent Design is an explanation of the origin of life that differs from Darwin's view. The reference book, *Of Pandas and People*, is available for students who might be interested in gaining an understanding of what Intelligent Design actually involves. With respect to any theory, students are encouraged to keep an open mind. The school leaves the discussion of the Origins of Life, to individual students and their families. As a Standards-driven district, class instruction focuses upon preparing students to achieve proficiency on Standards-based assessments.

A parent of one of the ninth-grade students sued when the local newspaper reported on the required statement, which had been written by elected officials in the community. The parent argued that this requirement to present intelligent design (ID) as an alternative explanation to evolution was a violation of the Establishment Clause of the First Amendment because it was creationism concealed in scientific language. The federal district court agreed, finding the mandatory statement to be an unconstitutional endorsement of a particular religious view by a local governmental entity.

The individuals who contributed $27 million for the development of the Creation Museum in Petersburg, Kentucky, and the self-reported three million individuals who visited the museum in its first decade disagree. Advocates for the teaching of creation in schools find the required teaching of evolution in high school biology classes to be a violation of their free exercise of religion rights protected under the same First Amendment.

Advocates of this version of creationism argue for a young earth theory, in which the earth was formed in six twenty-four-hour days and has only existed for six thousand years. How have we arrived at this impasse, where the federal courts determine how science can be taught in public schools?

This tension between some Christian faith communities and most scientists became visible with the publication of Charles Darwin's *On the Origin of the Species by the Means of Natural Selection* in 1860. Although many Christians were able to reconcile their vision of a personal, creating, and engaged God with Darwin's view of nature that evolves, competes, and allows for regular extinction, others saw Darwin's work as threatening to their worldview. The stories of creation in Genesis reveal a God who personally created humanity in His own image, while Darwin relates natural forces that do not demonstrate a clear evolutionary path to humanity but instead follow a process that results in species extinction, deadly competition, and slow changes in response to altering environments.

For many Christians—particularly fundamentalists and some evangelicals for whom a literal interpretation of the Bible is central to their faith—the threat that liberalism and modernism has against their values and morality is both existential and essential. As one creation advocacy group notes, "If Christians doubt what at first appears to be insignificant details of Scripture, then others may begin to look at the whole Bible differently, eventually doubting the central tenets of the Christian faith, namely the life, death, and resurrection of Jesus Christ. Thus the historicity of Scripture is quite important" (Answers in Genesis n.d.).

This struggle between faith and reason as the best means of making the most sense of the world became visible in the early twentieth century. In the so-called Scopes Monkey Trial, in which a Tennessee law (Butler Act of 1925) criminalized the teaching of evolution in the public schools, advocate William Jennings Bryant and others perceived the state as protecting the rights of parents to teach their own children the tenets of their faith unhindered by outsiders. But after World War II, values had changed, and evolution had the support of the majority of natural scientists and was not seen as a conflict to Christianity by many followers of the faith (neither the Catholic Church nor mainline denominations find any conflict).

For others, particularly whites in smaller towns and in the Southern region of the United States, the capacity of the state—through mandatory public schooling—to teach their children in biology courses that their faith in the direct creation of Adam and Eve was fallacious and a myth became a cultural battle line. Scientists who believe that evaluation has been clearly demonstrated and rigorously supported by the scientific method do not understand why religious objectives should impact any aspect of science education.

The U.S. Supreme Court has addressed this issue twice. In 1968, *Epperson v. Arkansas* (393 U.S. 97) scrutinized a 1928 Arkansas law that prohibited any public school or university from teaching or using a textbook that advanced "the theory or doctrine that mankind ascended or descended from a lower order of animals." By 1968, only Arkansas and Mississippi still had such laws in effect; there had not been any record of prosecution in Arkansas. In this case, the court found that the sole purpose of the law was to prevent the teaching of a theory that disputed the divine creation of man and therefore violated the Establishment Clause of the First Amendment.

In 1987, the court returned to the issue in the case of *Edwards v. Aguillard* (482 U.S. 578). This case challenged Louisiana's "Balanced Treatment for Creation-Science and Evolution-Science in Public School Instruction Act" as violating the Establishment Clause of the First Amendment. By this time, advocates for a literal six-day creation explanation of the earth argued that when the theory of evolution was taught, "creation science" also had to be presented—out of fairness. Henry Morris, the founder of the Institution for Creation Research (ICR) developed a model that attempted to use scientific research to demonstrate the historicity of a moment of creation and the events of the Old Testament (e.g., global flood) as well as to discover a geological model that scientifically justifies creation.

The Supreme Court found that creation science did not possess validity in the peer-reviewed world of science and was therefore a state endorsement of religion that violated the First Amendment's Establishment Clause. As the majority opinion noted, "The Creationism Act is designed either to promote the theory of creation science which embodies a particular religious tenet by requiring that creation science be taught wherever evolution is taught or to prohibit the teaching of a scientific theory disfavored by certain religious sects by forbidding the teaching of evolution when creation science is not also taught."

By the 1990s, advocates of a literal interpretation of the Bible had regrouped and focused on developing constitutional arguments and rationales for their position. After the Supreme Court closed the door on creation in public schools, others developed a worldview known as intelligent design (ID). As a broader understanding of creationism, this approach accepts microevolutions and the interpretation that the earth may be older than six thousand years. As articulated by Phillip E. Johnson in 1990, creationism is understood to be religion in the classroom; ID, on the other hand, is the belief in a scientific theory—without an explicit religious focus—but one that recognizes the likelihood of an intelligent cause for creation, which may or may not have been a form of deity. However, the defeat of ID as a constitutional alternative to evolution in the public schools in *Kitzmiller v. Dover Area School District*, 400 F. Supp. 2d 707 (M.D. Pa. 2005), discussed in the opening of this essay, has caused this approach to slowly retreat from legislative agendas.

Answers in Genesis, a nonprofit organized to promote a creation-oriented perspective, developed a museum that retells natural history through a young-earth creationist lens and includes the Ark Encounter, a physical experience designed to demonstrate the literal truth of a global flood. With access to the public schools denied by the U.S. Constitution, creationist organizations such as Answers in Genesis have focused on the development of curriculum and direct attempts to influence the public through state-of-the-art museums and attractions, popular videos, and accessible books. Policy efforts have moved toward state and federal legislation supporting homeschooling and private and charter schools, all of which avoid a conflict with the First Amendment's Establishment Clause.

Further Reading

Answers in Genesis. n.d. "Why Does Creation Matter?" Accessed July 2, 2020. https://answersingenesis.org/why-does-creation-matter.

Conkin, Paul K. 1998. *When All the Gods Trembled: Darwinism, Scopes, and American Intellectuals*. New York: Rowman & Littlefield Publishers.

Fuller, Randall. 2017. *The Book That Changed America: How Darwin's Theory of Evolution Ignited a Nation*. New York: Viking Publishing.

Johnson, Phillip E. 1991. *Darwin on Trial*. Washington, DC: Regnery Gateway, Inc.

Larson, Edward J. 1997. *Summer for the Gods: The Scopes Trial and America's Continuing Debate over Science and Religion*. New York: Basic Books.

Morris, J. D. 1994. *The Young Earth*. Colorado Springs, CO: Creation-Life Publishers.

Scott, Eugenie C. 2009. *Evolution versus Creationism: An Introduction*. Berkeley: University of California Press.

Wise, Donald U. 1998. "Creationism's Geologic Time Scale." *American Scientist* 86 (2): 160–173.

Michelle D. Deardorff is the Adolph S. Ochs Professor of Government and Department Head, University of Tennessee at Chattanooga.

The First Amendment and the School House Gate: The Rise, Decline, and Uncertain Future of Student Speech Rights
Joshua Dunn

Three words describe the history of student free speech rights: *expansion, contraction*, and, today, *uncertainty*.

The modern era of student speech rights began with *Tinker v. Des Moines Independent Community School District* (393 U.S. 503, 1969), in which the U.S. Supreme Court famously held that students do not "shed their constitutional rights to freedom of speech or expression at the schoolhouse gate," and thus students may wear black armbands to protest. Fifty years later, *Tinker* remains the lodestar for analyses of students' free speech rights in school. It also signaled the dramatic expansion of student rights that would last for over a decade. Combined with other cases, such as *Goss v. Lopez* (419 U.S. 565, 1975) and *Wood v. Strickland* (420 U.S. 308, 1975), which granted new due process protections to students facing school discipline and reduced protections for school officials imposing punishments on students, the 1970s was marked by a prostudent orientation by the courts.

But this era of expansion would not last. In fact, *Tinker* itself pointed to the limits of student rights with the court by including two important caveats: speech that creates a "substantial disruption" of school activities or that "impinges upon the rights others" could be punished. In the 1980s, the Supreme Court began curtailing student rights with two important decisions: *Bethel School District v. Fraser* (478 U.S. 675, 1986) and *Hazelwood School District v. Kuhlmeier* (484 U.S. 260, 1988). In *Fraser*, school officials suspended a student for a nomination speech for student body vice president that was an "elaborate sexual metaphor. "Vulgar and lewd" speech, the court ruled, could be censored. More broadly, the court held that this kind of speech "would undermine the school's basic educational mission," but left that phrase undefined, creating potentially even greater latitude for restricting student speech. In *Kuhl-meier*, a school principal had forbidden the student newspaper from publishing two articles, one about teen pregnancy and another about divorce. Both articles anonymously quoted students from the school. The court upheld the decision of the principal because the paper was sponsored by the school. Such school-sponsored speech, it ruled, is not protected by *Tinker*.

These two decisions signaled that federal courts would be less solicitous toward claims of student speech rights. Other cases, such as *Vernonia School District 47J v. Acton* (515 U.S. 646, 1995), which sanctioned suspicionless drug testing of student athletes, and *Pottawatomie City v. Earls* (536 U.S. 822, 2002), which allowed suspicionless drug testing of all students participating in extracurricular activities, showed that the court had an increasingly jaundiced view of student rights in general.

The culminating case for this period of contraction was *Morse v. Frederick* (551 U.S. 393, 2007). This case centered on the suspension of Joseph Frederick, a Juneau, Alaska, high school student, for displaying a banner that read "BONG HiTS 4 JESUS." He had unfurled the banner as the Olympic torch passed by the school on its way to the Winter Games in Salt Lake City. The school had given students and faculty permission to leave class for the event. Detecting a celebration of drug use, the school's principal, Deborah Morse, confiscated the banner and suspended Frederick for ten days. Frederick sued the district and Principal Morse.

On very narrow grounds, the court ruled in favor of the school district. The court rejected the school district's position that schools should be able to censor all offensive speech: "After all much political and religious speech might be perceived as offensive to some." The issue for the court was that the banner could be "reasonably viewed as promoting illegal drug use" and that schools have an "important—indeed, perhaps compelling interest," in deterring student drug use. While the court limited this to "pro-drug speech, an apparently narrow category, it created an exception to a bedrock free speech principle, viewpoint neutrality, which the court had never done before. *Viewpoint neutrality* means that the government cannot censor or punish speech based on the motivating ideology of the speaker. Even in other school speech cases, the court had never allowed for this kind of discrimination. Prior to *Morse*, viewpoint-based restrictions have always been struck down. The fear was that even though the court said that this exception only applied to prodrug speech, school officials could expand it to other kinds of speech they claim is harmful.

Today, because of social media, student speech rights are marked by significant uncertainty. There are two doctrinal impulses pulling in opposite directions. As *Tinker* says, schools can punish student speech, but only if it will cause a substantial disruption or violate the rights of others. But as we have seen, since the 1980s, the judicial trend has been to give school officials more authority to determine what constitutes a substantial disruption and to increase the categories of speech—vulgar and lewd speech, school-sponsored speech, and prodrug speech—that schools can prohibit and punish. The question, which the court has yet to resolve, is to what extent schools can punish off-campus speech that might cause an on-campus disruption. Prior to the internet, students said all sorts of inflammatory things about their teachers and classmates. But for it to disrupt the educational process, it had to be brought onto campus. With the internet, entire student bodies, even the whole world, can read this kind of speech without anyone ever setting foot on campus.

So far, schools have punished students for, among other things, tweeting vulgarities on a school-provided laptop, creating fake MySpace pages, implying their principals are drunk and have hit on students and parents, encouraging fellow students to call school officials "douchebags" for canceling a "jamfest" on a personal blog, and sending a vulgar Snapchat picture about the cheerleading squad.

Lower federal courts have been divided on whether schools can punish this off-campus speech. When these splits occur in the federal circuit courts, the Supreme Court almost always tries to resolve the conflict. Empowering schools to punish this kind of speech is tempting, but deputizing school officials as all-purpose community hall monitors raises many troubling constitutional questions. When the Supreme Court finally does address the issue, it is unlikely that school officials will be allowed to reach beyond the schoolhouse gate.

Joshua Dunn is a professor and chair of the Department of Political Science and the director of the Center for the Study of Government and the Individual at the University of Colorado–Colorado Springs. He earned his PhD at the University of Virginia. He is author of Complex Justice: The Case of Missouri v. Jenkins *(2008);* From School House to Courthouse: The Judiciary's Role in American Education *(2009); and* Passing on the Right: Conservative Professors in the Progressive University *(2016).*

Mexican Americans and the First Amendment
Devin Fernandes

In the history of Mexican American activism, the Fourteenth Amendment and its equal protection guarantees loom large, certainly larger than the civil liberties protections of the First Amendment. Mexican Americans, like African Americans, pursued path-breaking legal challenges against systems of government discrimination on Fourteenth Amendment grounds throughout the first half of the twentieth century. In so doing, they achieved important though less well-known victories in cases such as *Mendez v. Westminster* (64 F. Supp. 544, 1947) and *Hernandez v. Texas* (347 U.S. 475, 1954), tackling segregation in schools and juries, respectively. In the present moment, Mexican American activism continues to focus on equality claims under the Fourteenth Amendment and a newer civil rights policy regime established by the Civil Rights Act of 1964 and the Voting Rights Act of 1965.

For its part, the First Amendment remains mostly a footnote in the history of Mexican American civil rights advocacy and receives only slight attention as a contemporary concern. If any-thing, it is more frequently the subject of criticism, described as being in tension—if not at odds—with civil rights agendas. There are clear reasons for this. Antidiscrimination laws have faced challenges on First Amendment grounds, and practitioners of bigotry often invoke freedom of expression as a shield. Noting that hate speech and other demonstrations of bigotry can have harmful effects that further marginalize minorities, some civil rights advocates have understandably called for placing greater limits on First Amendment liberties.

But the ongoing juxtaposition of civil rights and civil liberties overlooks the ways in which they have also been historically intertwined. Speech and assembly freedoms of the First Amendment have long been tools utilized by Mexican Americans and other minorities to press equality claims, and precisely for this reason, they have also been important objects of the civil rights struggle. For example, in their efforts to achieve greater equity, the United Farm Workers (UFW) of Cesar Chavez and Chicano student protestors in the 1960s regularly fought against vague "public disorder" crackdowns on their First Amendment freedoms. Not surprisingly, demands for free speech consistently appear in various Chicano movement organization platforms and manifestos.

Contemporary amnesia regarding this history doubtlessly reflects the progress made by civil rights advocates and others in contesting the most egregious restrictions on the right to protest. However, it also reflects changes to government institutions and the infrastructure of Mexican American advocacy organizations since the 1960s, formalizing civil rights agendas and the ways in which they are pursued. Major Mexican American organizations now regularly employ top-down advocacy strategies that rely more on insider games of influencing courts and administrative agencies than popular mobilization and contentious actions.

This dynamic has diminished the seeming relevance of First Amendment liberties in civil rights activism and done so at least partially by design. The creation of the Mexican American Legal Defense and Educational Fund (MALDEF), currently one of the most prominent advocacy organizations for Mexican Americans (and Latinos more generally), is instructive here. Although officially founded in 1968 by a group of San Antonio-based Mexican American attorneys, it could not have gotten off the ground without the financial sponsorship of the Ford Foundation. In the late 1960s, Ford had been behind the formation of a wave of new civil rights advocacy organizations for different minority groups to supplement its antipoverty work, believing that its efforts in that arena would go nowhere without tackling lingering patterns of racial and ethnic discrimination. With MALDEF, they hoped to provide the regular organizational representation for Mexican Americans to pursue civil rights litigation and achieve important new rights on par with *Brown v. Board of Education* (347 U.S. 483, 1954).

But Ford officials had another motivation as well. They hoped their support of groups such as MALDEF would offer an alternative to the increasingly radical minority political movements across the country amid growing social unrest. In their view, these movements were pursuing ineffective or even counterproductive political actions. By channeling minority concerns into formal political venues, they hoped to obviate the protests in the streets. Indeed, the original MALDEF grant application (primarily drafted by a Ford consultant) expressed the expectation that MALDEF would channel the protest energy constructively and the work of the Fund (MALDEF) would demonstrate that law, not illegal conduct, could bring results.

Despite such sentiments, the application also suggested that MALDEF might dedicate some of its docket to defend "the right to peaceful protest" under the First Amendment. Two possibilities included representing UFW organizers in Texas or followers of prominent New Mexican land grant activist Reies López Tijerina in the face of law enforcement harassment. In its early years, the group did ultimately maintain a First Amendment program and helped support the legal defense of activists participating in several notable school protests in Texas and East Los Angeles. But in the eyes of Ford officials, these types of cases made MALDEF look like a legal aid operation serving the private defense needs of individuals and groups. It did not align with the type of precedent-setting litigation they expected the organization to pursue. Under pressure, MALDEF leaders began complying with the expectations of their funders and slowly pulled back from this type of defense work to a docket that more selectively emphasized traditional civil rights concerns.

Such suspicions toward the protest movements of the day and serving their needs reflected a wider sense that First Amendment liberties were individual rights that did not represent the proper domain of a professional civil rights advocacy organization. In the view of Ford officials and their partners, violations of First Amendment freedoms should be challenged privately because the vindication of those claims would only affect the private parties involved. The cases would not reshape the law more broadly to generate new rights for Mexican Americans.

This impulse has helped instantiate the distinction between civil rights and civil liberties, especially as protest energies of the 1960s faded and professionalized advocacy organizations became more prominent actors. To be sure, First Amendment concerns have not been entirely disentangled from civil rights advocacy. Cesar Chavez and the UFW would continue mounting prominent First Amendment defenses of their boycotts and strikes into the 1990s. Likewise, MALDEF and others have successfully used First Amendment defenses more recently to challenge state English-only laws, bans on public school ethnic studies programs, and restrictions on day laborers' ability to solicit work, among other areas. However, such episodes have not reaffirmed the importance of the First Amendment as a matter of principle. In these cases, it has more typically been deployed instrumentally to defend the policy preferences of Mexican American groups. Nonetheless, as activists continue debating whether free speech rights have gone too far, it would be wise to keep in mind the historical and contemporary civil rights relevance of the First Amendment.

Devin Fernandes is an assistant professor in the Department of Political Science and Criminal Justice at California State University, Chico, where he teaches courses in interest groups and Latino politics. He earned his PhD from Johns Hopkins University.

The Supreme Court and Freedom of Religion
Timothy R. Johnson and Siyu Li

Congress shall make no law respecting an establishment of religion, or prohibiting the free exercise thereof . . ..

Any read of the First Amendment to the U.S. Constitution suggests that, literally, Congress cannot pass any laws that prohibit the free exercise of religion. The question is whether the deciding authority, the U.S. Supreme Court, has ever suggested such a literal interpretation. The short answer is no. The longer answer—how it has actually interpreted the clause—is the focus of this essay. Specifically, we seek to explain the development of law concerning freedom of religion by the court, including standards it has set to decide cases that involve government encroachment on this right and how such encroachments have changed over time.

We note first that the court did not directly speak about freedom of religion until its landmark case *Cantwell v. Connecticut* (310 U.S. 296, 1940). However, it did give clues that it did not believe the protection of this freedom was set in stone. Indeed, as early as *Reynolds v. United States* (98 U.S. 145, 1878), the justices allowed limits on religion by upholding a congressional law outlawing polygamy. They held that, although Congress could not outlaw the belief that polygamy is a "sacred obligation" of faith, it could regulate the actual practice of it and that people cannot avoid laws due to their religious beliefs. This was, in short, a very conservative standard, by which we mean that the government has broad leeway to regulate a given freedom.

Almost fifty years after *Reynolds*, the court liberalized its views of religious freedom. In *Pierce v. Society of Sisters* (268 U.S. 510, 1925), it accepted an appeal to determine whether Oregon's compulsory public education law (for children ages eight to sixteen) violated the free exercise of groups who wanted to educate children in religiously based private schools. The court agreed the law did so. In particular, the justices argued that "the fundamental theory of liberty upon which all governments in this Union repose excludes any general power of the State to standardize its children by forcing them to accept instruction from public teachers only." In other words, religious institutions have the freedom to teach, and parents may choose to send their children to those schools instead of publicly run schools.

The interesting part about *Reynolds* and *Pierce* is that neither specifically addressed the Free Exercise Clause. It was not until *Cantwell v. Connecticut* (310 U.S. 296, 1940) that it did so. In this case, Cantwell and his sons, members of the Jehovah's Witnesses sect, were playing records and distributing pamphlets to citizens walking the streets of New Haven, Connecticut. Two passersby took offense to Cantwell's anti-Catholic message, and the next day, he was arrested by the police for violating a state law prohibiting individuals from soliciting money for any cause without a license. The law required that those wanting to solicit must obtain a certificate of approval from the state's secretary of Public Welfare Council. The official could grant the permit if it was meant for a religious cause or for charity. However, if the official found that neither of these was the purpose of the solicitation, he could deny the certificate.

Neutral laws are fine, but the law in *Cantwell* did not meet this standard. Although general regulations on solicitation were legitimate, restrictions based on religious grounds were not. Because the statute allowed local officials to determine which causes were religious and which ones were not, it violated the First and Fourteenth Amendments. The court also held that, while the maintenance of public order was a valid state interest, it could not be used to justify the suppression of "free communication of views." Cantwell's message, while offensive to many, did not constitute "bodily harm" and was therefore protected religious speech.

The court further broadened its interpretation of the Free Exercise Clause after *Cantwell.* More than twenty years later, in *Sherbert v. Verner* (374 U.S. 398, 1963), the court utilized the compelling interest test to regulate religious actions. In short, this legal test means that if a law would inhibit religious freedoms in any way the government has to first prove why there is an important reason for doing so. In addition, *Sherbert* made clear that such regulations must impact freedom in the least restrictive way possible.

This view of religious freedom dominated the court's interpretation of these cases for almost three decades. Then, there was a sharp increase in the government's ability (and power) to regulate speech. Indeed, in *Employment Division v. Smith* (494 U.S. 872, 1990) the Rehnquist court changed course and ruled that states no longer need compelling reasons to pass laws that only *incidentally* impact religious freedom. That is, while they may give exemptions for religious practices that violate legitimate laws, doing so is not constitutionally required. This standard was not necessarily new, however. Indeed, it took the court full circle back to the type of standard it set out in *Reynolds.* (The one exception was the court's decision in *Church of the Lukumi Babalu Aye v. City of Hialeah* (508 U.S. 520, 1993), where it was clear to a unanimous court that the regulation of the nonmainstream religious sect was not based on legitimate government interests.)

Interestingly, the decision in *Smith* led to one of the most important separation of powers controversies between Congress and the court. In response to this increase in states' power, Congress passed the Religious Freedom Restoration Act of 1993 (RFRA), of which Title 42, Chapter 21B, Section 2000BB restored "the compelling interest test as set forth in *Sherbert v. Verner,* 374 U.S. 398 (1963)" and guaranteed "its application in all cases where free exercise of religion is substantially burdened."

Not to be deterred, the court heard *City of Boerne v. Flores* (521 U.S. 507, 1997) and used its power of judicial review to make clear that only the court decides to what precedents it must adhere. Certainly, the court won the day, and it continues to control laws that impact religious freedom. That said, its jurisprudential view varies depending on the policy in question. *Smith* may have been decided the way it was because the court was thinking about the legitimate regulation of illicit drug use and the ability of states to enact such regulations. However, on other issues, such as applying RFRA to the federal government more generally, the court has sided with protecting freedom of religion. Thus, *Gonzales v. O Centro Espirita Beneficente Uniao de Vegetal* (546 U.S. 418, 2006) and *Little Sisters of the Poor Home for the Aged v. Burwell* (578 U.S. ____, 2016) made it clear that the Roberts court is much more willing to uphold religious freedoms and disallow federal action.

In the end, the U.S. Supreme Court seems to protect religious freedoms whether it is more liberal (e.g., the Warren court) or conservative (e.g. the Roberts court). However, the avenue through which it accomplishes this goal (e.g., more or less government action) waxes and wanes based on the current political and legal environment.

Timothy R. Johnson is the Morse Alumni Distinguished Professor of Political Science at the University of Minnesota.

Siyu Li is a PhD candidate in the Department of Political Science at the University of Minnesota.

The First Amendment, Bible Reading, and the Use of "Under God" in the Pledge of Allegiance
Scott A. Merriman

Much ink has been spilled over the last sixty-six years since Bible reading and prayers were banned in the public schools, and more has been added with a controversy over whether to keep the phrase "under god" in the Pledge of Allegiance. With that in mind, both the original purpose of those acts and their original controversies need reconsideration.

The original purpose of Bible reading was not, as many today might suggest, to put God into the schools. While some might suggest that that is not the reason to read the Bible there now, the complaint that many have when the Bible was removed was that "they" (whoever "they" were) were "taking God out of the schools." However, the real purpose was more sectarian than religious. Bible reading was first emphasized in many places in the 1830s and 1840s concurrent with the rise in Irish immigration. Most Irish were Catholics, and the Catholics, in the eyes of the majority Protestants, had two strikes against them. First, they used a different (and therefore wrong in Protestant eyes) Bible; the Catholic Church used the Douay Version, while the Protestants generally used the King James Version (at the time). Second, Protestants also generally believed that the individual should read the Bible, but Catholics relied more on the priest. The Protestants thus wanted to force the Catholics to read the right Bible themselves and skip the priests, and they also hoped to convert a few. Catholics were outraged, and this resulted in riots and lawsuits. Many districts consequently shelved the idea. In other places, Catholics simply created their own schools.

A second wave of Bible reading (and a reemphasis of the first laws where they still existed) occurred in the 1940s and 1950s. These efforts were not aimed against the Catholics but another C—Communists. The argument was that "godless Communists" would be the only ones who would oppose religion, and so the best way to prove that the United States was not Communist was to prove that it was religious and therefore believed in the Bible (or at least the Torah, as some laws accommodated Judaism somewhat by reading from the Old Testament, which closely resembles the Torah). Those religious people who were of other faiths were sidelined here as well as those who felt that religion and the state should not be combined.

Bible reading (and prayer, sometimes composed on a state level) remained in schools until the early 1960s when Madelyn Murray O'Hair (founder of American Atheists) and others took cases all the way to the U.S. Supreme Court. O'Hair, frequently described as "the most hated woman in America," received most of the publicity, even though other cases were the ones that the Supreme Court used to strike down Bible reading and mandatory prayer.

Ever since, efforts have been underway to bring Bible reading back into American schools, including efforts by President Trump to allow or require classes on the Bible as a literary or historical work. That skips the Bible as religion of course and brings up many questions, including whether this is a backdoor to require the Bible to be read. It should also be noted that many schools already allow the Bible as literature but do not require it. Similar efforts have been undertaken to put up monumentally sized copies of the Ten Commandments in public places, claiming them as "foundational documents" rather than religious texts.

Those who favor tradition, or think they do, have had better luck with the Pledge of Allegiance and its assertion that the United States is "one nation under god." However, some assume that this phrase has always been there, and others defend it (or believe in it) as being put in there for religious reasons. Both are not the case. The original Pledge of Allegiance was written by a Christian Socialist and minister in the 1890s as a less militaristic alternative to another pledge, and it aimed to unify the country. The original hand salute, by the way, was very similar to the later Nazi salute. Religion, however, was no part of the pledge.

The phrase "under God" was not added to the pledge until the 1950s, as many argued that Communists could take the pledge as written, and they did not want that. Adding "under God" would both purge Communists and further set the United States apart from the USSR. (How Communists were both supposed to say the pledge in any form and mean it and still be a threat was unclear, as obviously Communists who did not mean the pledge could still say it with the phrase in and were not the target here.) "One Nation Under God" was also added to most U.S. currency in the 1950s.

Lawsuits started in the 1960s to remove the language, with the most frequent argument being that the phrase amounts to an establishment of religion. Cases have largely been unsuccessful, but the reasoning used did not satisfy religious conservatives either. The coinage and other uses of "In God we trust" has been upheld, as the courts have ruled that the language has become ceremonial and thus only has meaning in terms of honoring the country. What god is being trusted is never stated, and there cannot be only one as it is only ceremonial, one might think. Other uses have been held to be a secular national slogan.

Relatively recent efforts to challenge the pledge have run into difficulty, as no student is forced to say the pledge or that phrase, and so few have standing to challenge it. One parent, Michael Newdow, sued on his daughter's behalf but lost at the Supreme Court level because he did not have custody (*Elk Grove Unified School District v. Newdow*, 542 U.S. 1, 2004). Most other efforts have been struck down because students who do not want to participate do not have to. Thus, a uniting pledge without religion has been turned into a pledge for some with religion (perhaps) or a pledge for some with a secular national slogan.

Scott A. Merriman, PhD, is professor of history at Troy University, Alabama. He is the author of twelve books, including Religion and the State *(ABC-CLIO, 2009),* Religion and the Law in America *(ABC-CLIO, 2009), and* When Religious and Secular Interests Collide *(Praeger, 2017).*

When Speech Becomes Untrustworthy
John R. Vile

In his First Inaugural Address, Thomas Jefferson, who had questioned the constitutionality of the Alien and Sedition Act in the prior administration, observed that "error of opinion may be tolerated where reason is left free to combat it." Writing in *Federalist* No. 1, Alexander Hamilton said the issue of constitutional ratification boiled down to "whether societies of men are really capable or not of establishing good government from reflection and choice, or whether they are forever destined to depend for their political constitutions on accident and force."

Although the First Amendment is designed to foster such deliberation, these democratic hopes are being severely tested with the rise of new media outlets, epitomized by tweets, which seem far better designed to register emotion than to promote reasoned debate. These hopes are also being tested by a president who announced his improbable candidacy by claiming that foreign countries are "not sending their best" and asserting, with an exception for some "good people," that migrants are "bringing drugs," "bringing crime," and are "rapists." Moreover, in contrast to Jefferson's inaugural pleas ("We are all republicans, we are all federalists"), Trump has sought to impassion and consolidate his own narrow base rather than widening it, and he has consistently attacked mainline media as purveyors of "fake news" and "enemies of the people," even while continuing false and exaggerated claims.

This is hardly the first time in American history that partisan passions have run high, and there is a hoary adage that the way to tell whether a politician is lying is to see whether his lips are moving. During the early years of the nineteenth century (perhaps echoed in Trump's plan for the Washington, DC, Independence Day celebrations), members of the Democratic-Republican and Federalist Parties often celebrated the occasion separately, with one group heaping praise on George Washington as another praised Jefferson and one group lauding the piety of Adams and another decrying the alleged atheism of Jefferson (ironic since both were essentially Unitarians). One factor that apparently resolved some of the early tension was the mourning over the simultaneous deaths of Adams and

Jefferson on the fiftieth anniversary of the signing of the Declaration of Independence.

Presidents come and go, but American institutions remain; to date, they appear to be passing the stress test of the Trump presidency. To be sure, right-wing passion begets left-wing passion, and the media sometimes match Trump's exaggerations with their own. Some citizens have chosen to skip the news rather than sift through rival claims, and key Republican senators appear more defensive of party control than of their own legislative powers. The House of Representatives has, however, begun hearings and has issued subpoenas, while the Supreme Court has largely avoided direct confrontation.

One exception is the case of *Department of Commerce v. New York*, 588 U.S. ____, which the U.S. Supreme Court issued on the last day of its 2018–2019 session. Justice Samuel Alito correctly notes that "it is a sign of our time that the inclusion of a question about citizenship on the census has become a subject of bitter public controversy."

Governmental administrators must make thousands of decisions every day, and most are rarely questioned. When they are, courts are almost always deferential, especially when their decisions do not appear to violate explicit congressional instructions. In this case, however, when Trump's secretary of commerce, Wilbur Ross, announced that he was going to add a question about citizenship to the decennial census, he set off innumerable alarm bells. After reviewing thousands of pages of documents, the U.S. district court decided that Ross's decision was unreasonable and contrived and that it was designed to discourage immigrants from responding. This, in turn, would decrease congressional representation of, and funding for, areas with high immigrant populations.

Writing for a narrow 5–4 majority, Chief Justice Roberts acknowledged that Congress had given broad authority to the secretary of commerce to administer the Census and that it had used citizenship questions throughout most of U.S. history. Moreover, in contrast to the district court, Roberts decided that the secretary had made a reasonable choice between alternatives, which was his to make, without the benefit of judicial second-guessing. Having given the secretary the benefit of the doubt when passing through this gauntlet, however, Roberts suggested that some twelve thousand pages of evidence pointed to the fact that the reasons that the secretary had given were pretextual. In his words, "The evidence tells a story that does not match the explanation the Secretary gave for his decision." The secretary's stated purpose of seeking to better enforce the Voting Rights Act was contrived. The secretary had, in fact, solicited the request from the Department of Justice by which he had justified his own action.

The fascinating aspect of this opinion is that Justice Breyer and Justices Ginsburg, Sotomayor, and Kagan were willing to go even further, affirming both the district court's finding that the secretary's decision was not only pretextual but also "arbitrary, capricious, and an abuse of discretion." It is as though five justices were collectively announcing "liar, liar, pants on fire." I am reminded of Gunning Bedford of Delaware reportedly telling members of the delegates from the large states at the U.S. Constitutional Convention of 1787, "I do not, gentleman, trust you." Justice Thomas may be correct in thinking that this decision may be "an aberration—a ticket good for this day and this train only," but it is clearly a sign of the times.

American representative government assumes a people vigilant for their own liberties. It is based on their ability, at least in the long term, to judge truth over falsehood. The founders knew that public opinion was fickle. In writing to John Taylor on June 4, 1798, Thomas Jefferson observed that "a little patience, and we shall see the reign of witches pass over, their spells dissolve, and the people, recovering their true sight, restore their government to its true principles."

Prior to the last presidential election, a colleague and I suggested that Trump might win the election because of what we dubbed the "Mae West effect," that when facing two perceived evils, voters would chose the one not tried before. It will soon be time to reassess this decision in the 2020 presidential election. One can only hope that the nation will not be faced with the choice between two blatant prevaricators and that Jefferson's and Hamilton's expressed faith in the power of reason will prevail over deprecating characterizations of opponents and appeals to fear and passion.

John R. Vile, PhD, is a professor of political science and dean of the University Honors College at Middle Tennessee State University. He is the author of numerous books concerning the Supreme Court and the Constitution, including The Encyclopedia of the First Amendment, *2nd ed., 2 vols. (2008);* The Writing and Ratification of the U.S. Constitution *(2012);* The Men Who Made the Constitution *(2013);* Encyclopedia of Constitutional Amendments, *4th ed., 2 vols. (2015);* Immigration and Citizenship: A Documentary History *(2016);* A Companion to the U.S. Constitution and Its Amendments, *6th ed. (Praeger, 2017); and* Essential Supreme Court Decisions, *17th ed. (2018).*

Establishment of Religion by the Free Exercise Thereof
David L. Weddle

The First Amendment to the Constitution of the United States prevents Congress from passing laws establishing a national religion or prohibiting the free exercise of any religion. The framers believed that religious views are private opinions that should not determine government decisions about public good. Thomas Jefferson created the image of a "wall of separation between Church and State," and James Madison employed the more subtle metaphor of "the line of separation between the rights of religion and the Civil authority." The point of either image is to maintain a separation of individual beliefs and government actions.

The Constitution also stipulates that "no religious Test shall ever be required as a Qualification to any Office of public Trust under the United States" (Article VI). What the framers did not anticipate, however, is that religious advocates might use their right of free exercise to influence legislators and judges to enact and confirm their religious views as the law of the land. Through a wide array of media platforms, certain believers make up for the absence of an official religious test for public office by persuading others to impose a private religious test in deciding which candidates to support. Their appeals take the form of voter information guides that are handed out with clear endorsements of candidates who share conservative Christian values.

Recognizing the power of this informal religious test, every president in the modern era has been at pains to be photographed attending church and to end every address to the nation with the prayer, "God bless America." Although there is no legal religious test, the fact remains that we have never elected an avowed atheist to the office of president—and only one Catholic. For evangelical Christians, the only way to pass the unofficial test is to profess faith in Jesus Christ as Lord and to demonstrate loyalty to "Christian values." In the current administration, Secretary of State Mike Pompeo has passed the test with flying colors. Pompeo keeps an open Bible on his desk and has told various audiences that his view of the Middle East is shaped by the belief that Israel must occupy all of Palestine in fulfillment of prophecy. Where a choice is to be made between international law and the Book of Revelation, Pompeo chooses Christian scripture. His *free exercise* of religion leads to the *establishment* of his version of evangelical Christianity as the basis of national policy, at least on matters of global relations.

Nevertheless, the broader attempt to establish Christianity as the national religion of the United States proceeds by constitutional means of persuasion, using freedom of speech and press as well as the right to peacefully assemble to express grievances against existing policies. All these rights are legally and vigorously exercised by religious groups in the attempt to change American politics and culture according to their ideals.

For some Christians, however, the goal is nothing less than the fulfillment of a utopian dream of bringing the kingdom of God to the United States. They promote a form of Protestant Christianity called *dominion theology*.

Dominion theology is an umbrella term under which many different Christian views are gathered from Reformed theologians who seek to establish a Calvinist theonomy under the strict rule of biblical law to evangelicals who wish to bring about the kingdom of God *now* in the United States through political and legislative action. These groups differ from one another in many ways, but they agree that the whole of personal and social life should be unified under divine law. Accordingly, dominion leaders are not only active in electing members of the legislative branch who support their views but also in securing the appointment of members of the judicial branch who share their values. Religious conservatives want those values to guide legal decisions, and so they favor justices who interpret the Constitution in the same way they interpret the Bible: as a fixed text to be read literally with no deviation from the intention of the original framers. But even a "literal" reading, whether of the Bible or the Constitution, is already a form of interpretation. If the meaning of the text and its contemporary relevance were self-evident, we would need neither biblical commentators nor constitutional judges.

One defender of dominionist interpretation was David Chilton, who wrote the revealingly titled work *Paradise Restored: A Biblical Theology of Dominion* (1985). Chilton claims that the "hope of worldwide conquest for Christianity has been the traditional faith of the Church through the ages." He cites Jesus's command, "Let your light so shine before men, that they may see your good works and give glory your Father who is in heaven" (Matthew 5:13–16), and concludes, "This is nothing less than a mandate for the complete social transformation of the entire world. . . . We are commanded to live in such a way that someday all men . . . will become converted to the Christian faith."

The problem with this breathtaking ambition is twofold. First, as in all forms of theocracy, or "rule by God," God never appears to sit on the throne. Rather, a human authority represents God on earth and applies divine law. The distinction, then, between God's law and "man's law" collapses into a single interpretation of divine order. Theocracy inevitably relies on human representation. So, the thorny questions persist: Who speaks for God? Who enforces God's law? The answer is never "God" but someone who stands in for God and presumes divine authority—in short, a religious despot. On the ground of representing divine rule, the Protestant Reformer John Calvin approved the execution of Unitarian Michael Servetus in sixteenth-century Geneva, and colonial Puritans hanged Quakers on Boston Common.

Second, success in converting the world's population to evangelical Christianity would result in the elimination of every other religion on the planet. To put it starkly, the victory of universal Christian missions would be an ideological Final Solution. If everyone on the globe became a Christian, evangelicals would no longer face any "problem" from Jews, Muslims, Buddhists, Hindus, or any other religious community. All non-Christians would become extinct. Religious and cultural diversity would disappear through the aggressive evangelism required of every Christian by dominion theology.

The biblical basis for this audacious program is the mandate in Genesis 1:28 to "have dominion . . . over every living thing that moves upon the earth." Many evangelicals extend the conventional interpretation of this verse—that humanity has responsibility to care for the natural environment—to the claim that Christians should also supervise human culture. The goal is to establish the "lordship" (meaning of the Latin root *dominio*) of Christ over American public life.

Specifically, dominion evangelicals refer to seven mountains that represent spheres of civic activity, including family, media, government, business, entertainment, religion, and education. The scope of the project is based on biblical prophecy: "In days to come the mountain of the Lord's house shall be established as the highest of the mountains. . . . All the nations shall stream to it" (Isaiah 2:2). The prophet is speaking of the restoration of the Temple in the messianic age, when the entire world is expected to look to Jerusalem for divine instruction. Appropriating this reference to Israel's destiny, dominion theologians insist that it foretells the vocation of the United States to lead the world into the golden age of the kingdom of God on earth.

This ambition of making Christian beliefs and values the guiding principles of American polity—directing the executive, judicial, and legislative branches of government—is a direct challenge to the prohibition of the establishment of religion in the First Amendment. If dominion evangelicals are successful in their mission, the separation of religion and government would be erased. They would effectively *establish* their religion by their *free exercise* of it.

David L. Weddle, PhD (Harvard), is the professor emeritus of religion at Colorado College, where he taught courses on philosophy of religion, ethics, theology, and comparative religion. He is the author of Miracles: Wonder and Meaning in World Religions *(2011) and* Sacrifice in Judaism, Christianity, and Islam *(2017).*

The First Amendment and Native American Religion
David Zeh

In 1982, the U.S. Forest Service conducted its final environmental survey for the construction of a paved road through the Chimney Rock area of the Six Rivers National Forest in California. However, the Chimney Rock area is considered to be a sacred site for the Yurok, Karuk, and Tolowa tribes, which requires that the area remain private and untouched by civilization. The Northwest Indian Cemetery Protective Association filed suit, claiming that the construction of the road as well as harvesting timber in the surrounding area would permanently damage the sacred site. The group argued that damage done to the Chimney Rock area would be a direct violation of Indigenous rights under the Free Exercise Clause of the First Amendment.

By 1987, the *Lyng v. Northwest Indian Cemetery Protective Association* (485 U.S. 439, 1988) case had made its way to the U.S. Supreme Court. During the trial, Justice Sandra Day O'Connor cited the 1986 case *Bowen v. Roy* (476 U.S. 693), where two parents argued that their religious beliefs prevented their two-year-old daughter from receiving a Social Security number (SSN). The parents stated that the numerical identifier would "rob her of her spirit and prevent her from attaining greater spiritual power." The court ruled in a 5–3 decision that giving their daughter a SSN would not violate their freedom to express their religion. Based on the decision made during the *Bowen v. Roy* trial, Justice O'Connor was able to draw parallels between the two cases, and with a vote of 5–3, the court decided that the construction of the road did not violate rights under the Free Exercise Clause of the First Amendment.

It is fairly common that Native American religious beliefs are not taken seriously, especially in a society that is dominated by Christianity. This is mainly due to the drastic differences between their religious practices. For example, the tradition of using feathers during ceremonies has been practiced long before European contact. However, laws have prevented Native Americans from acquiring these feathers for religious purposes, which is a direct violation of their First Amendment right. It is also worth noting that, during Prohibition, the Catholic Church was given special permission to still serve wine during Communion.

Unfortunately, it is clear that Judeo-Christian religions have been favored over Native American beliefs and traditions. Barney Old Coyote of the Crow Nation describes the failure of the First Amendment, stating,

It is a bleak history of disrespect, ignorance, suppression and attempted eradication of Native beliefs and practices.

Such treatment by the White society could not have been so much the result of a conviction of the righteousness of their own faith—for they respected or at least tolerated other faiths in both the Old and New World. It must surely have rested in the belief that the "barbarism" and "savagery" of the Natives rendered their religious beliefs unworthy of any respect or consideration.

During a 2004 panel discussion on the American Indian Religious Freedom Act's impact, Suzan Shown Harjo discussed why it failed in protecting Chimney Rock as well as other sacred sites scattered across the country. Harjo had great insight on the American Indian Religious Freedom Act because she had previously helped develop and pass the law during her time as a congressional liaison for Indian affairs under the Carter administration in 1978. Her explanation was that the act only served as a policy statement and not as a true substantive law that would actually protect and preserve sacred sites. It was clear after the *Lyng* case that more legislation was needed to make a difference.

In 1990, the Native American Graves Protection and Repatriation Act (NAGPRA) was signed into law. It sought to protect indigenous human remains, funerary objects, and sacred objects that have a "cultural affiliation" with "presently existing" Indian tribes or Native Hawaiian organizations. However, this law was not met without controversy. Archaeologists who study Native American prehistory felt that this law would put an end to their field because they now had to repatriate artifacts back to their respected tribes. While some anthropologists found this law to be a nuisance, others saw it as a chance to reconcile the relationship between archaeologists and Native Americans. In a debate discussing NAGPRA's effect on archaeology, Larry Zimmerman states,

What steps should archaeologists who study native peoples take to ensure an amicable working relationship?

First, we should be activists in consulting with any community or group that might be affected by our work, and we shouldn't be doing it just because it is required by law or is politically correct. Rather, we should consult Native Americans because we recognize their valid interests in the past. Working with them, they will provide us with insights into our understanding of their past.

The *Lyng* decision also sparked major criticism over the American Indian Religious Freedom Act. The case clearly proved that the act would not defend religious rights for Native Americans and that changes needed to be made for the law to work properly. In 1994, Congress admitted to the federal government's failure to understand and protect sites that are sacred to Native Americans. The 1994 amendment to the American Indian Religious Freedom Act finally addressed and helped settle the issues that were made while drafting the original.

Further Reading

American Indian Religious Freedom Act (92 Stat. 459, 1978).

Harjo, Suzan Shown. 2004. "Keynote Address: The American Indian Religious Freedom Act: Looking Back and Looking Forward." *Wicazo Sa Review* 19 (2): 143–151.

Kelsey, Penelope, and Carpenter, Cari M. 2011. "'In the End, Our Message Weighs': Blood Run, NAGPRA, and American Indian Identity." *American Indian Quarterly* 35 (1): 56.

Zimmerman, Larry J. 1999. "Sharing Control of the Past." Archaeology Archive, February 26. Accessed July 2, 2020. https://archive.archaeology.org/online/features/native/debate.html.

David Zeh is a graduate of the University of Wisconsin–Oshkosh, with a dual major in anthropology and history. He has specialized in the Oneida Tribe in Wisconsin.

4 Profiles

Introduction

Many organizations and people have been and continue to be involved in the political conflict over First Amendment rights in the United States, an enduring issue in American politics. This chapter provides a list and brief descriptions of some of the leading players in the arena of that perennial political struggle. The chapter is structured as follows: organizations involved and then people involved.

Governmental Organizations

This section lists and briefly profiles a few major agencies and organizations involved, beginning with federal government offices and agencies. Virtually any of the cabinet-level departments of the U.S. government can, by their rules and regulations and implementation of federal laws, play a role in defining the fundamental freedoms specified by the First Amendment.

Attorney General and Solicitor General of the United States

The Office of the Attorney General of the United States (AG) was established by the Judiciary Act of 1789. Since then,

---

The United States Supreme Court Building at sunset in Washington, D.C. Supreme Court decisions, through the power of judicial review, have been the single most important protector of First Amendment freedoms. (Luckyphotographer/Dreamstime.com)

eighty-five attorneys general have served the country, and the eighty-fifth is William Barr. The AG's office gradually evolved over time to become the head of the U.S. Department of Justice (DOJ), when that department was created in 1870, making the attorney general the chief law enforcement officer of the federal government. The position is one of the four most important cabinet-level offices, and is seventh in the line for succession to the presidency.

The AG represents the United States in legal matters and gives legal advice to the president and the heads of the executive branch departments when asked to do so. In matters of exceptional gravity, the AG appears before the U.S. Supreme Court to argue the government's case, although that task is usually performed by the solicitor general of the United States. The AG is appointed by the president and confirmed by the U.S. Senate. As head of the DOJ, the office is arguably second only to the Supreme Court in impact on legal matters pertaining to the First Amendment rights.

The AG has fairly wide latitude in deciding whether to bring cases to federal court on the basis of constitutionality questions or issues. When a case is brought to the federal court level by other litigants challenging a law or government action on First Amendment grounds, the attorney general must represent the government's side, although the solicitor general is normally the person who actually presents the federal government's case.

The solicitor general (SG) is likewise appointed by the president and confirmed by the Senate (28 U.S.C. 505). The position was created by the Act of June 22, 1870 (16 Stat. 162, 1870). The SG determines the legal position that the federal government will take to the Supreme Court and supervises and conducts cases in which the government is a party. The office also files amicus curiae briefs in which the federal government has a significant interest, and in federal courts of appeal, the SG argues in most of the cases in which an amicus curiae brief has been filed. The SG's office reviews cases decided against the United States in federal district courts and approves every case in which the federal government files an appeal. Five solicitors general have gone on to serve on the Supreme Court and numerous others on U.S. courts of appeals.

In addition to deciding whether to bring a case, the AG may opt to submit an amicus curiae brief in cases involving First Amendment rights, even if the case does not involve a federal government act. When the AG deems challenges to state or local government actions on First Amendment constitutional grounds, they are likely of import to the national level as well.

Office of the President of the United States (POTUS)

The president of the United States (POTUS) is both the head of state and head of the federal government (the executive branch of the United States). By constitutional powers (Article II), the president directs all the departments and executive agencies and is the commander in chief of the armed forces. The office's constitutional powers include execution of all federal law; appointment of federal executive, diplomatic, regulatory, and judicial offices; and the conclusion of treaties with foreign powers (with the advice and consent of the Senate). The president can grant pardons, reprieves, and clemency and convenes and adjourns either or both houses of the Congress under extraordinary circumstances. The president increasingly sets the legislative agenda of the party to which the president is titular head and directs both foreign and domestic policy.

The president is elected indirectly by the people through the electoral college to a four-year term, and along with the vice president, the president is one of only two nationally elected federal officers. Since 1951, with adoption of the Twenty-Second Amendment, the president is limited to two terms. On January 20, 2017, Donald Trump was sworn in as the forty-fifth POTUS.

The president impacts First Amendment freedoms in the United States in several ways. The president appoints some eight thousand to fourteen thousand offices—ambassadors, cabinet members, and other federal officers—who by their actions and departmental rules and regulations may affect one's fundamental freedoms. President Franklin Delano Roosevelt established the Executive Office of the President (EOP) in 1939. The EOP is overseen by the White House chief of staff, and it has traditionally housed many of the president's closest advisers.

The president also affects First Amendment freedoms by executive orders, which are reviewable by federal courts and can be superseded by legislation enacted by Congress. Historically, the greatest impact has been through the president's power to nominate federal judges, including the U.S. courts of appeals and the U.S. Supreme Court. Arguably, the greatest historical impact has been through the president's appointment of the chief justice, five of whom are profiled in this chapter: Warren Burger, Charles Hughes, William Rehnquist, John Roberts, and Earl Warren, each of whom has been instrumental in several landmark Supreme Court decisions on cases involving the First Amendment.

Every president has the potential to play a powerful role in matters concerning First Amendment freedoms. This chapter profiles four presidents to exemplify the power of the office to affect fundamental freedoms: George W. Bush, Thomas Jefferson, Barack Obama, and Donald Trump.

Supreme Court of the United States (SCOTUS)

As indicated by the plethora of landmark decisions discussed herein, the Supreme Court of the United States (SCOTUS) is the government organization that has had the most profound impact on fundamental freedoms. The SCOTUS oversees the federal court system, which is composed of ninety-four district-level trial courts in twelve regional circuits and thirteen courts of appeals. The federal district courts are the workhorses of the federal judicial system in that almost every civil or criminal case heard in the federal courts starts at the district court level. These courts review petitions, hear motions, hold trials, and issue injunctions, all of which can have an impact on First Amendment freedom matters.

The federal court system was established by Article III of the U.S. Constitution, which states, "The judicial Power of the

United States shall be vested in one supreme Court, and in such inferior Courts as the Congress may from time to time ordain and establish." The SCOTUS was created in accordance with this provision and by authority of the Judiciary Act of September 24, 1789 (1 Stat. 73) which states its jurisdiction as follows:

> shall extend to all Cases, in Law and Equity, arising under the Constitution, the Laws of the United States, and Treaties made, or which shall be made, under their Authority, to all Cases affecting Ambassadors, other public Ministers and Consuls, to all Cases of admiralty and maritime Jurisdiction, to Controversies to which the United States shall be a Party, to Controversies between two or more States—between a State and Citizens of another State, between Citizens of different States, between Citizens of the same State claiming Lands under Grants of different States, and between a State, or the Citizens thereof, and foreign States, Citizens or Subjects.
>
> In all Cases affecting Ambassadors, other public ministers and Consuls, and those in which a State shall be Party, the Supreme Court shall have original Jurisdiction. In all the other Cases before mentioned, the Supreme Court shall have appellate jurisdiction, both as to Law and Fact, with such Exceptions, and under such Regulations as the Congress shall make.

The Supreme Court consists of the chief justice and eight associate justices as fixed by Congress (28 U.S.C. 1). The president appoints justices with the advice and consent of the Senate. Article III, Section 1, provides that federal justices, both of the Supreme Court and of inferior courts (district and appellate), "shall hold their offices during good behaviour" (i.e., lifetime appointment). Congress has from time to time conferred upon the Supreme Court power to prescribe rules of procedure to be followed by the lower courts of the United States (28 U.S.C. 2071).

As of 2019, the members of SCOTUS are the following: Chief Justice John Roberts Jr. and Associate Justices Clarence Thomas, Ruth Bader Ginsberg, Stephen Breyer, Samuel Alito Jr., Sonia Sotomayor, Elena Kagan, Neil Gorsuch, and Brett Kavanaugh. Retired justices that are still living are Sandra Day O'Connor, David Souter, John Paul Stevens, and Anthony Kennedy. This chapter profiles five chief justices: Warren Burger, Charles Hughes, William Rehnquist, John Roberts, and Earl Warren. Chief justices have particularly important impact in that they assign the justice among the majority who will write the court's opinion. This chapter also profiles six associate justices: four representing ideological ends, Ruth Bader Ginsberg and William Brennan on the liberal end and the late Antonin Scalia and Potter Stewart as conservatives, and two justices who often have been the swing vote between the conservative and liberal ideological spectrum of the justices, Sandra Day O'Connor and Anthony Kennedy.

The SCOTUS essentially gave itself the power of judicial review of the constitutionality of acts of the Congress, the president and executive branch departments and agencies, and of state governments in the *Marbury v. Madison* decision (5 U.S. 137, 1803). The court, and the opinion of its chief justice, John Marshall, affirmed for the first time the principle that the courts may declare an act of Congress void if it is inconsistent with the U.S. Constitution. William Marbury had been appointed a justice of the peace of the District of Columbia in the final hours of President James Madison's administration.

U.S. Department of Homeland Security (DHS)

The U.S. Department of Homeland Security (DHS) was established on November 25, 2002, under President George W. Bush in response to the 9/11 terrorist attacks. DHS merged twenty-two agencies into a single new department. It was the most significant reorganization of the federal government since the National Security Act of 1947, which created the U.S. Department of Defense (DOD). In 2017, DHS had a budget of $40.6 billion.

The current DHS acting secretary is Chad Wolf, who was appointed by President Donald Trump in November 2019. Wolf leads the third-largest cabinet-level department of the U.S. government, with a workforce of 240,000 in twenty-two component units, among which are included the Transportation Safety Administration (TSA), Customs and Border Protection (CBP), Immigration and Customs Enforcement (ICE), and U.S. Citizenship and Immigration Services (USCIS), each of which often involves rules, regulations, and enforcement actions that give rise to challenges on religious grounds (e.g., a "Muslim ban," anti-terrorism actions constituting racial profiling of religious minorities, conflict with cities and religious groups providing sanctuary to illegal immigrants). DHS is responsible for counterterrorism, cybersecurity, aviation security, border security, port and maritime security, the administration and enforcement of immigration laws, the protection of national leaders, the protection of critical infrastructure, response to disasters, and detection of and protection against chemical, biological, and nuclear threats to the homeland.

DHS has been criticized for its excessive bureaucracy, waste, and ineffectiveness. It has been alleged to use racial profiling against Muslim Americans and for surveillance of controversial imams and Muslim mosques. It has been charged with implementing the three travel bans imposed through executive order by President Trump, each of which has been challenged in federal district courts, resulting in stays or injunctions against the department from enforcing what two federal district courts (one in Washington and one in Hawaii) have ruled unconstitutional infringements of the rights of Islamic individuals. The third iteration of the travel ban was in the main upheld by the U.S. Supreme Court in *Trump v. Hawaii* (585 U.S. ____, 2018).

U.S. Department of Justice (DOJ)

The U.S. Department of Justice (DOJ) was established in 1870 by President Ulysses S. Grant. It is home to several divisions and bureaus that potentially involve the DOJ in First Amendment freedom matters and controversies. It assumed control of federal prisons in 1884 (being transferred from the U.S. Department of Interior). Racial and religious minorities in the federal prison system have at times involved the DOJ in religious freedom controversies. It established its Civil Rights Division in 1957. On occasion, civil rights have led to conflict with free exercise of religion or freedom of assembly, of the press, or of speech. In 1909, the DOJ's Environment and Natural Resources Division was established. Matters before that division have on occasion conflicted with religious freedom issues, for example, with claimed sacred sites of Native Americans versus the DOJ policy and rulings over oil pipelines. The DOJ established a National Security Division in 2007, which occasionally gets embroiled in controversies with Muslim Americans.

The DOJ houses several law enforcement agencies: the U.S. Marshals Service (USMS) (1789); the Federal Bureau of Investigation (FBI) (1908); the Federal Bureau of Prisons (BOP) (1930); the Bureau of Alcohol, Tobacco, Firearms and Explosives (ATF) (1972); the U.S. Drug Enforcement Agency (DEA) (1973); the Office of Inspector General (OIG) (1976); the Executive Office of Immigration Review (EOIR) (1983); the Office of Immigration Litigation (OIL) (1983); and the Office of Tribal Justice (OTJ) (1995). In 2015, the DOJ's budget was $31 billion.

The DOJ is led by the attorney general of the United States. Some recent AGs that have been involved in conflicts over religious freedom include Janet Reno (1993–2001), the first female AG, appointed by President Bill Clinton; Alberto Gonzales (2005–2007), appointed by President George W. Bush; Loretta Lynch (2015–2017), appointed by President Barack Obama; and Sally Yates, acting AG from January 20, 2017, to January 30, 2017, who was fired by President Donald Trump for refusing to defend the constitutionality of his travel ban against persons from six predominately Muslim countries by maintaining that the executive order was an unconstitutional infringement.

Nongovernmental Organizations

There are a plethora of nongovernmental organizations that have been involved in controversies and conflicts over First Amendment freedoms in American politics. Space constraints limit the discussion here to about a dozen such organizations that exemplify the category. Some are lobby groups that advocate for religious groups and free exercise, and others seek to defend the "absolute wall of separation" between church and state and are involved in Establishment Clause cases. Some have advocated on freedom of the press and free speech issues, and still others exemplify the think tank type of organization that does research on First Amendment freedom topics. Their profiles are presented here in alphabetical order.

Access Now

Access Now was founded in 2009 by Brett Solomon and Cameran Ashraf as an international nonprofit human rights and public policy advocacy group for open and free internet that promotes free speech, digital security, privacy, net discrimination, and business and human rights. It campaigns against internet shutdowns, online censorship, and governmental surveillance. It supports net neutrality and the use of encrypted and thoughtful cybersecurity laws and regulations.

Access Now challenges telecommunication companies on transparency reporting. It offers direct assistance and advice to activists, independent media, and civil society organizations. It runs an annual international conference, RightCon. It is part of a network of nonprofit organizations specializing in Tor anonymity networks via workshops and donations. It fights for open and secure communications for all.

Access Now's stated mission is to defend and extend digital rights of users by advocating for innovative policy, user engagement, and direct technical support. It has a staff of more than forty in ten locations around the world, particularly in New York and Washington, DC. As of 2018, it was funded at $5.1 million (AccessNow.org).

American-Arab Anti-Discrimination Committee (ADC)

The American-Arab Anti-Discrimination Committee (ADC) is a civil rights organization whose mission is to defend the civil rights of people of Arab descent and to promote the cultural heritage of American Arabs. The ADC was founded in 1980 by then U.S. senator James Abourezk (D-SD). It claims to be the largest Arab American grassroots organization in the country. The ADC supports the human and civil rights of all people and opposes racism, bigotry, and discrimination in any form. It is open to participation and support from people of all ethnic, racial, and religious backgrounds. Its objectives are to do the following: (1) defend and promote human rights and civil rights and liberties of Arab Americans and other persons of Arab heritage; (2) combat stereotyping and discrimination against and affecting the Arab American community; (3) serve as the public voice of the Arab American community on domestic and foreign policy matters and issues; (4) educate the American public to promote greater understanding of Arab history and culture; and (5) organize and mobilize the Arab American community to further its objectives. It claims members in all fifty states; there are about three million Americans who trace their roots to an Arab country.

The ADC sponsors a number of programs to combat discrimination and bias against Arab Americans, including stereotypes of Arabs and Muslims, and it is a member of the Leadership Council on Civil Rights. Cofounder Samer Khalaf, an attorney from New Jersey, became the ADC national president in 2013. Its distinguished advisory board has included Muhammad Ali; Queen Noor of Jordan; actor and voice actor Casey Kasem; U.S. Representatives John Conyers (D-MI), Darrell Issa (R-CA), and Nick Joe Rahall (D-WVA); former representative Paul Findley (R-IL); and Philip Saliba, the archbishop of New York and metropolitan of all North America for the Antiochian Orthodox Christian Church.

The Legal Department of the ADC offers counsel in cases of discrimination, defamation, and hate crimes, and it participates in selected litigation in hundreds of cases against airlines and employers for discrimination on the basis of ethnicity and national origin and against the U.S. government for discriminatory detentions without probable cause of Arabs and Muslims post-9/11. The ADC Communications Department challenges defamation, stereotyping, and bias in films, television, and news reporting, and its spokespeople are considered authoritative voices on Arab American affairs. Its Government Affairs Department works with the U.S. Congress, the White House, and the Departments of State and Justice to promote the interests of the Arab American community (i.e., by lobbying). It contributes to the NAAA-ADC Political Action Committee to support political candidates for federal office. Its Research Institute, begun in 1981, sponsors research studies, seminars, conferences and publications about discrimination faced by Arab Americans; promotes better understanding of Arab cultural heritage; and provides lesson plans, background articles, fact sheets, bibliographies, and other resources to educators.

The ADC offices suffered a series of violent attacks in 1985, among a series of attacks on mosques in Southern California. In 1991, during the Gulf War, it was targeted by violent anti-Arab telephone messages, and the ADC documented more than one hundred hate crimes against Arab Americans. The 1996 Antiterrorism and Effective Death Penalty Act and the Illegal Immigration Reform and Immigrant Responsibility Act allowed for the deportation of immigrants for minor offenses and allowed secret classified evidence and the denial of bond for those under threat of deportation.

One case involving the targeting of Arab Americans reached the U.S. Supreme Court, *Reno v. American-Arab Anti-Discrimination Committee* (525 U.S. 471, 1999). In its decision, delivered by Justice Antonin Scalia, joined by Chief Justice Rehnquist and Justices O'Connor, Kennedy, and Thomas, with concurring opinions by Justices Breyer and Stevens and a dissenting opinion by Justice David Souter, the Supreme Court denied the case on the basis of the federal courts being deprived of jurisdiction over the respondent's suit, upholding the general rule that revised procedures for removing aliens do not apply to noncitizen aliens.

American Atheists (AA)

American Atheists (AA) is a nonprofit activist civil rights and civil liberties organization that defends atheists and advocates for complete separation of church and state. It was formed in 1963 by Madalyn Murray O'Hair following her role in removing mandatory prayer in public schools (*Abington School District v. Schempp* [374 U.S. 203] and *Murray v. Curlett* [371 U.S. 944] [1963]). Its mission is to promote atheism and secular humanism and to oppose religion in the public sphere. In 2005, it formed the Godless Americans Political Action Committee (GAPAC) to endorse candidates who support the separation of church and state. The GAPAC opposes, but to date to no avail, Christmas being a federal holiday and any mention of God on currency or in the Pledge of Allegiance.

The organization is known for its antireligious billboards. In 2014, it launched an internet television channel on the Roku streaming media platform, offering twenty-four hours of programming alongside an on-demand service to "provide a breadth of content, from science to politics to comedy."All of their content is centered on the issue of freedom *from* religion." (Atheists.org/about).

The ADC won several important cases among some twenty-two cases in which it was a party between 1963 and 2012, all involving the separation of church and state issue: *Murray v. Curlett* (374 U.S. 203, 1963), challenging Bible reading and prayer recitation in Maryland public schools; *Murray v. U.S.* (487 U.S. 533, 1987), forcing the Federal Elections Commission to extend the fairness doctrine to atheists; *O'Hair v. Paine* (397 U.S. 531, 1970), challenging NASA's religious use of the space program in requiring astronauts to read the Bible during a space flight; *O'Hair v. Blumenthal* (462 F. Supp. 19, 1978), challenging the use of the phrase "In God We Trust" on U.S. currency; *O'Hair v. Hill* (641 F. 2nd 680, 1981), seeking the removal of a provision from the Texas Constitution requiring a belief in God of persons holding offices of public trust; *American Atheists Inc. and Daniel Cooney v. Bradford County, Florida* (LeMay 2018), challenging a display of the Ten Commandments on public property; and *American Atheists v. Port Authority of New Jersey and New York* (July 28, 2014, U.S. Court of Appeals, Second Circuit), protesting the placement of cross-shaped steel beams called the "World Trade Center cross" at the National September 11 Memorial and Museum.

American Civil Liberties Union (ACLU)

The American Civil Liberties Union (ACLU) is a nonpartisan nonprofit organization that was formed to defend and preserve the individual rights and liberties of every person in the United States by the Constitution and laws of the United States. It was founded in 1920, and as of 2020, it claims a national membership of over 1.5 million. The ACLU has an annual budget of more than $133 million and a staff of one hundred attorneys as well as several thousand volunteer attorneys.

The ACLU lobbies for policy positions that include opposition to the death penalty; support of same-sex marriage rights and the right of LGBT people to adopt; support of birth control and abortion rights; elimination of discrimination against women, minorities, and LGBT people; support of the rights of prisoners and opposition to torture; and opposition to government preference for religion over nonreligion or for particular faiths over others. The ACLU consists of two separate but closely affiliated nonprofits: the ACLU, a 501(c)(4) social welfare group, and the ACLU Foundation, a 501(c)(3) public charity. Both engage in civil rights litigation, advocacy, and education; however, only the 501(c)(3) donations are tax-deductible, and only the 501(c)(4) group can engage in unlimited political lobbying.

The ACLU often engages in cases supporting Native American rights and defense of Jehovah's Witnesses members (filing support in *Lovell v. City of Griffin* (303 U.S. 444, 1938), *Martin v. Struthers* (317 U.S. 141, 1943), and *Cantwell v. Connecticut* (310 U.S. 296, 1940)). The ACLU supported Jehovah's Witnesses in a couple of flag saluting cases, winning in *West Virginia State Board of Education v. Barnette* (319 U.S. 624, 1943). It led legal battles over the separation of church and state, including *Everson v. Board of Education* (330 U.S. 1, 1947), in which Justice Hugo Black wrote, "The First Amendment has erected a wall between church and state. . . . That wall must be kept high and impregnable." The ACLU prevailed in *McCollum v. Board of Education* (333 U.S. 203, 1948) and in *Engel v. Vitale* (370 U.S. 421, 1962). The ACLU participated in lobbying efforts to oppose the School Prayer Constitutional Amendment and the 1966 congressional vote on the proposed amendment, which failed to obtain the required two-thirds majority. The ACLU challenged but lost cases on state laws requiring commercial businesses to close on Sunday.

In 2017, the ACLU supported and filed amicus curiae briefs in the two federal district court challenges to President Trump's travel ban executive orders. In both cases (in Washington and Hawaii), the district court justice ruled against the travel ban as being unconstitutional Muslim bans.

Americans for Religious Liberty (ARL)

Founded in 1981, Americans for Religious Liberty (ARL) is a political organization that supports the constitutional principle of separation of church and state to guarantee religious and intellectual freedom, religiously neutral democratic public education, and individual freedom of conscience. It promotes its goals through publishing, litigation, coalition building, public speaking, and expert testimony before national and state legislative committees, and it regularly cooperates with a wide range of civil liberties, educational, religious, labor, and reproductive rights advocacy groups and organizations.

In 2016 through 2018, ARL lobbied against the Mexican border wall proposed by President Trump. In January 2015, it published a comprehensive analysis of school voucher and tuition tax credit plans, detailing their harm to public education, religious freedom, and democratic values and institutions based on decades of research and involvement with the school voucher issue. In 2013, the ARL filed an amicus curiae brief with the U.S. Supreme Court in the case of *Town of Greece v. Susan Galloway and Linda Stephens* (572 U.S. 565), which challenged as discriminatory the practice of town council prayer. In 2012, it opposed any form of aid to faith-based private schools. As part of its public relations campaign, it publishes the journal/newsletter *The Voice of Reason*.

The ARL has been involved in sixty actions in the courts, regularly using amicus curiae briefs in federal district courts and the Supreme Court and often working with other organizations in coalition briefs, for example, in *Lamont v. Woods* 948 F. 2d 825 (2d Cir. 1991), which was filed in the U.S. Second Court of Appeals in New York. Lamont involved a challenge to U.S. government aid to faith-based schools in other countries. Between 1983 and 1989, the U.S. Agency for International Development (USAID) distributed more than $14 million to faith-based schools in the Philippines, Egypt, Israel, Jamaica, South Korea, and Micronesia. The appeals court found such aid unconstitutional, and the Bush administration decided not to appeal.

Other cases the ARL supported include *Gonzales v. O Centro Espirita Beneficiente Uniao do Vegetal* (546 U.S. 418, 2006), *Cutter v. Wilkinson* (544 U.S. 709, 2005), and *Gonzales v. State of Oregon* (546 U.S. 243, 2005), in defense of Oregon's physician-assisted suicide. It was involved in a number of cases involving religion in public schools: *Bauchman v. West High School* (132 F.3d 542, 1997), *Chaudhuri v. State of Tennessee* (886 F. Supp. 1374, 1995), *Ingebretsen v. Jackson Public School District* (864 F. Supp. 1473, 1994), *Lee v. Weisman* (505 U.S. 577, 1992), and *Board of Education of the Westside Community*

Schools v. Mergens (496 U.S. 226, 1990). The ARL supported briefs in a number of cases in regard to religious displays in government buildings: *Van Orden v. Perry* (545 U.S. 677, 2005), *Freethought Society v. Chester County* (334 F.3d. 247, 2003), and *Capitol Square Review and Advisory Board v. Pinette* (515 U.S. 753, 1995). It supported challenges to tax aid to faith-based schools (mostly various voucher plans) in such cases as *Bush v. Holmes* (919 So.2d 392, 2006), which successfully challenged Florida's school voucher plan that the Florida Supreme Court ruled unconstitutional in 2006; *Zelman v. Simmons-Harris* (536 U.S. 639, 2002), challenging Ohio's school voucher plan; and *Agostini v. Felton* (521 U.S. 203, 1997), challenging tax aid to faith-based schools in New York.

Americans United for Separation of Church and State (AU)

Founded in 1947, the Americans United for Separation of Church and State (AU) is a broad coalition of religious, educational, and civic leaders that was first formed to oppose pending legislation in Congress that would have extended government aid to private religious schools. It was founded to activate a national focus pursuing goals on several fronts for the education (lobbying) of members of Congress and state and local legislators on the importance of maintaining church and state separation. State and local chapters were formed to work at the grassroots level. AU publishes a magazine, *Church and State*, to help educate the general public. These goals continue as central to AU's activities. In the 1960s, AU supported the Supreme Court's rulings striking down state and local government-sponsored prayer and Bible reading in public school laws and defended the rulings in public, arguing that no government had the right to compel children to take part in religious worship and that truly voluntary student prayer remained legal.

During the late 1970s, when the religious right began to rise as a political force in American politics with such groups as Jerry Falwell's Moral Majority and its allied groups vigorously attacking the church and state separation principle in the halls of Congress and in federal courts, AU fought their efforts. The Moral Majority targeted public schools for "takeover" campaigns to saturate the curriculum with fundamentalist theology. Again, AU fought their efforts.

In the 1980s, "education choice" advocates began their campaign for tax subsidies for religious education through school voucher programs and tuition tax credit plans. AU rallied to oppose those efforts and helped secure a string of court victories over the religious right and the pro-voucher allied groups. It organized Americans to speak out against the extreme and intolerant agenda of the religious right. In the 1990s, those forces regrouped under the leadership of TV evangelist Pat Robertson's Christian Coalition. The coalition focused heavily on local school board politics. The Christian Coalition advocated an end to public education and the "Christianization" of American politics, arguing that the nation was founded as "a Christian nation." AU launched an in-depth media campaign exposing and opposing the radical agenda of the Christian Coalition.

AU was soon opposing other religious right organizations, such as Focus on the Family, the Family Research Council, and the Alliance Defense Fund. AU continued opposing voucher plan initiatives at the state level and to block so-called faith-based initiatives in the federal government, although they failed to block the George W. Bush administration's efforts to establish such an office in the White House. AU continues to advocate that all Americans have the constitutionally protected right to practice the religion of their choice; to refrain from taking part in any religion, as their individual conscience dictates; and to uphold the principle that government at all levels must remain neutral on religious matters. It has also supported, by amicus briefs, cases of freedom of speech.

Throughout its history, AU has enjoyed the participation of many clergy members, but it is officially a nonsectarian and nonpartisan organization. AU works with Christians, Jews, Muslims, Buddhists, Hindus, Humanists, and those who profess religious beliefs or no belief. Its members are affiliated with Democrats, Republicans, Independents, and other political affiliations (e.g., Libertarians) who likewise espouse belief in the principle of religious liberty. AU continues to stress that the wall of separation must remain a high and firm barrier between the institutions of government and religion, that religious liberty is not secure when the government presumes to promote religion over non-religion or favors one faith over another, and that it is not secure when government uses public services intended for everyone, such as public schools, to indoctrinate or coerce participation in worship. AU stresses that religious liberty is not secure when federal or state taxes are used to forward someone's religion or when the government appropriates and displays the symbols of faith that not everyone shares; that government-sponsored religion is dangerous, unnecessary, bad for government, and bad for religion, and that it is wrong for government to interfere in what must always remain a deeply personal matter.

Bill of Rights Institute (BRI)

The Bill of Rights Institute (BRI) is a nonprofit educational organization that develops educational resources on American history and government, provides professional development opportunities to teachers, and runs student programs and scholarship contests. It promotes a conservative view of the U.S. Constitution. BRI was founded in 1999 by the Charles G. Koch Charitable Foundation.

In 2014, BRI began publishing *Documents of Freedom*, a free digital course on history, government, and economics, with excerpts from primary source documents, including the *Federalist Papers* and *Anti-Federalist Papers*, presidential speeches, Supreme Court cases, the founding documents, and a set of original essays espousing a conservative view of federalism, separation of powers, limited government, checks and balances, republican government, consent of the governed, natural rights, rule of law, due process, and such virtues as self-governance, humility, integrity, justice, perseverance, respect, contribution, and responsibility and freedom of the press. In 2006, it began a high school essay contest on civic values and a student-run program, the Constitutional Academy, which provides students with a six-week study of the U.S. Constitution in Washington, DC.

Center for the Study of Law and Religion (CSLR)

Founded in 1982, the Center for the Study of Law and Religion (CSLR) is an organized center at Emory University dedicated to studying the religious dimensions of law, the legal dimensions of religion, and the interaction of religious and legal ideas in institutions, norms, customs, and practices The center is founded on the assumptions that religion gives law its spirit and inspires adherence to ritual and justice and that law gives religion its structure and encourages its devotion to order and organization.

The CSLR engages thousands of scholars and students each year through its courses, degree programs, fellowships, research projects, and public programming. It publishes, through Cambridge University Press, a leading periodical, *Journal of Law and Religion*, as well as two book series, Law and Christianity and Law and Judaism. It works in the fields of faith, freedom, and the family; legal and political theory; and the place of religious legal systems in modern democracies.

The CSLR is interdisciplinary in perspective, bringing religious wisdom and traditions into greater conversation with law, public policy, and humane and social sciences. International in orientation, it seeks to situate debates in the United States over interdisciplinary issues of law and religion within an emerging global discourse. Its claimed mission is to help peoples of the world learn how law and religion can balance each other and stabilize society and politics. It offers six degree programs, pursues multiyear research projects, and has produced more than three hundred books, in addition to hosting major international conferences and distinguished lecture series.

In 1985, the center's founder, Emory president James T. Laney, convinced Harvard Law School's Harold J. Berman to join Emory as the first Robert W. Woodruff Professor of Law, and he then recruited John Witte Jr., a recent Harvard Law graduate and research assistant, to lead Emory's Law and Religion Program. In 1991, its conferences were launched into international prominence when eight hundred participants from five continents came together and when the conference's keynote addresses were presented by former U.S. president Jimmy Carter and Anglican archbishop Desmond Tutu. In 2000, the Pew Charitable Trust solidified the program's status with a $3.2 million grant; it officially became a Pew Center of Excellence and was renamed the Center for the Study of Law and Religion. In recent years, it has added the study of law and Asian religions; law, religion, and immigration; and religion, state, and housing. It is supported with some $20 million in grant funding as well as the generous university endowment of the center's general operations.

Council on American-Islamic Relations (CAIR)

The mission of the Council on American-Islamic Relations (CAIR) is to enhance understanding of Islam, encourage dialogue, protect civil liberties, empower American Muslims, and build coalitions to promote justice and mutual understanding. It is a grassroots civil rights and advocacy group and is noted as the largest Muslim civil liberties organization. Its national headquarters is in Washington, DC, on Capitol Hill, and it has several regional offices.

CAIR began in 1994. Through media relations, government relations, education, and advocacy, it promotes an Islamic perspective to ensure the Muslim voice is represented and to empower the American Muslim community and encourage its participation in political and social activism. It espouses the following core principles: (1) support for free enterprise, freedom of religion, and freedom of expression; (2) protection of civil rights of all Americans, regardless of faith; (3) support for domestic policies that promote civil rights, diversity, and freedom of religion; (4) opposition to domestic policies that limit civil rights and permit racial, ethnic, or religious profiling; (5) alliance with groups, religious or secular, that advocate justice and human rights in the United States and around the world; (6) support for foreign policies that help create free and equitable trade, encourage human rights, and promote representative government based on socioeconomic justice; (7) the belief that the active practice of Islam strengthens the social and religious fabric of the United States; (8) condemnation of all acts of violence against civilians by any individual, group, or state; (9) encouragement of dialogue between faith communities both in the United States and worldwide; and (10) support of equal and complementary rights and responsibilities for men and women.

CAIR's Civil Rights Department provides counsels, mediates, and advocates on behalf of Muslims and others who have experienced religious discrimination, defamation, or hate crimes, and it protects and defends the constitutional rights of American Muslims. The Government Affairs Department conducts and organizes lobbying efforts on issues related to Islam and Muslims, monitors legislation and other government activities, and responds on behalf of the American Muslim community. CAIR's representatives have testified before Congress and have sponsored activities to bring Muslim concerns to Capitol Hill. CAIR issues action alerts to generate grassroots response to critical social, political, and media-related issues, providing an e-mail list to be a source of information and news for the American Muslim community.

CAIR's research team conducts empirical research studies relevant to the American Muslim community, gathering and analyzing data for its annual civil rights reports, and publishes a North American Muslim resource guide: *Muslim Community Life in the United States and Canada*. CAIR offers internships to students and other interested individuals to gain experience in media relations, political activism, or civil rights work.

CAIR regularly sponsors conferences, seminars, and workshops and training seminars for government and law enforcement agencies, media professionals, and the academic community. It also provides training to the Muslim community for activists in media relations, public speaking, lobbying, and civil rights. It sponsors voter registration drives and participation in the political arena. It participates in ongoing outreach and interfaith relations.

First Amendment Coalition (FAC)

The First Amendment Coalition (FAC) is a nonprofit organization dedicated to advocacy of freedom of the press, free speech, open government, and public participation in civic affairs. It was founded in 1988 and has its headquarters in San Rafael, California. Its executive director is David Snyder. FAC acts locally, statewide, and nationally. It strives to advance freedom of the press and freedom of speech through education, advocacy, and litigation to prevent unnecessary government secrecy and to resist censorship of all kinds.

FAC won a legal victory in its yearlong effort to enforce California's police transparency law when an appellate court held the public had the right to see police misconduct records held by the California state attorney general on local police offices across the state. FAC and public news outlet sued California attorney general Xavier Becerra over his refusal to turn over records sought by the FAC in response to the California Public Records Act, SB 1411, that went into effect on January 1, 2019. AG Becerra's office is appealing the decision to the California Supreme Court.

FAC's President is Peter Scheer. FAC coauthored California Proposition 59, the Sunshine Amendment to the California Constitution enacted by voters in 2004. FAC's case was sparked by the arrest of journalist Bryan Carmody by the San Francisco Police Department (SFPD). In seeking its search warrant, the SFPD failed to inform the judge issuing the warrants that Carmody was a journalist. The SFPD executed searches on his home property, office, and telephones from May through September 2019. FAC has cases pending against CALPERS, Santa Clara County, and the California State Legislature (firstamendmentcoalition.org).

Freedom Forum Institute (FFI)

The Freedom Forum Institute (FFI) is a nonprofit, nonpartisan 501(c)(3) foundation that fosters First Amendment freedoms for all. It was founded in 1991 by Al Neuharth and is headquartered in Washington, DC. It is an advocacy organization that seeks to raise awareness of First Amendment freedoms through education, advocacy, and action. It sponsors public policy forums and programs on freedom of assembly and association, such as the Al Neuharth Free Spirit and Journalism Conference, the Chips Quinn Scholars, and the Al Neuharth Award for Excellence in Media.

FFI is affiliated with the Al Neuharth Media Center at the University of South Dakota, the Overby Center for Southern Journalism and Politics at the University of Mississippi, the John Seigenthaler Center at Vanderbilt University, and Newseum Ed. It sponsors the Women's Leadership on the Political Stage meeting that featured Valerie Jarrett, and it hosts the Free Expression Awards gala that recognizes individuals for courageous acts and contributions to free and fearless expression (freedomforum.org).

Freedom from Religion Foundation (FFRF)

The Freedom from Religion Foundation (FFRF) was founded in 1978. It is a nonprofit 501(c)(3) educational organization whose purpose is to support the separation of church and state, nontheism, atheism, and secularism. It has chapters in all fifty states and claims more than 23,500 members as the largest national organization for nontheists. It educates the public on matters related to atheism, agnosticism, and nontheism. It publishes a newspaper, *Freethought Today*, and since 2006, the Freethought Radio Network has produced the *Freethought Radio* show. Annually, it spends more than $1 million on legal fees, education, outreach, publishing, broadcasting, and sponsored events. Legal fees primarily support amicus curiae briefs for cases supporting separation of church and state that involve government entities, and it has a paid staff of twenty-two, including five full-time attorneys and two legal fellows.

Since 2011, FFRF has supported "hardship grants" for clergy as they leave their faith. In 2013, it announced, in partnership with the Secular Student Alliance, an educational program for students on their religious rights and assistance in rectifying violations. In 2015, it began a new charitable arm, NonBelief Relief, Inc., as a humanitarian agency for atheists, agnostics, freethinkers, and their supporters seeking to remediate conditions of human suffering on a global scale, whether as a result of natural disasters, human actions, or adherence to religious dogma. In 2004, it challenged the constitutionality of the White House Office of Faith-Based and Community Initiatives, but in 2007, the Supreme Court ruled 5–4 that taxpayers do not have the right to challenge the constitutionality of expenditures made by the executive branch.

In 2007, FFRF won a suit challenging a State of Indiana Family and Social Services Administration program that hired a Baptist minister at an annual salary of $60,000, and the program was ended. It backed cases challenging aid to faith-based programs in health care and the use of chaplains to treat patients in drug and alcohol treatment programs as violations of the Establishment Clause. In 2004 and 2005, it supported successful challenges to state education programs holding weekly Bible classes. It has brought or supported cases challenging criminal justice programs, religion in the public sphere, employment issues, prayer in government schools, tax exemptions, and cases against the IRS and FEC for not enforcing electioneering laws in violation of the First Amendment. In 2013, it won a Florida case and was allowed to hang a banner at the capital after a nativity scene was placed by a private group. It won cases in Illinois,

Washington, Wisconsin, Rhode Island, and Texas over plaques and signs placed in state capitals.

Freedom House

Freedom House is an independent watchdog organization dedicated to the expansion of freedom and democracy. It is a government-funded, nongovernmental 501(c)(3) organization that conducts research and advocacy on freedom of the press, political freedom, and human rights. It was founded in 1941 by Eleanor Roosevelt and Wendell Willkie. Freedom House exemplifies the think tank research institute approach and is headquartered in Washington, DC. Its president is Michael Abramowitz. It has revenues of over $30 million, and supports a staff of 150 with field offices in a dozen countries. In 2018, the U.S. government provided Freedom House with more than $35 million, 88 percent of its annual revenues.

In the 1940s, Freedom House sponsored the radio programs *Voice of Freedom* and *Our Secret Weapon*, which were established to counter Axis radio propaganda. In the 1950s, it was highly critical of McCarthyism, and in the 1960s, it supported the civil rights movement and later the Solidarity movement in Poland. It publishes *Freedom of the Press*, an annual survey of media independence around the world with numerical ratings for 196 countries. It also publishes *Freedom on the Net*, analytical reports and numerical ratings of internet freedom for countries worldwide. Its findings are used by governments, international organizations, academics, and news media outlets in many countries. Since 2002, Freedom House has published eighty-five special reports.

Free Speech Center

The Free Speech Center is one of several such centers established around the country. It is located at Middle Tennessee State University in Murfreesboro. There is a similar center located in Alexandria, Virginia. The Free Speech Center at Middle Tennessee State University oversees One for All, a national nonpartisan and nonprofit educational effort to build understanding of and respect for all five freedoms of the First Amendment. One for All is an interactive site that focuses on all five freedoms: press, speech, religion, assembly, and the freedom to petition the government for a redress of grievances. The Free Speech Center also publishes the *First Amendment Encyclopedia*, a collection of more than fifteen hundred articles on various First Amendment topics, reviews of court cases, and the history of First Amendment freedoms. It is headed by Professor John Vile.

Human Rights House Foundation

The Human Rights House Foundation is an international organization that began in Oslo, Norway, in 1989, and still has its headquarters there, with regional offices in Brussels and Tbilisi (Georgia). It operates sixteen houses in Eastern Europe, Western Europe, the Caucuses, and the Balkans and has a presence in the following countries: Armenia, Azerbaijan, Belarus, Crimea, Croatia, Georgia, Norway, Poland, the Russian Federation, Serbia, Ukraine, and the United Kingdom.

The Human Rights House Foundation works to protect, empower, and support human rights defenders and their organizations locally and unites them in an international network of Human Rights Houses. It was founded on the idea that the success and knowledge from one organization can help inspire and enable others and that this does not stop at country borders. Since 1989, it has built an international network of Human Rights Houses to promote the fundamental freedoms of assembly, association, and expression and the right to be a human rights defender. The organization works in consultation with the United Nations and with the Council of Europe.

Jehovah's Witnesses (JW)

The Jehovah's Witnesses (JW) is a millenarian Christian denomination with nontrinitarian beliefs distinct from mainstream Christianity. JW claims membership of about 8.5 million members in 240 lands and just over 20 million attendees at their annual memorials of Christ's death. They meet in roughly 120,000 congregations and have held more than ten million home Bible courses.

JW's members are noted for their aggressive door-to-door preaching and distribution of literature (*The Watchtower* and *Awake*). They refuse to serve in the military, and they refuse blood transfusions. They consider secular society corrupt and under the influence of Satan and limit their social interactions with non-Witnesses. Similar to the Old Order Amish, they use congregational disciplinary action, including *disfellowshipping*, their term for formal expulsion and shunning.

JW's conscientious objection to military service and refusal to salute the flag has engendered the most conflict between JW and governments, mostly at the local or state levels. They consider saluting the flag as a form of false worship and have fought, and won, a court challenge to compulsory flag salute laws (*West Virginia State Board of Education v. Barnette*, 319 U.S. 624, 1943). In the *Barnette* decision, the court ruled they had the right "not to speak," in this case meaning the symbolic speech of the flag salute. They have been involved in numerous Supreme Court cases challenging state and local laws on the basis of the Establishment Clause and Free Exercise Clause. Even in cases they lost, their legal challenges have helped shape jurisprudence with respect to the First Amendment and freedom of religion and free speech matters. JW members have been the victims of a number of hate crimes.

Knight First Amendment Freedom Institute

The Knight First Amendment Freedom Institute of Columbia University is a think tank institute that on occasion also uses litigation, as it did in the 2017 New York federal appeals court case that successfully argued that President Donald Trump could not block people from his Twitter account simply because he disagreed with the opinions they expressed. The institute was established in 2016 by Columbia University and the James L. Knight Foundation to combat threats to freedom of speech and press arising from evolving technologies, the privatization of the public square, the expansion of government surveillance and secrecy, and the demonization of the media. It defends freedom of speech and press in the digital age through strategic litigation, research, and public education.

National Committee for Public Education and Religious Liberty (PEARL)

The National Committee for Public Education and Religious Liberty (PEARL) is a coalition composed of more than fifty grassroots, civic, educational, and religious groups committed to keeping public schools free of religious indoctrination and discrimination. It is noted for its vigilant opposition to the teaching of creationism in public schools. PEARL maintains that allowing the teaching of creationism would result in opening a virtual Pandora's box that would require teachers to teach religious or less-than-scientific views on other topics, presenting students with a dizzying array of religious doctrines.

PEARL argues that *Everson v. Board of Education* (330 U.S. 1, 1947) clearly establishes that to teach creationism would violate the Establishment Clause of the First Amendment because it puts government-run schools in the position of establishing religion by using their power to teach children compelled to attend school. It argues that such violation is based on the precedents set by the legal tests from *Lemon v. Kurtzman* (403 U.S. 602, 1971) and by *Edwards v. Aguillard* (482 U.S. 578, 1987). PEARL concludes that for both educational and constitutional grounds, creationism should not be taught in public schools.

Seventh-Day Adventist Church (SDA)

The Seventh-day Adventist Church (SDA) is a Protestant Christian denomination that was founded in 1863 in Battle Creek, Michigan, by Joseph Bates, James and Ellen White, and John Nevins Andrews as a branch of the Millerite movement. It claims just more than twenty million members in 81,500 churches and seventy thousand companies organized into thirteen world divisions from two hundred countries. It runs 175 hospitals, 136 nursing homes, and a humanitarian aid organization, the Adventist Development and Relief Agency (ADRA). SDA has more than five thousand primary schools and two thousand secondary schools. It proudly proclaims itself as a denomination *sola scriptura*—believing that the Bible is the only standard of faith and practice for Christians. It espouses twenty-eight fundamental beliefs organized into six categories, adopted at its General Conference in 1980, with an eleventh belief added in 2005. It is distinguished by its observance of Saturday as the Sabbath and by its belief in the imminent Second Coming of Jesus Christ (his advent). It is also known for its emphasis on diet and health, a "holistic" understanding of the person, the promotion of religious liberty, and conservative principles and lifestyle.

SDA is the largest of several Adventist groups emerging from the Millerite movement in upstate New York in the 1840s, a phase of the Second Great Awakening. As the early Adventist movement coalesced in its beliefs, the question of the biblical day of rest and worship arose within the movement. Joseph Bates was the foremost advocate that Sabbath keeping should be stressed and should be the biblical day of rest—Saturday, rather than Sunday.

In the 1870s, SDA turned to missionary work and the holding of revivals, and it had grown rapidly by 1900. It espouses Trinitarian Protestant theology with a premillennial and Arminian emphasis. SDA is considered evangelical, conducts baptism by full immersion, and believes in creation having taken place in six literal (twenty-four-hour) days. The modern creationist movement was started by Adventist George McCready Price, having been inspired by one of Ellen White's visions. A number of its distinctive beliefs and doctrines are: (1) the Law of God is "embedded in the Ten Commandments," which bind Christians today; (2) the Sabbath should be observed on the seventh day of the week, from Friday sunset to Saturday sunset; (3) Jesus Christ will return to earth after a time of trouble and that the Second Coming will be followed by a millennial reign of the saints in heaven; (4) humans are an indivisible unity of body, mind, and spirit; that humans do not possess an immortal soul and that there is no consciousness after death (referred to as "soul sleep"). Its members further believe that the wicked will not suffer eternal torment in hell but will instead be permanently destroyed. They believe in the Great Controversy—i.e. the struggle between Jesus Christ and Satan. They hold that evil began in heaven when an angelic being (Lucifer) rebelled against the Law of God.

SDA has been involved in a number of U.S. Supreme Court cases involving the First Amendment's Establishment and Free Exercise Clauses and the right of assembly.

People: Governmental Stakeholders

This chapter profiles one attorney general, five U.S. presidents, eleven justices of the U.S. Supreme Court, and two U.S. senators as examples of the governmental stakeholders. They are arranged alphabetically by their last name.

William Brennan (1906–1997), Associate Justice of the Supreme Court

William Brennan was an associate justice of the U.S. Supreme Court from 1956 to 1990, the seventh-longest-serving justice and a leader of the court's liberal wing. He was nominated to the court by President Dwight Eisenhower and succeeded by Justice David Souter.

Brennan was born in Newark, New Jersey, in 1906, the son of Irish immigrants. He graduated from the University of Pennsylvania in 1928 with a BS in economics and earned his LLB from Harvard University. Brennan served as a major in the U.S. Army during World War II (1942–1945). After the war, he was an associate justice of the New Jersey Supreme Court (1951–1956), appointed by Governor Alfred Driscoll.

During his time at the U.S. Supreme Court, Brennan wrote 1,360 opinions, second only to Justice William Douglas. He wrote the majority opinion in several landmark decisions concerning First Amendment rights. In a 6–3 ruling in *Roth v. United States* (354 U.S. 476, 1957), the court essentially redefined what constitutes obscene material that was thereby unprotected by the First Amendment. Brennan's majority opinion, concurred in by Chief Justice Earl Warren and Justices Felix Frankfurter, Harold Burton, Tom Clark, and Charles Whitaker, held that obscenity was not within the area of constitutionally protected free speech. Justices Hugo Black, William Douglas, and John Harlan were in dissent. The *Roth* decision held that materials were "utterly without redeeming social importance" and that the test to determine obscenity was "whether the average person, applying contemporary community standards, the dominant theme of the material taken as a whole appeals to prurient interest."

Brennan wrote the majority opinion in two unanimous free speech cases in 1964. In *New York Times Co. v. Sullivan* (376 U.S. 254), the court ruled that the freedom of speech protection of the First Amendment restricted American public officials from suing for defamation. In *Garrison v. Louisiana* (379 U.S. 64), the decision overturned the defamation conviction of Louisiana district attorney Jim Garrison, ruling that the libel law used to convict him was unconstitutional.

In *Village of Skokie v. National Socialist Party* (432 U.S. 43, 1977), in a 5–4 decision, the court ruled that the Illinois Supreme Court improperly denied the Nationalist Socialist Party's request to stay a district court's injunction. The ruling held that Illinois must provide strict procedural safeguards, including appellate review, to deny a stay of an injunction, thereby denying the Nazi Party of its protected First Amendment right.

In *Texas v. Johnson* (491 U.S. 397, 1989) and a related case, *United States v. Eichman* (496 U.S. 310, 1990), the court invalidated prohibitions on desecrating the American flag, which at the time were enforced in forty-eight states. Brennan wrote for the five-justice majority that Gregory Lee Johnson's act of flag burning was protected symbolic speech under the First Amendment. Brennan's opinion was joined in by Justices Thurgood Marshall, Harry Blackmun, Antonin Scalia, and Anthony Kennedy. The dissenters were Chief Justice William Rehnquist and Justices Byron White, Sandra Day O'Connor, and John Paul Stevens.

After retiring from the Supreme Court, Brennan taught at the Georgetown University Law Center. A much-respected jurist died in Arlington, Virginia, in 1997 at the age of ninety-one.

Warren Burger (1907–1995), Chief Justice of the Supreme Court

Warren Burger was the fifteenth chief justice of the U.S. Supreme Court and the longest-serving chief justice of the twentieth century (1969–1986). He was appointed by President Richard Nixon. During his term as chief justice, twenty-one cases involving religious freedom questions were ruled on, and Burger wrote the majority opinion on ten of them and assigned the justice who wrote the majority opinion for the other eleven. Burger strove for achieving comfortable margins or consensus on the bench, and during his tenure, only nine of those twenty-one cases were decided 5–4. He disappointed President Nixon, who expected him to reverse the decisions of the court under Chief Justice Earl Warren. Burger voted with the majority, for example, in *Roe v. Wade* (410 U.S. 113, 1973), which established women's constitutional right to have abortions.

Warren Burger wrote the majority opinion in two landmark decisions on free press and free speech. In *Nebraska Press Association v. Stuart* (427 U.S. 539, 1976), Burger's majority opinion emphasized the principle of "prior restraint." The court held unconstitutional the use of prior restraint on media coverage of criminal trials. Burger wrote, "Prior restraint on speech and publication are the most serious and least tolerable infringements on First Amendment rights." In *Bethel School District #43 v. Fraser* (478 U.S. 675, 1986), a 7–2 ruling, Burger's majority opinion held that the First Amendment does not prevent a school district from disciplining a high school student for giving a lewd speech at a school-sponsored high school assembly.

Warren Burger was born in St. Paul, Minnesota, in 1907. He attended the University of Minnesota and the St. Paul College of Law, earning his JD magna cum laude in 1931. He was an early and effective supporter of Dwight David Eisenhower for president, and upon his election as president in 1952, Eisenhower appointed Burger as assistant attorney general in the Civil Rights Division of the U.S. Department of Justice (DOJ). Burger was appointed to U.S. Court of Appeals for the District of Columbia by President Dwight D. Eisenhower in 1965, and he served there until his appointment to the U.S. Supreme Court in 1969.

Burger was conservative, and he advocated the literal, strict-constructionist reading of the U.S. Constitution. Under his leadership, the court delivered many conservative decisions, but a few liberal decisions as well, such as on abortion, capital punishment, religious establishment, and school desegregation. Notably, Burger led the court to a 9–0 decision in *United States v. Nixon* (418 U.S. 683, 1974), which ruled that the White House Watergate tapes had to be released to Congress for investigating the scandal and considering articles of impeachment. He was not a popular chief justice among his colleagues, as described in the thinly disguised John Grisham legal thriller novel *The Brethren* (2000).

Burger retired in 1986, and in 1988, he received the prestigious Presidential Medal of Freedom. He died of a heart attack on June 25, 1995, at the age of eighty-six (Frank 1995).

George W. Bush (1946–), President of the United States

George W. Bush served as the nation's forty-third president (2001–2009). He became a wartime president in the aftermath of the terrorist attacks on September 11, 2001. The attacks put his "compassionate conservatism" domestic agenda on hold. One of his key domestic policy campaign promises was the establishment, by executive order, in January 2001, of the White House Office of Faith-Based and Community Initiatives (OFBCI). The initiative sought to strengthen faith-based community organizations and expand their capacity to provide federally funded social services. The ACLU was strongly critical of the OFBCI, asserting it violated the Establishment Clause by using tax money to fund religion. The White House formulated certain restrictions on the use of such funds to avoid violations of the Establishment Clause.

President Bush's impact on freedom of religion issues was also significant in several post-9/11/2001 actions. In 2001, he pushed for and Congress passed the USA PATRIOT Act of October 26, 2001. The act gave the federal government sweeping powers to combat terrorism, including "enhanced interrogation," that critics contend were used against Muslims. Even more sweeping was the Homeland Security Act of 2002 (116 Stat. 2135). The U.S. Department of Homeland Security (DHS) has been embroiled in many actions and policies that critics contend involve racial and ethnic profiling against Muslim Americans as well as the current controversial travel bans against immigrants and refugees from Muslim countries. Finally, President George W. Bush indirectly impacted freedom of religion through his appointment, in 2005, of John Roberts as chief justice of the U.S. Supreme Court.

Ted Cruz (1970–), United States Senator

Potentially any member of Congress can have an impact on First Amendment freedom issues through the legislation they sponsor. Space limitations here are such that Senator Ted Cruz is being profiled to exemplify the role that senators can play in the issue in part because he is an avowed advocate of the religious right and Senate champion of their views and positions. He serves on the Senate Judiciary Committee and has authored some eighty U.S. Supreme Court briefs and argued forty-three oral arguments, nine of which were before the U.S. Supreme Court.

In private practice for five years, Cruz led the large firm's Supreme Court and National Appellate Litigation practice. As solicitor general of Texas (2003–2008), appointed by then attorney general of Texas Greg Abbott, Cruz was the state's youngest and first Hispanic solicitor general. He successfully defended U.S. sovereignty against the United Nations in *Medellín v. Texas* (552 U.S. 491, 2008), the Second Amendment right to keep and bear arms, the constitutionality of the Texas Ten Commandments monument, the constitutionality of the words "under God" in the Pledge of Allegiance, the constitutionality of Texas's Sexually Violent Predator Civil Commitment law, and the Texas congressional redistricting plan. He drafted the amicus curiae brief for the *District of Columbia v. Heller* (554 U.S. 570, 2008) and won in 5–4 decisions the *Van Orden v. Perry* (545 U.S. 677, 2005) case and the *Elk Grove Unified School District v. Newdow* (542 U.S. 1, 2004).

Ted Cruz was born in 1970 in Calgary, Canada, of Cuban descent. He earned a BA from Princeton University and a JD from Harvard University in 1995, graduating magna cum laude and having served as editor of the *Harvard Law Review*. He clerked for Chief Justice William Rehnquist, where he worked on matters related to the National Rifle Association (NRA) and helped prepare testimony for the impeachment proceedings against President Bill Clinton.

From 1999 to 2003, Cruz served as the director of the Office of Policy Planning for the Federal Trade Commission and as associate deputy attorney general of the United States in the U.S. Department of Justice (DOJ). He was the domestic policy adviser to George W. Bush's 2000 presidential campaign.

In 2004–2009, Cruz was adjunct professor at the University of Texas School of Law in Austin, Texas, where he taught U.S. Supreme Court Litigation. He is the first Hispanic to serve as U.S. senator from Texas.

Ted Cruz was elected the thirty-fourth senator from Texas in 2012 and was successfully reelected in a close race in 2016. In 2012, he served as vice chair of the National Republican

Senatorial Committee. In the Senate, he serves on the Committee on the Judiciary and on its Subcommittee on Immigration, Refugees and Border Security.

Senator Cruz is notably strongly pro-life, and he has pushed to defund Planned Parenthood. He opposes same-sex marriage as well as civil unions. With the support of the Alliance Defense Fund and its Pulpit Initiative, Senator Cruz has sponsored a bill in the U.S. Senate to repeal the Johnson Amendment.

Senator Cruz was a candidate for the Republican presidential nomination in 2016, being backed by the religious right and several evangelical PACs. He lost to Donald Trump, being the last of Trump's opponents to withdraw from the race.

He is the author of the 2015 book *A Time for Truth: Reigniting the Promise of America.*

Ruth Bader Ginsburg (1933–2020), Associate Justice of the Supreme Court

Ruth Bader Ginsburg (RBG) was appointed to the U.S. Supreme Court in August 1993 by President Bill Clinton, filling the seat vacated by Justice Byron White. She was the unquestioned leader of the court's liberal block, regularly joined by Justices Stephen Breyer, Sonia Sotomayor, and Elena Kagan. Since her appointment to the high court, RBG participated in fourteen decisions on religious freedom cases, eight of which were 5–4 votes in which she voted with the minority. Throughout her long legal career, she had notably been an advocate against gender discrimination, serving, for example, as the first female member of the *Harvard Law Review*. She wrote the dissenting opinion in the 5–4 *Ledbetter v. Goodyear Tire and Rubber Company* (550 U.S. 618, 2007) decision. In her dissent, she called on Congress to undo the "improper interpretation of the law" and was vindicated when Congress passed and President Obama signed into law, as his very first act, the Lilly Ledbetter Fair Pay Act of 2009.

Justice Ginsburg earned her BS from Cornell, attended Harvard Law, and received her LLB from Columbia Law School, where she graduated first in her class. She clerked for Edmund Palmieri, a judge of the U.S. District Court for the Southern

District of New York (1959–1961). From 1961 to 1963, Justice Ginsburg was a research associate and then associate director of the Columbia Law School Project on International Procedure, living abroad in Sweden to do research for her book on Swedish Civil Procedure. In 1963, she became a professor at Rutgers University Law School. In 1972, she began teaching at Columbia Law, the first female to earn tenure there. She directed the Women's Rights Project for the ACLU, successfully arguing six landmark cases before the U.S. Supreme Court. In 1977–1978, she was a fellow at the Center for Advanced Study in the Behavioral Sciences at Stanford University. In 1980, President Jimmy Carter appointed Justice Ginsburg to the U.S. Court of Appeals for the District of Columbia. She served on the court until President Clinton appointed her to the U.S. Supreme Court in 1993.

Ruth Bader was born in Brooklyn, New York, in 1933. Although she disagreed with Justice Scalia on virtually every case they ruled on, they were friends in their personal lives, sharing a love for the opera. They did vote together on four religious freedom decisions. Justice Ginsburg had initially planned to retire in 2016, assuming that Secretary Hillary Clinton had won the presidency. She had wanted the first woman president to appoint her successor. When President Trump beat Clinton in the electoral college (despite losing the popular vote by three million votes), Justice Ginsburg stayed on the Court, hoping to last beyond Donald Trump's first term. However, she did not make it. Ruth Bader Ginsburg died of pancreatic cancer on September 18, 2020, much revered and respected by her fellow justices on both sides of the ideological divide on the Supreme Court.

Alberto Gonzales (1955–), Attorney General of the United States

Alberto Gonzales served as the eightieth attorney general of the United States, the first Hispanic appointed to the office, serving from 2005 to 2007. In *Gonzales v. O Centro Espirita Beneficente Uniao do Vegetal* (546 U.S. 418, 2006), the court decided 8–0 against the attorney general, ruling that the government had failed to meet its burden under the Religious Freedom Restoration Act (1993) and the Controlled Substances Act (1970) to ban the importation and use of *hoasca*, a hallucinogenic tea, in religious ceremonies.

Alberto Gonzales was born in 1955. He was educated at the United States Air Force Academy and Rice University (a BA degree in 1979) and earned his JD from Harvard Law School in 1982. He practiced corporate law in Texas and taught law as an adjunct professor at the University of Houston Law Center. He served as Texas's one hundredth secretary of state (1997–1999). He served as general counsel to then Texas governor George W. Bush and as a justice of the Supreme Court of Texas in 1999. President Bush appointed him White House counsel in 2001. In 2005, President Bush appointed him attorney general of the United States.

Alexander Hamilton (1755–1804), Secretary of the Treasury

Alexander Hamilton was a Revolutionary War hero and one of the most influential Founding Fathers. He was the founder and publisher of a major New York newspaper, the *New York Post*. Hamilton is considered one of the founders of the Federalist Party and of the U.S. Coast Guard as well as founder of the Bank of New York and the First Bank of the United States. He played a leading role in defending and ratifying the U.S. Constitution as a major author of *The Federalist Papers*.

Hamilton was born in 1755 in the British West Indies on the Caribbean island of Nevis. He came to the New York Colony in 1772 at the age of seventeen and studied at Kings College (now Columbia University). He led an artillery company in the Continental Army and then served on the staff of General George Washington. He fought in eight major battles or engagements in the war, notably as a hero in the Battle of Yorktown (1781) that led British general Cornwallis to surrender. He rose to the rank of major general.

Hamilton studied law and passed the New York bar in 1787. He was one of three delegates from New York to the

Constitutional Convention in 1788–1789. After convincing John Jay and James Madison to join with him, Hamilton conceived of and supervised the writing of a series of essays, under the pseudonym Publius, that came to be known as *The Federalist Papers*. Hamilton wrote fifty-one of the eighty-five essays. He forcefully argued for the separation of powers, a system of checks and balances, and an independent judiciary.

Hamilton served as secretary of the treasury in President George Washington's administration (1789–1795), during which time he led the establishment of the U.S. Mint, the use of both silver and gold as currency, and creation of the U.S. Bank. He was the most influential cabinet secretary and the main political opponent of Thomas Jefferson. Hamilton is credited as one of the founders of the Federalist Party, and he supported passage of the Alien and Sedition Acts. However, as publisher of the *New York Post* newspaper, he was a strong proponent of freedom of the press.

In the 1804 case of *People v. Croswell* (3 Johns. Cas. 337, N.Y.), the New York State Supreme Court justices were deadlocked over whether the truth of statements could be used as a defense against libel. In English common law, established by the Star Chamber courts, truth of statements could not be used in defense against seditious libel. Alexander Hamilton's arguments in favor of "the truthful statement defense" were written into New York state constitutional law, as "truthful statements cannot be libelous."

Hamilton was also a political opponent of Aaron Burr, and his opposition to Burr led him to convince members of the Federalist Party in the House of Representatives in the contested 1800 presidential election to back Jefferson over Burr for president. Hamilton was behind a series of anti-Burr articles published in 1804 when Burr ran for governor of New York. Burr challenged Hamilton to an "honor duel," in which he shot Hamilton, who died of his wounds the next day (Chernow 2004; Hamilton 2017; LeMay 2017; Zentner and LeMay 2020).

Charles Evan Hughes (1862–1948), Chief Justice of the Supreme Court

Charles Hughes was an American statesman, serving as the eleventh chief justice of the Supreme Court, the thirty-sixth governor of New York (1907–1910), and the forty-fourth secretary of state. He was also the Republican presidential nominee in 1916. He served as chief justice from 1930 to 1941, having been nominated to the court by President Herbert Hoover. He served as the secretary of state from 1921 to 1925, being appointed by President Warren Harding and also serving under President Calvin Coolidge. Hughes was an associate justice of the court from 1910 to 1916, appointed by President Taft.

Hughes was born in Glenn Falls, New York, in 1862, and he died in 1948 at the age of eighty-six. He received a BA from Brown University and an LLB from Columbia University. In 1910, he was unanimously confirmed as an associate justice and worked closely with Justices John Marshall Harlan and Oliver Wendell Holmes. In 1930, he was confirmed as chief justice by a vote of 52 to 26. During his term as chief justice, the Supreme Court was often divided by the conservative "Four Horsemen" and the liberal "Three Musketeers."

Chief Justice Hughes wrote the majority opinion in the landmark case *Near v. Minnesota* (283 U.S. 697, 1931), in which the court laid down the principle that prior restraint on publication violated the First Amendment. In *DeJonge v. Oregon* (299 U.S. 353, 1937), Hughes wrote the majority opinion (8–0) that an Oregon state law violated the Due Process Clause of the Fourteenth Amendment and the First Amendment rights of free speech and assembly by prohibiting the meeting, in a public place, of the Communist Party. He also wrote the majority opinion (7–2) in *Stromberg v. California* (283 U.S. 359, 1931), wherein, for the first time, the court struck down a state law on the basis of incorporation of the Bill of Rights. Hughes joined the majority in *Minersville School District v. Gobitis* (310 U.S. 586, 1940), by an 8–1 decision, in which the court upheld a law that public schools could require students to salute the American flag. Chief Justice Hughes opposed the court-packing effort by President Franklin Roosevelt in 1937. (Parrish 2002; Simon 2012).

Thomas Jefferson (1743–1826), President of the United States

Thomas Jefferson was one of the Founding Fathers, the principle author of the Declaration of Independence, the nation's first secretary of state (1789–1794), second vice president (1797–1801), and third president (1801–1809). He spent five decades of his life in public service.

In 1774, Jefferson drafted Virginia's delegation to the First Continental Congress. He was an early advocate of the total separation of church and state and the coauthor (with James Madison) of the Virginia Statute for Religious Liberty in 1786. He was Virginia's representative to the Second Continental Congress in 1775 and was one of the greatest proponents of the Bill of Rights, especially the First Amendment rights of freedom of the press, speech, and religion. In a letter to Lafayette in 1823, he wrote about the need for the freedom of the press: "The only security of all is a free press. The force of public opinion cannot be resisted when permitted freely to be expressed. The agitation it produces must be submitted to. It is necessary to keep the water pure."

Thomas Jefferson was born in Virginia in 1743, and he died there (at Monticello) on July 4, 1826. He attended William and Mary College, and as draftsman of the Declaration of Independence, he was known as the "Apostle of Liberty." He was also instrumental in crafting the Bill of Rights.

As president, he was responsible for the Louisiana Purchase (1803, from France), which essentially doubled the territory of the United States and added a significant population of Catholics (from the Spanish and the French colonies) to the American population at a time when Catholics were still highly suspected as to their loyalty and were often discriminated against by the nation's Protestant majority. He negotiated the purchase despite the fact that the Constitution made no provision for the acquisition of new land. The addition of so many Roman Catholic adherents to the population led to clashes with state government laws that at the time still legalized established churches (Anglican).

After leaving the presidency, where he was succeeded by his friend, James Madison, he retired to his estate at Monticello. He is justly considered the "Father of the University of Virginia" in that he spearheaded the legislative campaign for its charter; he secured the location of its campus, designed its buildings, planned its curriculum, and served as its first rector (*Papers of Thomas Jefferson* 1950).

Anthony Kennedy (1936–), Associate Justice of the Supreme Court

Associate Justice Anthony M. Kennedy was appointed to the U.S. Supreme Court by President Ronald Reagan in 1988, and he served until his retirement in 2018. In many respects, Kennedy replaced Justice Sandra Day O'Connor in the role of swing vote between the conservative and liberal wings of the court. He participated in twenty-one cases involving religious freedom issues and wrote the majority opinion in five of those cases: *Lee v. Weisman* (505 U.S. 577, 1992), *Church of the Lukumi Babalu Aye, Inc. v. City of Hialeah* (508 U.S. 520, 1993), *Rosenberger v. West Virginia* (1995), *Arizona Christian School Tuition Organization v. Winn* (563 U.S. 125, 2011), and *Town of Greece v. Galloway* (572 U.S. 565, 2014). His was the swing vote in four cases: *Zobrest v. Catalina Foothills School District* (509 U.S. 1, 1993), *Rosenberger v. Rector and Visitors of the University of Virginia* (515 U.S. 819, 1995), *Arizona Christian School Tuition Organization v. Winn* (563 U.S. 125, 2011), and *Town of Greece v. Galloway* (572 U.S. 565, 2014).

Kennedy graduated with honors from Stanford University, and in his senior year, he studied at the London School of

Economics. He earned his LLB from Harvard Law School and went into private practice in California (1961–1975), during which time he worked as a lobbyist for the Republican Party of California with Ed Meese, through whom he met then governor Ronald Reagan. He taught constitutional law at the McGeorge School of Law, University of the Pacific from 1965 to 1968. Kennedy served on the board of the Federal Judicial Center (1987–1988) and on two committees of the Judicial Conference of the United States, including chairing the Committee on Pacific Territories from 1982 to 1990.

Through Reagan, he was recommended to President Gerald Ford and was appointed to the U.S. Court of Appeals for the Ninth Circuit in 1975, making him the youngest federal appellate judge at the time. After President Reagan's failed attempt to name Robert H. Bork to the high court, President Ronald Reagan nominated Anthony Kennedy as an associate justice, and he was unanimously confirmed by the Senate. Kennedy was sworn in on February 18, 1988, filling the seat of Justice Lewis Powell Jr. He soon established himself as a proponent of individual rights. He wrote the majority opinion in *Romer v. Evans*, which invalidated a provision of the Colorado Constitution denying homosexuals the right to bring local discrimination claims. In *Lawrence v. Texas* (539 U.S. 558, 2003), he wrote the majority opinion declaring unconstitutional a Texas law that criminalized sodomy between two consenting adults of the same sex. He soon became known as the swing vote between the liberal and conservative camps of the other eight justices. He voted to guarantee the right to same-sex marriage and wrote the majority opinion in the 5–4 landmark decision in *Obergefell v. Hodges* (576 U.S. 644, 2015), despite his being a devout Roman Catholic. In 2010, he voted to uphold the Affordable Care Act in the court's 6–3 ruling in the case.

Joseph Lieberman (1942–), United States Senator

Former senator Joseph Lieberman (D-CT and I-CT) graduated from Yale University in 1964 and received his LLB from

Yale in 1967. He was a practicing attorney from 1964 to 1980. In his political career, Lieberman served in the Connecticut State Senate from 1970 to 1980. He then served as attorney general of the state from 1983 to 1988. He was elected to the U.S. Senate in 1988, serving there until 2014. In 2000, Senator Lieberman ran as the vice-presidential running mate to Al Gore and for reelection to the U.S. Senate. He lost the vice presidency but won reelection to his Senate seat.

Important to First Amendment freedom matters, Senator Lieberman was the author of the bill to establish the U.S. Department of Homeland Security (DHS) in 2002, with all its adverse implications for Muslim Americans and freedom of association. (Post-2001, thousands of Muslim Americans were detained and many held for months without access to lawyers simply on the grounds that they were Muslims—guilt by association). In 2016, Lieberman was briefly considered by President Donald Trump for nomination to be the U.S. attorney general (LeMay 2018).

James Madison (1751–1836), President of the United States

James Madison was an American statesman, lawyer, diplomat, philosopher, Founding Father, and the fourth president of the United States (1809–1817). Madison, along with his lifelong friend, Thomas Jefferson, is considered the "Father of the Constitution."

Madison is generally acknowledged to have taken the lead at the Second Constitutional Convention, and he notably drafted the Bill of Rights and cowrote (with John Jay and Alexander Hamilton) the *Federalist Papers* that argued the justification for the Constitution and the Bill of Rights. He was also the author of the Virginia Plan at the Constitutional Convention. He was a member of the U.S. House of Representatives (1789–1797) and the fifth secretary of state (1801–1809), serving in the Jefferson administration. With Thomas Jefferson, he helped cofound the Democratic-Republican Party, which advocated the end of the Alien and Sedition Acts and for freedom of the press, freedom of speech, and freedom of assembly—all of which were threatened by the acts.

Madison received a BA from Princeton University in 1771. He also served as a colonel in the Virginia militia (1775–1776). A Deist, Madison argued for Virginia's disestablishment of the Anglican Church in the 1770s and 1780s. He immersed himself in the liberalism of the Enlightenment.

In Congress, Madison supported the system of checks and balances and the separation of church and state, and he proposed a series of constitutional amendments to protect individual liberties that became the Bill of Rights, which he introduced on June 8, 1789, with its provisions protecting freedom of religion, speech, and press and the right of peaceful assembly. The ten amendments were ratified on December 15, 1796.

As president, Madison led the United States through the War of 1812. He appointed two justices to the U.S. Supreme Court: Gabriel Duvall and Joseph Story. He left office in 1817, at age sixty-five, and retired to his Montpelier estate. He helped Thomas Jefferson establish the University of Virginia, and after Jefferson's death, he served as its second rector. James Madison died of congestive heart failure in June 1836 at the age of eighty-five.

Barack Obama (1961–), President of the United States

Barack H. Obama served as the forty-fourth, and first African American, president of the United States from 2009 to 2017. He was born in Hawaii in 1961. He was educated at Occidental College, Columbia University (BA), and Harvard Law School (JD) and was the first African American editor of the prestigious *Harvard Law Review*.

Barack Obama worked his way through college with financial help from scholarships and student loans. When he was president, he mentioned that it took him and his wife, Michelle, years to pay off all their student loans. After graduation from Columbia University, he moved to Chicago, where he worked with a group of churches to help rebuild communities devastated by the closure of local steel plants. He attended Harvard Law and then returned to Chicago to lead a voter registration drive and teach constitutional law at the University of Chicago, remaining active as a community organizer. He served in the Illinois State Senate (2005–2008), sponsoring a bill that was the first major ethics reform law in twenty-five years. He is the author of several books, notably *Dreams of My Father* (1995), *The Audacity of Hope* (2008), *Change We Can Believe In* (2008), and *Of Thee I Sing* (2010). In 2008, Lisa Rogak's *Barack Obama in His Own Words* was published.

A devout Christian, Barack Obama attended the Trinity United Church of Christ. During his presidency, he continued the Office of Faith-Based and Community Initiatives begun by President Bush, renaming it the White House Office of Faith-Based and Neighborhood Partnerships, and appointed an advisory council composed of religious and secular leaders and scholars.

In terms of his impact on First Amendment freedoms, Obama notably appointed two associate justices to the U.S. Supreme Court: Sonia Sotomayor (2009) and Elena Kagan (2010). He emphasized LGBT rights and same-sex marriage, and he ended the Defense of Marriage Act, all of which drew harsh criticism and opposition from the religious right.

President Obama was awarded the Nobel Peace Prize in 2008 and the Profile in Courage Award in 2017.

Sandra Day O'Connor (1930–), Associate Justice of the Supreme Court

Sandra Day O'Connor is notable as the first woman appointed to the U.S. Supreme Court. Throughout her judicial career, she was considered to be a moderate conservative, and on the Supreme Court (1981–2006), she often provided the swing vote between the conservative and progressive (liberal) blocs. She participated in thirty-three decisions dealing with religious freedom cases and wrote the majority opinion in two cases:

Lyng v. Northwest Indian Cemetery Protective Association (485 U.S. 439, 1988) and *Westside Community Board of Education v. Mergens* (496 U.S. 226, 1990). Importantly, Justice O'Connor provided the swing vote on six cases: *Lee v. Weisman* (505 U.S. 577, 1992), *Rosenberger v. Rector and Visitors of the University of Virginia* (515 U.S. 819, 1995), *Mitchell v. Helms* (530 U.S. 793, 2000), *Zelman v. Simmons-Harris* (536 U.S. 639, 2002), *McCreary County v. American Civil Liberties Union* (545 U.S. 844, 2005), and *Van Orden v. Perry* (545 U.S. 677, 2005). She also provided the swing vote in a case upholding the abortion rights ruling in *Roe v. Wade* (410 U.S. 113, 1973).

Sandra Day O'Connor was born in El Paso, Texas, in 1930. She received her BA and LLB from Stanford University. She was elected to two terms in the Arizona State Senate. She served as the deputy county attorney of San Mateo County, California, from 1952 to 1953 and as a civilian attorney for Quartermaster Market Center, Frankfurt, Germany, from 1954 to 1957. From 1958 to 1960, she was in private practice in Maryvale, Arizona.

O'Connor served as the assistant attorney general of Arizona (1965–1969) and was appointed to the Arizona State Senate in 1959 and reelected to two terms. In 1975, she was elected a judge of the Maricopa County Superior Court and served in that capacity until 1979, when she was appointed to the Arizona Court of Appeals. President Ronald Reagan appointed her as an associate justice of the U.S. Supreme Court in 1981, where she served for twenty-four years until she retired in January 2006. Since her retirement, Justice O'Connor has continued her judicial service by hearing cases in the U.S. courts of appeals. In 2009, President Obama awarded her with the nation's highest civilian honor, the Presidential Medal of Freedom.

William Rehnquist (1924–2005), Chief Justice of the Supreme Court

William Rehnquist served on the U.S. Supreme Court for thirty-three years, as associate justice from 1972 to 1986 and as chief justice from 1986 to 2005. During his years as associate justice, he often wrote dissenting opinions, sometimes solo dissents. As chief justice, he often wrote the majority opinion and impacted the court by managing its docket. On religious freedom, he wrote, "Just because an action is religiously motivated, does not make it consequence-free for society, and should not make it consequence-free under society's laws." A consistently conservative voice on the court, he supported the death penalty and opposed gay rights. In 1973, as an associate justice, Rehnquist opposed the decision in *Roe v. Wade*.

As chief justice, William Rehnquist managed the court over eighteen decisions involving freedom of religion cases. He wrote the majority opinion in several decisions that were decided by 5–4 votes. In *Stone v. Graham* (449 U.S. 39, 1980), the court ruled that a Kentucky law was an unconstitutional violation of the Establishment Clause of the First Amendment because it lacked a nonreligious legislative purpose. In *Bowen v. Kendrick* (487 U.S. 589, 1988), the court upheld the Adolescent Family Life Act that applied the three-part test set forth in *Lemon v. Kurtzman*: (1) it had a secular purpose, (2) it neither advanced nor inhibited religion, and (3) it did not excessively entangle government in religion. In *Zobrest v. Catalina Foothills School District* (509 U.S. 1, 1993), the court held that under the Individuals with Disabilities Education Act (IDEA), the public school board was required to provide on-site services of a sign language interpreter to a hearing-impaired student in a private religious school. In *Zelman v. Simmons-Harris* (536 U.S. 639, 2002), the court upheld an Ohio program that used high school vouchers, ruling that the program did not violate the Establishment Clause, even if the parents could use the vouchers to send their child to a private religious school. In *Valley Forge Christian College v. Americans United for the Separation of Church and State* (454 U.S. 464, 1982), the court upheld the Flast test for taxpayer standing, ruling that the plaintiffs lacked standing as taxpayers. In *Mueller v. Allen* (463 U.S. 388, 1983), Rehnquist's majority opinion upheld the constitutionality of a Minnesota state law that allowed a tax deduction for parents for school expenses, including those for private secular and religious schools.

As an associate justice, Rehnquist dissented in *Wallace v. Jaffree* (472 U.S. 38, 1985), contending that the founders' intent to erect a "wall of separation" between church and state was misguided. Rehnquist dissented, arguing the school-authorized "one minute period of silence for meditation or voluntary prayer" was voluntary in nature, and he opposed the majority's peripheral reasoning in its use of the Lemon test. In *Committee for Public Education and Religious Liberty v. Nyquist* (413 U.S. 756, 1973), the court invalidated a New York state law providing grants to parochial schools for maintenance and repairs of school facilities. He dissented, arguing that the tax exemption was to prevent government oppression of religion via taxation, not for the promotion of religion. And in *Meek v. Pittenger* (421 U.S. 349, 1975), he concurred in part and dissented in part but concluded that the textbook loan program is constitutionally indistinguishable from the program upheld in *Board of Education v. Allen* (392 US 236, 1968). Finally, in *Hustler Magazine, Inc. v. Falwell* (485 U.S. 46, 1988), Rehnquist wrote the majority opinion (8–0) that the First Amendment and the Fourteenth Amendment prohibit public figures from recovering damages.

William Rehnquist was born in Milwaukee, Wisconsin, in 1924. He graduated from Harvard University (BA and MA in political science) and earned his JD from Stanford Law School, graduating in the same law class as Sandra Day O'Connor. He served in the U.S. Army Air Forces during World War II.

As chief justice, he presided over the impeachment trial (in the U.S. Senate) of President Bill Clinton and the *Bush v. Gore* election decision (531 U.S. 98, 2000). He died in September 2005 of thyroid cancer.

John Roberts (1955–), Chief Justice of the Supreme Court

John Roberts Jr. was appointed chief justice of the U.S. Supreme Court by President George W. Bush in 2005. In six religious freedom cases where he presided as chief justice, four were decided 5–4, and in two cases, Chief Justice Roberts wrote the majority opinions. In *Gonzales v. O Centro Espirita Beneficiente Uniao do Vegetal* (546 U.S. 418, 2006), the court upheld (8–0) that the Brazil-based U.D.V. church was properly granted an injunction under the Religious Freedom Restoration Act (1993) against criminal prosecution for its sacramental use of a hallucinatory substance—*hoasca* tea—because the government failed to demonstrate a compelling interest in prohibiting its use. In *Hosanna-Tabor Evangelical Lutheran Church and School v. Equal Employment Opportunity Commission* (565 U.S. 171, 2012), the court ruled unanimously that federal discrimination laws do not apply to religious organizations' selection of religious leaders.

Chief Justice Roberts wrote the majority opinion in the 5–4 decision in *Morse v. Frederick* (551 U.S. 393, 2007), which held that the First Amendment does not prevent educators from suppressing, at or across the street from a school for a school-sponsored event, student speech that is reasonably viewed as promoting illegal drug use (that is, the smoking of marijuana).

Chief Justice Roberts attended Harvard College (BA, 1976) and Harvard Law School (JD, 1979). He was a law clerk for Associate Justice William Rehnquist in 1980. He was the special assistant to the attorney general in the U.S. Department of Justice (DOJ) from 1981 to 1982 and served as associate counsel to President Ronald Reagan in the White House Counsel's Office from 1982 to 1986. He was principle deputy solicitor general for the DOJ from 1989 to 1993. He also practiced law in Washington, DC.

Roberts served on the U.S. court of appeals in 2003, appointed by President George W. Bush, before being appointed to the U.S. Supreme Court by President Bush and confirmed as chief justice in 2005. Roberts ruled on two landmark legislative cases: reaffirming the legality of the Affordable Care Act by siding with the liberal wing of the court along with the swing vote of Associate Justice Anthony Kennedy. He voted his conservative views in the minority on the issue of same-sex marriage; the decision made same-sex marriage legal in all fifty states. It has been roundly opposed by the religious right but is supported by a majority of Americans in postdecision public opinion polls.

Chief Justice Roberts was born in Buffalo, New York, in 1959. His family moved to Long Beach, Indiana. He attended Notre Dame Elementary school there and La Lumiere boarding school in La Porte, Indiana, where he excelled as a wrestler, becoming regional champion.

Antonin Scalia (1936–2016), Associate Justice of the Supreme Court

Associate Justice Antonin Scalia (1936–2016) was unquestionably the leading voice of the conservative bloc on the high court. He participated in twenty-four decisions on religious freedom cases. Justice Scalia wrote the majority opinion in several: *Employment Division v. Smith* (494 U.S. 872, 1990), *R. A. V. v. City of St. Paul* (505 U.S. 377, 1992), and *Capitol Square Review & Advisory Board v. Pinette* (515 U.S. 753, 1995). He was the forceful articulator of the judicial principle of "original interpretation," or "strict construction," and argued forcefully against what he labeled "judicial activism," yet he was an activist on several decisions in which his conservative philosophy outweighed judicial precedent, court tradition, or any language in the Constitution and cases in which the justices voted 5–4 along political party lines: *Gore v. Bush* (531 U.S. 98, 2000) and *Citizens United v. Federal Election Commission* (558 U.S. 310, 2010).

Antonin Scalia was born in New Jersey in 1936. He was a lifelong devout Roman Catholic. He earned his AB from Georgetown University and the University of Fribourg, Switzerland, and his LLB from Harvard Law School. He served as a Sheldon Fellow of Harvard University (1960–1961). Upon graduating from Harvard Law, he went into private practice in Cleveland, Ohio, for several years before becoming a professor of law at the University of Virginia (1967–1971). He went on to teach law at the University of Chicago (1977–1982) and as a visiting professor of law at Georgetown University and Stanford University. Justice Scalia was chair of the American Bar Association's Section of Administrative Law (1981–1982) and the conference section chair (1982–1983).

In the federal government, Scalia was general counsel of the Office of Telecommunications Policy (1971–1972), chair of the Administrative Conference of the United States (1972–1974), and assistant attorney general for the Office of Legal Counsel (1974–1977). In 1982, President Ronald Reagan appointed Scalia to the U.S. Court of Appeals for the District of Columbia Circuit (the appeals court from which the most justices have moved up to the Supreme Court). In 1986, President Reagan appointed him as an associate justice of the U.S. Supreme Court, and he took his seat in September 1986.

Justice Antonin Scalia died suddenly of a heart attack on February 13, 2016. He was succeeded by Neil Gorsuch, who is considered a "strict constructionist" judge, firmly in the tradition of Justice Scalia and likely to vote as Scalia would have on several freedom of religion cases on the court's docket.

Potter Stewart (1915–1985), Associate Justice of the Supreme Court

Potter Stewart was born in 1915 in Michigan. He received his BA from Yale University, from which he also earned his LLB degree and where he served as editor of the *Yale Law Journal*. Potter Stewart served in the U.S. Navy during World War II.

Stewart was appointed to the Sixth Circuit Court of Appeals by President Eisenhower and served on the appellate court from 1954 to 1958. President Eisenhower appointed Stewart to the U.S. Supreme Court in 1958, and he served on the court until 1981. He was a conservative on the Warren court, often writing dissenting opinions. In an obscenity case, *Jacobellis v. Ohio* (378 U.S. 184, 1964), Stewart concurred with the majority opinion. At issue was whether the State of Ohio could ban the showing of a film, *The Lovers*, that the state deemed obscene. Justice Potter Stewart wrote that hard-core pornography was excepted from free speech protection, but in this case, he determined the film was not hard core, famously stating that "hard-core pornography" was hard to define, but "I know it when I see it."

Justice Stewart wrote the majority opinion in four cases. In *Bates v. Little Rock* (361 U.S. 616, 1960), in a unanimous 9–0 decision, the court ruled on the freedom of association to advocate ideas and air grievances as protected by the First Amendment and the Fourteenth Amendment's Due Process Clause that bars state action that might suppress those principles. Daisy Bates was president of the Arkansas NAACP.

In *Edwards v. South Carolina* (372 U.S. 229, 1963), by an 8–1 vote, the court held that the Due Process Clause of the Fourteenth Amendment allows the First Amendment's right to petition to extend to the states as well as the federal government. Edwards had been arrested for breach of peace, but Stewart's majority opinion found that the South Carolina law infringed on free speech, free assembly, and the freedom to petition for redress of grievances. His opinion was joined in by Chief Justice Earl Warren and Justices Hugo Black, William Douglas, John Harlan, William Brennan, Byron White, and Arthur Goldberg. Only Justice Tom Clark dissented.

In *Shuttlesworth v. Birmingham* (394 U.S. 147, 1969), the court struck down a Birmingham ordinance that prohibited holding a parade or procession on city streets without first obtaining a permit. Justice Stewart's opinion and the court found that the permit denial was not to control traffic but to censor ideas.

Finally, in *Coates v. City of Cincinnati* (402 U.S. 611, 1971), the court invalidated a city ordinance against loitering that negatively affected freedom of assembly. Justice Stewart's majority opinion was that the city ordinance's use of the words "annoying conduct" violated the Due Process Clause and the First Amendment as too vague and an infringement on freedom of assembly and association.

Justice Stewart retired from the Supreme Court in June 1981, and he died in 1985 in New Hampshire (Frank 1995; Woodward and Armstrong 1979).

Donald J. Trump (1946–), President of the United States

Donald J. Trump was elected the forty-fifth president of the United States in 2016 and was sworn into office in January 2017. He has had a notable impact on First Amendment freedom issues, including on religion (free exercise and establishment issues) and the press (attacks on the press as "fake news") and his attacks on the Federal Bureau of Investigation (FBI) and the U.S. Department of Justice (DOJ). His administration policies and executive orders involve a significant policy shift toward the conservative right. He nominated two hard-right conservative justices, Neil Gorsuch and Brett Cavanaugh, to the U.S. Supreme Court and a sizable number of conservative judges to federal district and appellate courts.

Significantly, President Trump has issued three executive orders attempting to enforce a (Muslim) travel ban; two were ruled unconstitutional in two federal district courts, but the third iteration was upheld by the U.S. Supreme Court

Earl Warren (1891–1974), Chief Justice of the Supreme Court

Earl Warren was the fourteenth chief justice of the U.S. Supreme Court (1953–1969) and arguably the most impactful chief justice with respect to issues of civil rights and civil liberties, especially concerning First Amendment freedoms. He presided over sweeping changes in constitutional law related to areas of race relations, criminal procedure, and legislative apportionment. President Dwight Eisenhower appointed him the interim chief justice to the Supreme Court in 1954.

Warren wrote the unanimous opinion in *Brown v. Board of Education of Topeka, Kansas* (347 U.S. 483, 1954), which declared unconstitutional the separation of public school students by race, overturning the "separate but equal" doctrine that had prevailed since the *Plessy v. Ferguson* (163 U.S. 537) decision in 1896. In *Watkins v. United States* (354 U.S. 178, 1957), he led the court in upholding the right of a witness to refuse to testify before a congressional committee and several opinions concerning federal and state loyalty and security investigations during the anti-communism and subversion hysteria of the 1950s.

Chief Justice Warren wrote the majority opinion in two landmark First Amendment decisions: *Gregory v. City of Chicago* (394 U.S. 111, 1969) and *United States v. O'Brien* (391 U.S. 367, 1968). In *Gregory*, Warren's majority opinion (9–0) upheld the First Amendment rights of comedian and civil rights activist Dick Gregory to peaceful civil rights protest against the overzealous actions of the Chicago Police Department's attempt to "quell an anticipated civil disorder." The unanimous court found that the "march was, in fact, peaceful and orderly." In the *O'Brien* case, the issue was over symbolic speech—the act of burning a draft card. Warren's majority opinion held that because the government has an important interest in an effective draft system, the First Amendment does not void a law against burning a draft card, as the act of burning a draft card does not implicate a substantial speech interest. Warren wrote, "This Court will not strike down an otherwise constitutional statute on the basis of an alleged illicit legislative motive."

The civil rights legacy of the Warren court, that the court should be a vessel for social change in the field of civil liberties and civil rights, reflected Warren's liberal judicial activism and interpretation of the Constitution—including the First Amendment—in an "open-ended manner," reading its provisions as potential solutions to contemporary social problems (Frank 1995).

People: Nongovernmental Stakeholders

Any one of dozens of nongovernmental activists on the issue of First Amendment freedoms in American politics could be profiled. Space considerations limit the profiles here to seven: two representing the religious right movement and the pro-freedom of expression side of the freedom of religion conflict, two representing atheism and the freedom from religion and upholding the Establishment Clause, one representing labor and the Socialist Party, and two representing the middle and the think tank and academic perspective on the matter.

Eugene Debs (1855–1926)

Eugene V. Debs was a labor organizer and five-time Socialist Party candidate for president between 1900 and 1920. He was born in Terre Haute, Indiana, the son of immigrants from Alsace, France, who came to the United States in 1849. Debs left home at age fourteen to work in railroad shops and later as a locomotive fireman. He organized a lodge of the Brotherhood of Locomotive Fireman in 1875, and in 1880, he was elected its national secretary and treasurer. Debs was a city clerk in Terre Haute from 1879 to 1883 and a member of the state legislature from 1885 to 1887. He was an advocate of industrial unionism then being promoted by the Knights of Labor rather than craft unionism. In 1893, Debs became president of the American Railway Union. He was sentenced to six months in jail in 1895 for leading the Pullman Palace Car Company strike.

Debs worked for the Populist presidential candidate, William Jennings Bryan, in 1896. He was converted to socialism in 1897 by Victor Berger. Debs helped establish the Socialist Party of America and was its presidential candidate in 1900 and again in 1904. He helped found the Industrial Workers of the World (IWW) in 1905. He was the Socialist nominee for president in 1908, and in 1912, he ran on the party's ticket against Democrat Woodrow Wilson. He opted not to run in 1916. In 1920, he ran again, winning his largest popular vote (just over 915,000) while serving time in prison for violation of the Espionage Act of 1917. Debs and many socialists and IWW members were imprisoned for sedition because they opposed the U.S. entry into World War I. He was released from prison by presidential order in 1921. Harsh prison conditions affected his health and led to his poor health thereafter.

Debs was a dynamic public speaker. After 1920, he essentially earned his living as a lecturer and contributor to various periodicals. His best-known writings are *Unionism and Socialism*, a 1904 pamphlet, and *Walls and Bars*, a 1927 book. Debs died in Elmhurst, Illinois, in October 1926 at age seventy-one (Ginger and Davis 2007; Salvatore 2007).

James Dobson (1936–)

James Dobson founded Focus on the Family in 1977, and he led the organization until 2003. Since 2010, his radio show *Family Talk* has been broadcast on over three hundred stations nationwide. In the 1980s, Dobson was considered to be the conservative social movement leader and the most influential evangelical leader, often considered the successor to Jerry Falwell and Pat Robertson.

Dobson is a psychologist with a PhD from Southern California University (1967). In the 1980s, he produced *Focus on the Family* as a daily radio program broadcast to over seven thousand stations and in a dozen languages, with a claimed audience of 220 million. It was also carried on about sixty television stations daily. He resigned as president and CEO of the Focus on the Family organization in 2003, citing philosophical differences with his successor, Jim Daly. Dobson is a strong proponent of traditional marriage, with the husband as the breadwinner and the wife as homemaker and mother, and he recommends women with children remain focused on mothering until the children are eighteen. He is adamantly opposed to same-sex marriage.

Madalyn Murray O'Hair (1919–1995)

Once known as the "Pope of Atheism" and called "the most hated woman in America," Madalyn O'Hair was an avowed atheist, a lifelong champion of the separation of church and state, and a notable feminist. She was the litigant in the U.S.

Supreme Court case *Murray v. Curlett* and its consolidated case *Abbington School District v. Schempp* (232 Md 368 and 374 U.S. 203, 1963), in which the court, in its 8–1 decision, ruled that required Bible reading and recitation of the Lord's Prayer in public schools violated the Establishment Clause of the First Amendment. With those judicial victories, she became the nation's most famous atheist.

Murray O'Hair founded the American Atheists in 1963 and remained its leading spokesperson for thirty years, appearing on radio and television and authoring three books: *What on Earth Is an Atheist* (1973), *Freedom under Siege* (1974), and *An Atheist Epic* (1989).

Murray O'Hair was born in 1919 in Pennsylvania. She died in September 1995, murdered along with her two children. She was married twice: to Richard O'Hair and to John Roths. She earned a BA from Ashland College and a JD from the South Texas College of Law. In 2013, the first "atheist monument" was erected, and it contained quotes from Benjamin Franklin, Thomas Jefferson, and Madalyn Murray O'Hair.

In 1995, Murray O'Hair disappeared in San Antonio, Texas, along with $500,000 in American Atheist funds. A note was left saying she and her two adult children would be away temporarily. For a time, it was suspected that she stole the funds and fled to New Zealand, but police eventually arrested David Waters, an ex-convict who worked for the American Atheist organization. He and an accomplice had kidnapped Madalyn, John Garth Murray, and Robin Murray O'Hair. They forced Madalyn to withdraw the funds and then killed and buried them. He led authorities to their grave site in 2001.

Ron Reagan (1958–)

Ron Reagan is an avowed atheist and the public spokesperson for the Freedom from Religion Foundation. In the foundation's radio and television ads, Reagan describes himself as "an unabashed atheist, not afraid of burning in hell." He is the son of conservative Republican president Ronald Reagan and Nancy Reagan and authored a book, *My Father at 100: A Memoir* (2011), in which he addresses his father's Alzheimer's disease.

Politically, Reagan is registered as an independent. He is a radio host on the Air America radio network and a frequent political commentator/consultant for MSNBC, including a stint in 2005 as cohost of the talk show *Connected: Coast to Coast with Monica Crowley*. He briefly hosted a late-night television talk show, *The Ron Reagan Show* (2008–2010). He is on the board of the Creative Coalition, a politically active organization founded in 1989 that mobilizes entertainers and artists to advocate for First Amendment rights and causes as a 501(c)(3) nonprofit public charity. He spoke at the 2004 Democratic National Convention and endorsed and worked for Barack Obama's presidential bid in 2008. In the 2016 presidential primaries, he endorsed Vermont senator Bernie Sanders.

Reagan was born in 1958 in Los Angeles, California. He declared his atheism to his parents at age twelve. He attended Yale University but dropped out to become a ballet dancer, joining the Joffrey Ballet Company. The Freedom from Religion Foundation named him to its Honorary Board of distinguished achievers. He is an outspoken opponent of the conservative Christian right movement's attempts to repeal the Johnson Amendment and their support of school voucher programs for financial aid to religious-based schools.

Ralph Reed (1961–)

Ralph Reed is the founder and chairman of the Faith and Freedom Coalition, a former adviser to the Bush-Cheney presidential campaigns of 2000 and 2004, and a leading voice of the conservative Christian right movement. He is credited with founding and serving as the CEO of the Christian Coalition in 1989–1997, widely considered one of the most successful public policy lobbying organizations.

The Faith and Freedom Coalition is primarily a fundraising and political contribution organization that supports conservative Republicans and emphasizes a religious freedom agenda. It claims over one million members. It was founded in 2009 by Reed, who also established the Faith and Freedom Foundation, a 501(c)(3) organization that promotes political lobbying to enact legislation favorable to the religious right and political activism.

Reed was born in Virginia in 1961. He earned his AB from the University of Georgia (1985) and his PhD from Emory University (1989), majoring in history for both degrees. He started and led the Georgia College Republicans.

In the early 1980s, Reed moved to Washington, DC, and along with Jack Abramoff and Grover Norquist formed a "triumvirate" of political activists. He became a born-again Christian activist in 1983. He led Students for America, a conservative activist group, before founding the Christian Coalition, which organized Pat Robertson supporters. In 1996, the Federal Election Commission (FEC) brought enforcement actions against the Christian Coalition for violating federal campaign laws, and Reed resigned as its executive director. In 2005, he became embroiled in the Abramoff Indian gaming scandal.

Reed ran for the Georgia Republican Party chairmanship in 2001, and he led the party to electoral success in 2002. He ran unsuccessfully for lieutenant governor of Georgia in 2006.

Melissa Rogers (unknown–)

Melissa Rogers is a nonresident senior fellow in Governance Studies at the Brookings Institute, and she previously served as executive director of the Pew Forum on Religion and Public Life. She was also the special assistant to the president in the White House Office of Faith-Based and Neighborhood Partnerships under President Barack Obama. She was the inaugural chair of its advisory council.

Rogers earned her BA from Baylor University and her JD from the University of Pennsylvania Law School. She coauthored a book on religion and law for Baylor University Press entitled *Freedom and the Supreme Court* (2008). She directed the Center for Religion and Public Affairs at Wake Forest University Divinity School and also served as the general counsel of the Baptist Joint Committee for Religious Liberty.

Rogers's area of expertise at the Brookings Institute includes the First Amendment's religion clauses, religion in American public life, and the interplay of religion, policy, and politics. She well exemplifies the activist in religious freedom from the think tank perspective

John Witte Jr. (1959–)

John Witte Jr. is another example of a freedom of religion stakeholder who represents the think tank approach to the issue. He is the director of the Center for the Study of Law and Religion at Emory University and the Robert F. Woodruff Professor of Law and a McDonald Distinguished Professor at Emory. His areas of expertise include American legal history, human rights, law and religion, marriage and family law, and religious liberty. A prolific scholar, he has authored 230 articles, 15 journal symposia, and 30 books.

Professor Witte was born in 1959 in Canada. He earned his BA from Calvin College in 1982 and his JD from Harvard Law School in 1985. He was selected twelve times by Emory law students as the Most Outstanding Professor.

Witte has given the McDonald Lecture at Emory University on the topic "Separation of Church and State: There Is No Wall." Among his hundreds of articles, the following topics are of special note: "The Legal Challenges of Religious Polygamy in the USA"; "Lift High the Cross? Religion in Public Spaces"; "Sex May Be Free, but Children Come with a Cost"; "Keeping the Commandments"; and "Can America Still Ban Polygamy?"

Among his thirty books, some recent books, published since 2010, include the following: *Christianity and Human Rights: An Introduction* (Cambridge University Press, 2010); *Religion and Human Rights: An Introduction* (Oxford University Press, 2012); *From Sacrament to Contract: Marriage, Religion, and*

Law in the Western Tradition (Westminster John Knox Press, 2nd ed., 2012); *No Establishment of Religion: America's Original Contribution to Religious Liberty* (Oxford University Press, 2012); *The Western Case for Monogamy over Polygamy* (Cambridge University Press, 2015); and *Texts and Contexts in Legal History: Essays in Honor of Charles Donahue* (The Robbins Collection, 2016).

John Peter Zenger (1697–1746)

John Zenger was a German-born immigrant who came to the New York Colony at the age of thirteen. He was indentured for eight years as a printer's apprentice to William Bradford, a pioneer printer, and Zenger started his own printing business in 1726. He became a noted printer and journalist in New York, publishing the *New York Weekly Journal* (1720–1746), in which he ran a series of articles that opposed the policies of the colonial governor, William Cosby. Zenger was arrested, imprisoned for ten months, and tried for seditious libel in 1875. In the 1870s, English common law, established by the Star Chamber, provided that the truth was no defense for seditious libel. Zenger's defense lawyer, Andrew Hamilton, argued that the jury should consider the truth of Zenger's printed statements. Zenger was acquitted of libel by the jury on the grounds that his charges were based on fact, thereby establishing as a key consideration in libel cases that truthful information cannot be libelous—a principle that has been used in libel cases ever since.

Zenger's account of his trial, published in 1836 in the *New York Weekly Journal*, was widely circulated in both the American colonies and in England. In 1804, in *People v. Croswell*, Alexander Hamilton used the precedent of *Zenger v. Cosby* in defending Croswell of libel charges versus President Thomas Jefferson, who likewise argued that truthful information cannot be libelous.

Zenger died in July 1746 in New York at the age of forty-eight (Vile 2008; Editors of Encyclopaedia Britannica 2020).

Further Reading

Books

Allitt, Patrick. 2008. *Religion in America since 1945: A History.* New York: Columbia University Press.

Chernow, Ron. 2004. *Alexander Hamilton.* New York: Penguin.

Editors of Encyclopaedia Britannica. 2020. "John Peter Zenger." *Encyclopædia Britannica.* Accessed July 2, 2020. https://www.britannica.com/biography/John-Peter-Zenger.

Frank, John. 1995. *The Justices of the United States Supreme Court: Their Lives and Major Decisions.* Philadelphia: Chelsea House.

Friedman, Leon. 1978. *The Justices of the United States Supreme Court: Their Lives and Major Decisions.* Philadelphia: Chelsea House.

Ginger, Ray, and Mike Davis. 2007. *The Bending Cross: A Biography of Eugene Victor Debs.* Chicago: Haymarket Books.

Hamilton, Alexander. 2017. *The Essential Hamilton: Letters and Other Writings.* Edited by Joanne Freeman. New York: Library of America.

Jefferson, Thomas. 1950. *The Papers of Thomas Jefferson.* Princeton, NJ: Princeton University Press.

LeMay, Michael. 2017. *The American Political Party System: A Reference Handbook.* Santa Barbara, CA: ABC-CLIO.

LeMay, Michael. 2018. *Homeland Security: A Reference Handbook.* Santa Barbara, CA: ABC-CLIO.

Parrish, Michael. 2002. *The Hughes Court: Justices, Rulings, and Legacy.* Santa Barbara, CA: ABC-CLIO.

Salvatore, Nick, ed. 2007. *Eugene V. Debs: Citizen and Socialist.* Champaign: University of Illinois Press.

Simon, James. 2012. *FDR and Chief Justice Hughes: The President, the Supreme Court, and the Epic Battle over the New Deal.* New York: Simon and Schuster.

Vile, John R. 2008. *The First Amendment Encyclopedia.* Accessed July 2, 2020. https://mtsu.edu /first-amendment/encyclopedia.

Zentner, Scot, and Michael LeMay. 2020. *Party and Nation.* Lanham, MD: Lexington Books.

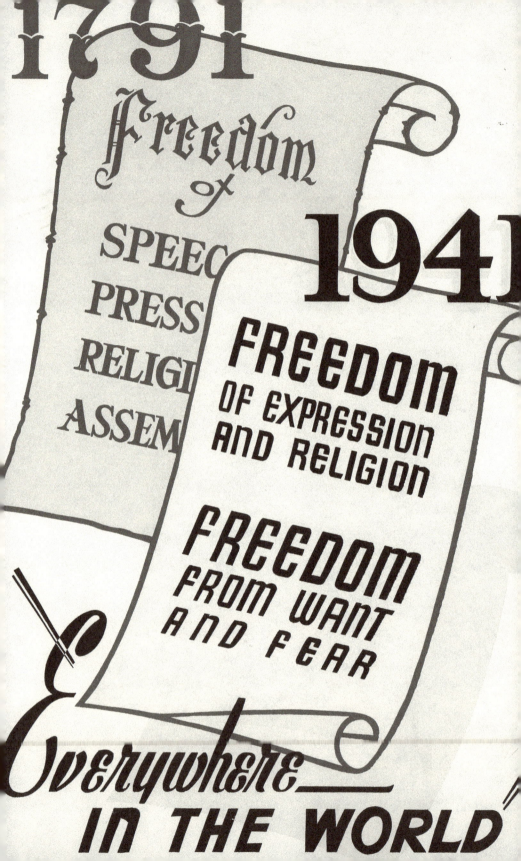

5 Data and Documents

Introduction

Public policy related to First Amendment freedoms has been advanced by enactment of laws, presidential actions, and especially U.S. Supreme Court rulings. This chapter presents a synopsis of critical actions, both legislative and judicial, that have collectively set national policy on the fundamental freedoms citizens enjoy as a result of the First Amendment. In its first section, this chapter presents data in tables and figures. These are followed by a primary documents section that presents excerpts from some key federal legislative actions on the topic, excerpts of several landmark Supreme Court decisions, and presidential executive orders or a veto message pertaining to the topic. The documents are presented in chronological order.

Data

Table 5.1. Religious Freedom Supreme Court Cases

Table 5.1 lists the major U.S. Supreme Court cases dealing with religious freedom issues. The cases are organized by those dealing with challenges based on the Establishment Clause and then those based on the Freedom of Expression Clause. Within each category, cases are listed by the nature of the problem at issue in the case, in alphabetical order.

A Federal Art Project poster showng freedom of speech, press, religion, assembly (1791) as well as Freedom of expression and religion, and freedom from want and fear (1941). (Library of Congress)

Table 5.1

Establishment Clause

Religions Involved

Anglican, Congregational, Roman Catholic, Evangelical, Latter-day Saints

Cases

1. Aid to Church-Related Schools: *Pierce v. Society of Sisters* (268 U.S. 510, 1925); *Cochran v. Louisiana State Board of Education* (281 U.S. 370, 1930); *Everson v. Board of Education* (330 U.S. 1, 1947); *Abington School District v. Schempp* (374 U.S. 203, 1963); *Board of Education v. Allen* (392 U.S. 236, 1968); *Lemon v. Kurtzman* (403 U.S. 602, 1971); *Tilton v. Richardson* (403 U.S. 672, 1971); *Committee for Public Education and Religious Liberty v. Nyquist* (413 U.S. 756, 1971); *Meek v. Pittenger* (421 U.S. 349, 1975); *Roemer v. Board of Public Works of Maryland* (426 U.S. 736, 1976); *Wolman v. Walter* (433 U.S. 229, 1977); *Committee for Public Education and Religious Liberty v. Regan* (444 U.S. 646, 1980); *Mueller v. Allen* (463 U.S. 388, 1983); *Aguilar v. Felton* (473 U.S. 402, 1985); *Grand Rapids School District v. Ball* (473 U.S. 373, 1985); *Zobrest v. Catalina Foothills School District* (509 U.S. 1, 1993); *Zelman v. Simmons-Harris* (536 U.S. 639, 2002); *Arizona Christian School Tuition Organization v. Winn* (563 U.S. 125, 2011).

2. Religion in Public Education: *McCollum v. Board of Education* (330 U.S. 203, 1948); *Zorach v. Clauson* (343 U.S. 306, 1952); *Engel v. Vitale* (370 U. S. 421, 1962); *Abington School District v. Schempp* (374 U.S. 203, 1963); *Epperson v. Arkansas* (393 U.S. 97, 1968); *Stone v. Graham* (449 U.S. 39, 1980); *Rosenberger v. Rector and Visitors of University of Virginia* (515 U.S. 819, 1995); *Agostini v. Felton* (473 U.S. 402, 1997); *Mitchell v. Helms* (530 U.S. 793, 2000).

3. Government-Sponsored Religious Displays: *Lynch v. Donnelly* (465 U.S. 668, 1984); *Board of Trustees of Scarsdale v. McCreary* (471 U.S. 83, 1985); *County of Allegheny v. American Civil Liberties Union Greater Pittsburgh Chapter* (492 U.S. 573, 1989); *McCreary County v. American Civil Liberties Union of Kentucky* (545 U.S. 844, 2005); *Van Orden v. Perry* (545 U.S. 677, 2005).

4. Prayers in Public Schools: *Wallace v. Jaffree* (472 U.S. 38, 1985); *Lee v. Weisman* (505 U.S. 577, 1992); *Santa Fe Independent School District v. Doe* (530 U.S. 290, 2000); *Elk Grove Unified School District v. Newdow* (542 U.S. 1, 2004).

5. Sabbatarian Laws (Blue Laws): *McGowan v. Maryland* (366 U.S. 420, 1961); *Braunfeld v. Brown* (366 U.S. 599, 1961); *Gallagher v. Crown Kosher Super Market of Massachusetts, Inc.* (366 U.S. 617, 1961); *Estate of Thornton v. Caldor, Inc.* (472 U.S. 703, 1985).

6. Religious Institutions Functioning as Government Agency: *Larkin v. Grendel's Den, Inc.* (459 U.S. 116, 1982); *Bowen v. Kendrick* (487 U.S. 589, 1988); *Board of Education of Kiryas Joel Village School v. Grumet* (512 U.S. 687, 1994).

Table 5.1 (continued)

7. Tax Exemption to Religious Institutions: *Walz v. Tax Commission of the City of New York* (397 U.S. 664, 1970); *Bob Jones University v. United States* (461 U.S. 574, 1983); *Texas Monthly, Inc. v. Bullock* (489 U.S. 1, 1989).

8. Legislative Chaplains/Prayers: *Marsh v. Chambers* (463 U.S. 783, 1983); *Town of Greece v. Galloway* (572 U.S. 565, 2014).

9. Standing to Sue: *Flast v. Cohen* (392 U.S. 83, 1968); *Valley Forge Christian College v. Americans United for Separation of Church and State* (454 U.S. 464, 1982).

10. Teaching Creationism in Public Schools: *Edwards v. Aguillard* (482 U.S. 578, 1987).

11. Unequal Government Treatment of Religious Groups: *Larson v. Valente* (456 U.S. 228, 1982).

Free Exercise Clause
Religions Involved
Amish/Mennonites, JW, LDS

Cases

1. Solicitation by Religious Groups: *Cantwell v. Connecticut* (310 U.S. 296, 1940); *Minersville School District v. Gobitis* (310 U.S. 586, 1940); *Cox v. New Hampshire* (312 U.S. 569, 1941); *Jones v. City of Opelika-I* (316 U.S. 584, 1942); *Marsh v. Alabama* (326 U.S. 501, 1946); *Murdock v. Pennsylvania* (319 U.S. 105, 1943); *Jones v. City of Opelika-II* (319 U.S. 103, 1943); *West Virginia State Board of Education v. Barnette* (319 U.S. 624, 1943); *Prince v. Massachusetts* (321 U.S. 158, 1944); *Heffron v. International Society for Krishna Consciousness* (452 U.S. 640, 1981).

2. Religious Tests for Public Benefits/Services: *Chaplinsky v. New Hampshire* (315 U.S. 568, 1942); *Torcaso v. Watkins* (367 U.S. 488, 1961); *McDaniel v. Paty* (435 U.S. 618, 1978); *Thomas v. Review Board of the Indiana Employment Security Division* (450 U.S. 707, 1981); *Goldman v. Weinberger* (475 U.S. 503, 1986); *Bowen v. Roy* (476 U.S. 693, 1986).

3. Free Exercise and Public Education: *Wisconsin v. Yoder* (406 U.S. 205, 1972); *Widmar v. Vincent* (454 U.S. 263, 1981); *Board of Education of the Westside Community Schools v. Mergens* (496 U.S. 266, 1990); *Lamb's Chapel v. Center Moriches Union Free School District* (508 U.S. 384, 1993); *Rosenberger v. Rector and Visitors of the University of Virginia* (515 U.S. 819, 1995).

4. Religion versus the Right to Work: *Sherbert v. Verner* (374 U.S. 398, 1963); *Trans World Airlines v. Hardison, Inc.* (432 U.S. 63, 1977); *Ohio Civil Rights Commission v. Dayton Christian Schools* (477 U.S. 619, 1986); *Corporation of the Presiding Bishop of the Church of Jesus Christ of Latter-Day Saints v. Amos* (483 U.S. 327, 1987); *Employment Division v. Smith* (494 U.S. 872, 1990).

(continued)

Table 5.1 (*continued*)

5. Government Intrusion into Church Controversies: *United States v. Ballard* (322 U.S. 78, 1944); *Kedroff v. Saint Nicholas Cathedral* (344 U.S. 94, 1952); *Presbyterian Church v. Hull Church* (393 U.S. 440, 1969); *Jones v. Wolf* (443 U.S. 595, 1979); *Hosanna-Tabor Evangelical Lutheran Church and School v. Equal Employment Opportunity Commission* (565 U.S. 171, 2012).

6. Free Exercise versus Eminent Domain: *Lyng v. Northwest Indian Cemetery Protective Association* (485 U.S. 439, 1988); *City of Boerne v. Flores* (521 U.S. 507, 1997).

7. Free Exercise versus Freedom of Speech: *R. A. V. v. City of St. Paul* (505 U.S. 377, 1992); *Gonzales v. O Centro Espirita Beneficente Uniao do Vegetal* (546 U.S. 418, 2006).

8. Polygamy: *Reynolds v. United States* (98 U.S. 145, 1878); *Davis v. Beason* (133 U.S. 333, 1890).

9. Ritual Sacrifice of Animals: *Church of Lukumi Babalu Aye v. City of Hialeah* (508 U.S. 520, 1993).

Table 5.2. Key Supreme Court Cases on First Amendment Issues

Table 5.2 presents landmark U.S. Supreme Court cases dealing with freedom of assembly/association, freedom of the press, and freedom of speech. In each category, the cases are listed in order of the date the Supreme Court decided the case.

Table 5.2

Freedom of Assembly/Association Issues

1. *De Jonge v. Oregon* (299 U.S. 353, 1937). The court overturned Oregon's syndicalism law ruling that state governments may not violate constitutional right to peaceable assembly and further developed the legal concept of "symbolic speech." The decision overturned *United States v. Cruikshank* (92 U.S. 542, 1876).

2. *Hague v. Committee for Industrial Organization* (307 U.S. 496, 1939). The court ruled, 5–2, that banning a group from holding a political meeting in a public place violated the group's freedom of assembly under the First Amendment and set the precedent for the "public forum" doctrine. It was a landmark decision for labor organizations and the use of public spaces.

3. *Thomas v. Collins* (323 U.S. 516, 1945). In a 5–4 vote, the court ruled that a Texas law violated the First and Fourteenth Amendments' right to free speech and assembly by use of previous restraint to assemble and that such laws can only be justified by a "clear and present danger" to public welfare.

Table 5.2 (continued)

4. *National Association for the Advancement of Colored People v. Alabama* (357 U.S. 449, 1958). The court ruling unanimously held that Alabama's attempt to force the NAACP to turn over its membership list violated its freedom of association and was protected by the Fourteenth Amendment's Due Process Clause.

5. *Bates v. City of Little Rock* (361 U.S. 516, 1960). The court ruled unanimously that the rights of Daisy Bates and the NAACP to advocate ideas and air grievances were protected by the First and Fourteenth Amendments' Due Process Clause against state laws that suppressed that principle.

6. *Edwards v. South Carolina* (372 U.S. 229, 1963). The court ruled, 8–1, that the Due Process Clause of the Fourteenth Amendment extends the free petition clause of the First Amendment to states and that the South Carolina law infringed on Edwards's right of free assembly and freedom to petition for redress of grievances.

7. *Cox v. Louisiana* (379 U.S. 536, 1965). In a 7–2 decision, the court struck down a Louisiana law defining "breach of peace" as unconstitutionally vague and overly broad in scope and had no "uniform, consistent, and non-discriminatory standards" for granting exceptions to the general law.

8. *Carroll v. President and Commissioners of Princess Anne* (393 U.S. 175, 1968). The court unanimously struck down a ten-day injunction by a Maryland court against the National States Rights Party, a white supremacist group, on the basis of its use of prior restraint, which was held unconstitutional on freedom of assembly grounds.

9. *Shuttlesworth v. Birmingham* (394 U.S. 147, 1969). In its 7–1 decision, the court struck down a Birmingham ordinance prohibiting holding parades and processions on city streets without first obtaining a permit on the basis that the permit denial was not to control traffic but to censure ideas.

10. *Gregory v. City of Chicago* (394 U.S. 111, 1969). The court unanimously upheld the First Amendment rights to peaceful civil rights protest against the City of Chicago's police department's overzealous actions in attempting to quell "an anticipated civil disorder" when in fact the march was peaceful and orderly.

11. *Coates v. City of Cincinnati* (402 U.S. 611, 1971). In its 6–3 decision, the court ruled that the Cincinnati city ordinance against loitering violated freedom of assembly and the law's use of the words "annoying conduct" was too vague and was therefore an unconstitutional infringement of the freedom of assembly and association.

12. *Lloyd Corporation v. Tanner* (407 U.S. 551, 1972). In a 5–4 decision, the court reversed a Ninth Circuit Court ruling holding that Donald Tanner and other Vietnam War protestors who were handing out handbills inside the Lloyd Center Mall in Portland, Oregon, were not protected by the First Amendment because the protest was not related to the mall's operation and that the protestors did not have a First Amendment right to distribute handbills within a privately owned mall.

(continued)

Table 5.2 *(continued)*

13. *National Socialist Party v. Village of Skokie* (432 U.S. 43, 1978). The court ruled, 5–4, that strict procedural safeguards—including that of appellate review—must be in place when a lower court (the Illinois Supreme Court) intends to enforce a prohibition on free speech and assembly, in this case by denying the Nazi Party members' right to assemble and march down the streets of Skokie.

14. *Rotary International v. Rotary Club of Duarte* (481 U.S. 537, 1987). The court found that Rotary International did not have a First Amendment right to exclude women, affirming the judgment of the Court of Appeals of California respecting a state statute requiring business establishments to admit women members.

15. *Madsen v. Women's Health Center, Inc.* (512 U.S. 753, 1994). The court sustained the constitutionality of the clinic's right to a thirty-six-foot buffer zone and noise-level provision, finding that they burdened no more than necessary the rights of the abortion protestors' free speech and assembly rights to serve the injunction's goals, but it held against a three hundred–foot no-approach zone, thus affirming in part and reversing in part a Florida Supreme Court ruling on the matter.

16. *Hurley v. Irish-America Gay, Lesbian and Bisexual Group of Boston* (515 U.S. 557, 1995). In a unanimous decision, the court upheld the right of groups to determine what message their activities convey to the public and were thus permitted to exclude groups if those groups presented a message contrary to the one the organizing group wanted to portray. In this case, for the Irish Saint Patrick's Day Parade, the South Boston Allied War Veterans, a group of unincorporated private citizens, who had the parade permit, could exclude the Irish-American Gay, Lesbian and Bisexual Group of Boston from marching in the parade.

17. *Boy Scouts of America v. Dale* (530 U.S. 640, 2000). In a 5–4 decision, the court held that it was the constitutional right to freedom of association for the BSA to exclude a homosexual person from membership despite a New Jersey state law requiring equality of treatment, thereby reversing a New Jersey Supreme Court ruling that the public accommodation law required the BSA to readmit assistant scoutmaster James Dale, who had come out as a homosexual and had been expelled from the organization as a result.

18. *Christian Legal Society v. Martinez* (561 U.S. 661, 2010). The court upheld, 5–4, against a First Amendment challenge that the policy of the University of California, Hastings College of Law, governing the official recognition of student groups, which required the groups to accept all students regardless of their status or beliefs, to obtain recognition is a reasonable viewpoint-neutral condition on access to the forum.

Freedom of the Press Issues

1. *Rex v. Zenger* or *Crown v. Zenger* (1735) (Judiciary of New York Colony). The jury in the case ruled and thereby set the precedent for the principle that "truthful information cannot be seditiously libelous."

Table 5.2 *(continued)*

2. *People of New York v. Croswell* (3 Johns. Cas. 337, N.Y. 1804). In a defamation case, the judges deadlocked over whether the truth of statements could be introduced as defense against libel. A subsequent New York law stipulated that truthful statements cannot be libelous.

3. *Near v. Minnesota* (283 U.S. 697, 1931). In a 5–4 decision, the court held that prior restraint on publication violated freedom of press guaranteed by the First Amendment.

4. *New York Times Co. v. Sullivan* (376 U.S. 254, 1964). By a unanimous decision, the court ruled that freedom of speech protection in the First Amendment restricts the ability of American public officials to sue for defamation.

5. *Garrison v. Louisiana* (379 U.S. 64, 1964). In a unanimous decision, the court overturned the defamation conviction of Louisiana district attorney Jim Garrison, holding that the criminal libel law used to convict him was unconstitutional.

6. *Curtis Publishing v. Butts* (388 U.S. 130, 1967) and *Associated Press v. Walker* (389 U.S. 28, 1967). In a 5–4 decision, the court ruled in favor of Wally Butts versus the *Saturday Evening Post*, holding that although news organizations are protected from libel when printing allegations against public officials, they are not so protected when the allegations are against private individuals.

7. *New York Times Co. v. United States* (403 U.S. 713, 1971). In a 6–3 vote, the court made it possible for the *New York Times* and the *Washington Post* to publish the then classified Pentagon Papers without risk of government censorship or punishment.

8. *Nebraska Press Association v. Stuart* (427 U.S. 539, 1976). In a unanimous decision, the court held unconstitutional the use of prior restraint on media coverage during criminal trials.

9. *Zacchini v. Scripps-Howard Broadcasting* (433 U.S. 562, 1977). In a 5–4 vote, the court decided that broadcasting an entire act was different from reporting on an event and held in favor of Zacchini.

10. *Hustler Magazine, Inc. v. Falwell* (485 U.S. 46, 1988). In this landmark 8–0 decision, in which Justice Anthony Kennedy took no part, the court held that the First and Fourteenth Amendments prohibited public figures from recovering damages, in this case for alleged defamation involving an ad parody.

11. *Hazelwood School District v. Kuhlmeier* (484 U.S. 260, 1988). In a 5–3 vote, the eight-member court held that public school curricular student newspapers that have not been established as forums for student expression are subject to a lower level of First Amendment protection than independent student expression or newspapers, by policy or practice, established as forums for student expression.

(continued)

Table 5.2 *(continued)*

Freedom of Speech Issues

1. *Schenck v. United States* (249 U.S. 47, 1919). The court unanimously ruled in favor of the U.S. government upholding the Espionage Act of 1917, holding that Charles Schenk, in distributing flyers criticizing the draft and urging persons to resist the draft, did not have his First Amendment right to freedom of speech violated because draft resistance during a time of war posed a clear and present danger.

2. *Abrams v. United States* (250 U.S. 616, 1919). In a 7–2 decision, the court upheld the 1918 Amendment to the Espionage Act of 1917 making it a crime to urge the curtailment of production of materiel necessary to wage war against Germany with the intent to hinder the progress of the war, ruling that the defendants' freedom of speech was not violated.

3. *Debs v. United States* (249 U.S. 211, 1919). In a unanimous opinion, the court upheld the conviction of Eugene Debs for a public speech urging his audience to interfere with military recruitment during World War I. The court found that Debs's sympathy for individuals convicted of opposing the draft and obstructing recruitment was analogous to the situation in the *Schenk* decision, and thus Debs's conviction was valid.

4. *Gitlow v. New York* (268 U.S. 652, 1925). In a 7–2 decision, the court held that the First Amendment's freedom of speech and the Fourteenth Amendment's Due Process Clause extended to the governments of U.S. states, requiring them to be held to the same standards in regulating speech.

5. *West Virginia State Board of Education v. Barnette* (319 U.S. 624, 1943). The court, by its 6–3 ruling, held that the West Virginia state law requiring compulsory flag saluting violated the First Amendment and was therefore unconstitutional.

6. *Tinker v. Des Moines Independent Community School District* (393 U.S. 503, 1969). The court decided, 7–2, that the wearing of black armbands by students to protest the Vietnam War was pure speech and thus protected by the First Amendment.

7. *Brandenburg v. Ohio* (395 U.S. 444, 1969). Brandenburg, a Ku Klux Klan leader, made a speech at a Klan rally and was later convicted under an Ohio syndicalism law. The court's per curiam opinion held that the Ohio law violated Brandenburg's right to free speech, and the court established a two-part test to evaluate speech: (1) that the speech was intended to incite imminent lawless action, and (2) that the speech was likely to incite or produce such action. The court found the Ohio syndicalism law overly broad and thus in violation of the U.S. Constitution.

8. *United States v. O'Brien* (391 U.S. 367, 1968). The court ruled 7–1 for the United States that a criminal prohibition against burning a draft card did not violate the First Amendment's guarantee of free speech.

Table 5.2   *(continued)*

9. *Cohen v. California* (403 U.S. 15, 1971). In a 5–4 decision, the court found for Paul Cohen that the California law violated his freedom of expression protected by the First Amendment, reasoning that the expletive emblazoned on his jacket, while provocative, was not directed at anyone and that there was no evidence that it provoked some sort of physical action. Justice Harlan's majority opinion stated that "one man's vulgarity is another's lyric" and that the freedom of speech clause protects two elements of speech: (1) emotive (the expression of emotion) and (2) cognitive (the expression of ideas).

10. *Buckley v. Valeo* (424 U.S. 1, 1976). The court ruled per curiam that Federal Election Campaign Act limitations on personal or family expenditures by a candidate violated freedom of speech and were unconstitutional.

11. *Virginia State Board of Pharmacy v. Virginia Citizens Consumer Council, Inc.* (425 U.S. 748, 1976). The court ruled, 7–1, that the state could not limit pharmacists' right to provide information about prescription drug prices, as the state law violated "commercial speech" under the First Amendment.

12. *Bates v. State Bar of Arizona* (433 U.S. 350, 1977). The court ruled, 5–4, the right of lawyers to advertise their services as protected commercial speech.

13. *Island Trees School District v. Pico by Pico* (457 U.S. 853, 1983). For the first time, the court addressed the issue of the removal of books from public school libraries, holding that the motivation of a book's removal must be central in determining unconstitutionality. If the purpose is purely to eliminate a diversity of ideas for nationalistic, political, or religious reasons, it violates the First Amendment, but if the board can point to nondiscriminatory reasons, such as vulgarity or educational unsuitability, they are granted wide discretion in removing public school library books.

14. *Bethel School District v. Fraser* (478 U.S. 675, 1986). The court ruled, 7–1, that the First Amendment did not prevent a school district from disciplining a high school student for giving a lewd speech at a high school assembly.

15. *Hazelwood School District v. Kuhlmeier* (484 U.S. 260, 1988). The court held, 5–3, that educators—in this case the high school principal—did not offend the First Amendment by exercising editorial control over the content of a student's speech so long as their actions were "reasonably related to legitimate pedagogical concerns."

16. *Texas v. Johnson* (491 U.S. 397, 1989). The court, in a 5–4 decision, invalidated a Texas law's prohibition on desecrating the American flag, which at the time was enforced in forty-eight states, holding that the act of flag burning was protected "symbolic speech" under the First Amendment.

17. *R. A. V. v. City of St. Paul* (505 U.S. 377, 1992). The court unanimously struck down the St. Paul Bias-Motivated Crime Ordinance and reversed the conviction of a teenager for burning a cross on the lawn of an African American family, holding that the St. Paul ordinance was facially unconstitutional.

(continued)

Table 5.2   (continued)

18. *Reno v. American Civil Liberties Union* (521 U.S. 844, 1997). The court unanimously ruled that the anti-indecency provision of the 1996 Communication Decency Act violated the First Amendment.

19. *Watchtower Bible and Tract Society v. Village of Stratton* (536 U.S. 150, 2002). The court, in an 8–1 decision, struck down an ordinance making it a misdemeanor to canvass or solicit door-to-door without a permit, holding that the ordinance violated the First Amendment's protection of anonymous political speech, religious and political canvassing, and pamphleteering.

20. *United States v. American Library Association* (539 U.S. 194, 2003). The court ruled, 6–3, that the U.S. Congress has the authority to require public schools and libraries receiving E-Rate discounts to install web-filtering software as a condition of receiving federal funding and that the Children's Internet Protection Act is not unconstitutional.

21. *Virginia v. Hicks* (539 U.S. 113, 2003). The court unanimously ruled that a policy of the Richmond Redevelopment and Housing Authority barring nonresidents from a housing community unless they could demonstrate a legitimate business or social purpose for being on the premises was facially invalid under the First Amendment's overbreadth doctrine.

22. *Virginia v. Black* (538 U.S. 343, 2003). The court struck down, 6–3, a Virginia law against cross burning based on the fact that the Virginia statute making cross burning "prima facie" evidence of intent to intimidate, arguing that the law blurs the distinction between prosecution of "threats of intimidation" with the Klan's protected "message of shared ideology."

23. *Ashcroft v. American Civil Liberties Union* (535 U.S. 564, 2002). The case concerned the 1998 Child Online Protection Act (COPA) that severely restricted any speech on the internet that is "harmful to minors" and imposed steep fines and prison terms for violators. The court held, 8–1, that COPA should be enjoined because it likely violates the First Amendment and that there are less restrictive alternatives to COPA.

24. *Morse v. Frederick* (551 U.S. 393, 2007). In a 5–4 ruling, the court held that the First Amendment does not prevent educators from suppressing, at or across the street from a school-supervised event, student speech that is reasonably viewed as promoting illegal drug use.

25. *Citizens United v. Federal Election Commission* (558 U.S. 310, 2010). In a 5–4 ruling, the court held that the free speech clause of the First Amendment prohibits the government from restricting independent expenditures for political communications by corporations, including nonprofit corporations and labor unions, and other associations.

26. *Janus v. American Federation of State, County, and Municipal Employees* (585 U.S. ____, 2018). In a 5–4 decision, the court ruled to bar public sector unions from charging "agency fees" to the public employees for whom they negotiate pay increases and benefits if those employees decline to join the union as full members. The *Janus* decision overturned a 1977 decision, *Abood v. Detroit Board of Education* (431 U.S. 209, 1977).

DOCUMENTS

The Maryland Toleration Act (1649)

This document presents the Maryland Toleration Act of 1649. It was enacted to protect the Catholic minority in the Maryland Colony from the Protestant majority. Although it only lasted a short time, it is important in that it provided modest protection for the Catholic minority and set a precedent to which other religious minorities, other colonies, and ultimately the United States in its First Amendment freedoms could refer.

Forasmuch as in a well governed and Christian Common Wealth matters concerning Religion and the honor of God ought in the first place to bee taken, into serious consideration and endeavorured to bee settled, Be it therefore ordered and enacted by the Right Honourable Cecilius Lord Baron of Baltemore absolute Lord and Propietary of this Province with the advise and consent of this Generall Assembly:

That whatsoever person or persons within this Province and the Islands thereunto belonging shall from henceforth blaspheme God, that is Curse him, or deny our Saviour Jesus Christ to bee the sonne of God, or shall deny the holy Trinity the father sonne and holy Ghost, or the Godhead of any of the said Three persons of the Trinity, or the unity of the Godhead, or shall use or utter any reproachfull Speeches, words or language concerning the said Holy Trinity, or any of the said three persons thereof, shalbe punished with death and confiscation or forfeiture of all his or her lands and goods to the Lord Proprietary and his heires.

And bee it also Enacted by the Authority and with the advise and assent aforesaid, That whatsoever person or persons shall from henceforth use or utter any reproachfull words or Speeches concerning the blessed Virgin Mary the Mother of our Saviour of the holy Apostles or Evangelists or any of them shall in such case for the first offence forfeit to the said Lord Proprietary and his heirs Lords and Proprietaries of this

Province the summe of five pound Sterling or the value thereof to be Levyed on the goods and chattels of every such person soe offending, but in case such Offender or Offenders, shall not then have goods and chattels sufficient for satisfying of such forfeiture, or that the same bee not otherwise speedily satisfied that then such Offender or Offenders shalbe publiquely whipt and bee imprisoned during the pleasure of the Lord Propri-etary or the Lieutenant or cheife Governor of this Province for the time being. And that every such Offender or Offenders for every second offense shall forfeit tenne pound Sterling or the value thereof to bee levied as aforesaid, or in case such Offender or Offenders shall not then have goods and chattels within this Province sufficient for that purpose then to bee publiquely and severely whipt and imprisoned as before is expressed. And that every person or persons before mentioned offending herein a third time, shall for such third Offence forfeit all his lands and Goods and bee for ever banished and expelled out of this Province.

And be it also further Enacted by the same authority and advise and assent that whatsoever person or persons shall from henceforth upon any occasion of Offence or otherwise in a reproachful manner or Way declare call or denominate any person or persons whatsoever inhabiting, residing, traffiqueing, trading, or comerceing within This Province or within any the Ports, Harbors, Creeks, or Havens to the same belonging an heritick, Scismatick, Idolator, puritan, Independent, Prespite-rian popish prest, Jesuite, Jesuited papist, Lutheran, Calvenist, Anabaptist, Brownist, Antinomian, Barrowist, Roundhead, Separatist, or any other name or terme in a reproachful manner relating to matter of Religion shall for every such Offence for-feit and loose the somme of tenne shillings sterling or the value thereof to bee levied on the goods and chattels of every such Offender or Offenders, the one half thereof to be forfeited and paid unto the person and persons of whom such reproachful words are or shalbe spoken or uttered, and the other half thereof to the Lord Proprietary and his heires Lords and Proprietaries of this Province. But if such person or persons who shall at any time utter or speake any such reproachful words or Language shall not have Goods or Chattells sufficient and overt within this Province to bee taken to satisfie the penalty aforesaid or that the same bee not otherwise speedily satisfied, that then the person or persons soe offending shalbe publickly whipt, and shall suffer imprisonment without baile or maineprise [bail] until hee, shee or they respectively shall satisfy the party soe offended or grieved by such reproachful Language by asking him or her respectively forgivens publiquely for such his Offence before the Magistrate or cheife Officer or Officers of the Towne or place where such Offence shall be given.

And be it further likewise Enacted by the Authority and consent aforesaid That every person or persons within this Province that shall at any time hereafter prophane the Sabbath or Lords day called Sunday by frequent swearing, drunkenness or by any uncivill or disorderly recreacion, or by working on that day when absolute necessity doth not require it shall for every such first offence forfeit 2s 6d sterling or the value thereof, and for the second offence 5s sterling or the value thereof, and for the third offence and soe for every time he shall offend in like manner afterwards 10s sterling or the value thereof. And in case such offender and offenders shall not have sufficient goods or chattels within this Province to satisfy any of the said Penalties respectively hereby imposed for prophaning the Sabbath or Lords day called Sunday as aforesaid, That is Every such case the partie soe offending shall for the first and second offence in that kinde be imprisoned till hee or shee shall publickly in open Court before the cheife Commander Judge or Magistrate, of that County Towne or precinct where such offence shalbe committed acknowledge the Scandall and offence he hath in that respect given against God and the good and civill Government of this Province, And for the third offence and for every time after shall also bee publickly whipt.

And whereas the inforceing of the conscience in matters of Religion hath frequently fallen out to be dangerous

Consequence in those commonwealths where it hath been practiced, And for the more quiet and peaceable government of this Province, and the better to preserve mutuall Love and amity amongst the Inhabitants thereof, Be it Therefore also by the Lord Proprietary with the advise and consent of this Assembly Ordeyned and enacted (except as in this present Act is before Declared and sett forth) that noe person or persons whatsoever within this Province, or the Islands, Ports, Harbors, Creekes, or havens thereunto belonging professing to believe in Jesus Christ, shall from henceforth bee any waies troubled, Molested or discountenanced for or in respect of his or her religion nor in the free exercise thereof within this Province or the Islands thereunto belonging nor any way compelled to the beliefe or exercise of any other Religion against his or her consent, soe as they be not unfaithfull to the Lord Proprietary, or molest or conspire against the civill Governement established or to bee established in this Province under him or his heires. And that all and every person and persons that shall presume Contrary to this Act and the true intent and meaning thereof directly or indirectly either in person or estate willfully to wrong or disturbe trouble or molest any person whatsoever within this Province professing to believe in Jesus Christ for or in respect his or her religion or the free exercise thereof within this Provence other than is provided for in this Act that such person or persons soe offending, shalbe compelled to pay treble damages to the party soe wronged or molested, and for every such offence shall also forfeit 20s sterling in money or the value thereof, half thereof for the use of the Lord Proprietary, and his heires Lords and Proprietaries of this Province, and the other half for the use of the party soe wronged or molested as aforesaid, Or if the partie soe offending as aforesaid shall refuse or bee unable to recompense the party soe wronged, or to satisfy such fine or forfeiture, than such Offender shalbe severely punished by publick whipping and imprisonment during the pleasure of the Lord Proprietary, or his Lieutenant or cheife

Governor of this Province for the tyme being without baile or maineprise.

And bee it further alsoe Enacted by the authority and consent aforesaid That the Sheriff or other Officer or Officers from time to time to bee appointed and authorized for that purpose, of the County Towne or precinct where every particular offence in this present Act conteyned shall happen at any time to bee committed and whereupon there is hereby a forfeiture fine or penalty imposed shall from time to time distraine and seise the goods and estate of every such person soe offending and aforesaid against this present Act or any party thereof, and sell the same or any party thereof for the full satisfaction of such forfeiture, fine, or penalty as aforesaid, Restoring unto the partie soe offending the Remainder or overplus of the said goods or estate after such satisfaccion soe made as aforesaid. The freemen have assented.

Source: Available online at http://www.let.rug.nl/usa/docu ments/1600-1650/the-maryland-toleration-act-1649.php.

The Virginia Statute for Religious Freedom (1786)

Virginia was the first state to enact a law for religious freedom. It was drafted by Thomas Jefferson in 1777, introduced into the Virginia General Assembly in 1779, and enacted into the state's law in 1786. It served as a model for the First Amendment and for subsequent states when they disestablished their official state religions.

Well aware that the opinions and belief of men depend not on their own will, but follow involuntarily the evidence proposed to their minds, that Almighty God hath created the mind free, and manifested his supreme will that free it shall remain by making it altogether insusceptible of restraint; that all attempts to influence it by temporal punishments, or burthens, or by civil incapacitations, tend only to beget habits of hypocrisy and meanness, and are a departure from the plan of the holy author of our religion, who being lord both of body and mind, yet chose not to propagate it by coercions on either, as was in his Almighty power to do, but to extend it by its influence on reason alone; that the impious presumption of legislators and rulers, civil as well as ecclesiastical, who, being themselves but fallible and uninspired men, have assumed dominion over the faith of others, setting up their own opinions and modes of thinking as the only true and infallible, and as such endeavoring to impose them on others, hath established and maintained false religions over the greatest part of the world and through all time: That to compel a man to furnish contributions of money for the propagation of opinions which he disbelieves and abhors, is sinful and tyrannical; that even the forcing of him to support this or that teacher of his own religious persuasion, is depriving him of the comfortable liberty of giving his contributions to the particular pastor whose morals he would make his pattern, and whose powers he feels most persuasive to righteousness; and is withdrawing from the ministry those temporary rewards, which proceeding from an approbation of their personal conduct, are an addition incitement to earnest and unremitting labours for the instruction of mankind; that our civil rights have no dependence on our religious opinions, any more than our opinions in physics or geometry; that therefore the proscribing any citizen as unworthy the public confidence by laying upon him an incapacity of being called to offices of trust and emolument, unless he profess or renounce this or that religious opinion, is depriving him injuriously of those privileges and advantages to which, in common with his fellow citizens, he has a natural right; that it tends also to corrupt the principles of that very religion it is meant to encourage, by bribing, with a monopoly of worldly honours and emoluments, those who will externally profess and conform to it; that though indeed these are criminal who do not withstand such temptation yet neither are those innocent who lay the bait in their way; that the opinions of men are not the object of civil government, nor under its jurisdiction; that to suffer the civil magistrate to intrude his powers into the field of opinion and to restrain the profession or propagation of principles on supposition of their ill tendency is a dangerous fallacy, which at once destroys all religious liberty, because he is being of course judge of that tendency will make his opinions the rule of judgment, and approve or condemn the sentiments of others only as they shall square with or differ from his own; that it is time enough for the rightful purposes of civil government for its officers to interfere when principles break out into overt acts against peace and good order; and finally, that truth is great and will prevails if left to herself; that she is the proper and sufficient antagonist to error, and has nothing to fear from the conflict unless by human interposition disarmed of her natural weapons, free argument and debate; errors ceasing to be dangerous when it is permitted freely to contradict them.

We the General Assembly of Virginia do enact that no man shall be compelled to frequent or support any religious worship, place, or ministry whatsoever, nor shall be enforced, restrained, molested, or burthened in his body or goods, nor shall otherwise suffer, on account of his religious opinions or belief; but that all men shall be free to profess, and by argument to maintain, their opinions in matters of religion, and that the same shall in no wise diminish, enlarge, or affect their civil capacities.

And though we well know that this Assembly, elected by the people for the ordinary purposes of legislation only, have no power to restrain the acts of succeeding Assemblies, constituted with powers equal to our own, and that therefore to déclassé this act irrevocable would be of no effect in law; yet we are free to declare, and do declare, that the rights hereby asserted are of the natural rights of mankind, and that if any act shall be hereafter passed to repeal the present or to narrow its operation, such act will be an infringement of natural right.

Source: Julian P. Boyd, ed. *The Papers of Thomas Jefferson.* Vol. 2, *1777–18 June 1779.* Princeton, NJ: Princeton University Press, 1950, pp. 545–553.

Constitutional Provisions

Key provisions of the U.S. Constitution, in Article VI and in the First and Fourteenth Amendments, are cited here in their entirety.

Article VI (1787)

All Debt contracted and Engagements entered into, before the Adoption of this Constitution, shall be as valid against the United States under this Constitution, as under the Confederation.

This Constitution, and the Laws of the United States which shall be made in Pursuance thereof, and all Treaties made, or which shall be made, under the Authority of the United States, shall be the supreme Law of the Land, and the Judges in every State shall be bound thereby, any Thing in the Constitution or Laws of any State to the Contrary notwithstanding.

The Senators and Representatives before mentioned, and the Members of the several State Legislatures, and all executive and judicial Officers, both of the United States and of the several States, shall be bound by Oath or Affirmation, to support this Constitution, but no religious Test shall ever be required of a Qualification to any Office or public Trust under the United States.

First Amendment (1789)

Freedom of religion, speech, and the press, rights of assembly and petition.

Congress shall make no law respecting an establishment of religion, or prohibiting the free exercise thereof; or abridging the freedom of speech, or of the press, or the right of the people to peaceably to assemble, and to petition the Government for a redress of grievances.

Fourteenth Amendment (1868)

Section 1. All persons born or naturalized in the United States, and subject to the jurisdiction thereof, are citizens of the United States and of the State wherein they reside. No State shall make or enforce any law which shall abridge the privileges and immunities of citizens of the United States; nor shall any State deprive any person of life, liberty, or property, without due process of law; nor deny any person within its jurisdiction the equal protection of the laws.

. . .

Section 5. The Congress shall have the power to enforce, by appropriate legislation, the provisions of this article.

Source: U.S. National Archives. Available online at https://www.archives.gov/founding-docs/bill-of-rights.

Letter from James Madison to Edward Livingston (July 10, 1822)

James Madison, who along with Thomas Jefferson was the principal author of the Bill of Rights, wrote a letter in July 1822 to Edward Livingston about the latter's Report to the Legislature of the State (Louisiana) on the subject of a penal code. In his letter, excerpted here to its main points about freedom of religion, Madison expounds on his own thoughts on that lofty principle.

To Edward Livingston

Montpellier, July 10, 1822

Dear Sir,

I was favored some days ago with your letter of May 19, accompanied by a copy of your Report to the Legislature of the State on the subject of a Penal Code.

I should commit a tacit injustice if I did not say that the Report does great honor to the talents & sentiments of the Author. It abounds with ideas of conspicuous value, and presents them in a manner equally elegant & persuasive. . . .

I observe with particular pleasure the view you have taken of the immunity of Religion from Civil Jurisdiction, in every case where it does not trespass on private rights or the public peace. This has always been a favorite point to me: and it was not with my approbation, that the deviation from it took place in Congress when they appointed Chaplains to be paid from the national Treasury. It would have been a much better proof to their Constituents of their pious feelings, if the members had contributed for that purpose, a pittance from their own pockets. As the precedent is not likely to be rescinded, the best that can now be done may be, to apply to the Constitution, the maxim of the law, de minimis non curat.

There has been another deviation from the strict principle, in the Executive Proclamations of fasts and festivals; so far at least as they have spoken the language of *injunction*, or have lost sight of the equality of *all* Religious Sects in the eye of the Constitution. Whilst I was honored with the Executive Trust [the presidency], I found it necessary on more than one occasion to follow the example of predecessors. But I was always careful to make the Proclamations absolutely indiscriminate, and merely recommendatory; or rather mere *designations* of a day, on which all who thought proper might *unite* in consecrating it to religious purposes, according to their own faith & forms. In this sense, I presume, you reserve to the Government a right to *appoint* particular days for religious worship throughout the State; without any particular sanction *enforcing* the worship. I know not what may be the way of thinking on this subject in Louisiana. I should suppose the Catholic portion of the people, at least, as small and even unpopular Sect in the U.S., would rally, as they did in Virginia, when religious liberty was a Legislative topic, to its broadest principle.

Notwithstanding the general progress made within the last two Centuries in favor of this branch of liberty, and the full establishment of it, in some parts of our Country, there remains in others, a strong bias towards the old error, that without some sort of alliance or coalition between Government and Religion, neither can be duly supported. Such indeed is the tendency to such a Coalition, and such its corrupting influence on both the parties, that the danger can not be too carefully guarded against. And in a Government of opinion, like ours, the only effectual guard must be found in the soundness & stability of the general opinion on the subject. Every new & successful example therefore of a perfect separation between ecclesiastical & Civil matters is of importance. And I have no doubt that every new example will succeed, as every past one has done, in shewing that Religion & Govt. will both exist in greater purity, the less they are mixed together. It was the belief of all Sects at one time that the establishment of Religion by law was right & necessary; that the true Religion ought to be established to the exclusion of all others; and that the only question to be decided was, which was the true Religion. The example of Holland proved that a toleration of Sects dissenting from the established Sect, was safe and even useful. The example of the Colonies now States, which rejected Religious establishment altogether, proved that all Sects might be safely & advantageously put on a footing of equal & entire freedom. And a continuance of their example since the Declaration of Independence has shewn, that its success in Colonies was not to be ascribed to their connection with the parent Country. If a further confirmation of the truth could be wanted, it is to be found in the examples furnished by the States, which have abolished their religious Establishments. I can not speak particularly of any of the cases excepting that of Virginia, where it is impossible to deny that Religion prevails with more zeal, and a more exemplary priesthood, than it ever did when established and patronized by Public authority. We are teaching the World the great truth, that Governments do better without Kings and Nobles than with them. The merit will be doubled by other lesson, that Religion flourishes in greater purity, without than with the aid of Government.

My pen, I perceive, has rambled into reflections for which it was not taken up. I recall it to the proper object of thanking

you for your very interesting pamphlet, and of tendering you my respects & good wishes.
James Madison

Source: David B. Mattern, J. C. A. Stagg, Mary Parke Johnson, and Anne Mandeville Colony, eds. *The Papers of James Madison*. Retirement Series. Vol. 2, *1 February 1820–26 February 1823*. Charlottesville: University of Virginia Press, 2013, pp. 542–545.

Missouri Governor Lilburn W. Boggs's Order of Extermination, Missouri Executive Order Number 44 (1838)

A black stain on religious tolerance in the United States was the Missouri Executive Order Number 44 of Governor Lilburn W. Boggs, commonly known as the Order of Extermination, in which, pursuant to the order, hundreds of Mormon civilians were, as applicable, attacked, lynched, looted, tarred, raped, and murdered. The order is presented here verbatim and in its entirety.

Headquarters of the Militia
City of Jefferson, Oct. 27, 1838
General John B. Clark:
Sir, Since the order of this morning to you, directing you to cause four hundred mounted men to be raised within your division, I have received by Amos Reese, Esq., of Ray county, and Wiley C. Williams, Esq., one of my aids, information of the most appalling character, which entirely changes the face of things, and places the Mormons in the attitude of an open and avowed defiance of the laws, and of having made war upon the people of this state. Your orders are, therefore, to hasten your operation with all possible speed. The Mormons must be treated as enemies, and must be exterminated or driven from the state if necessary for the public peace—their outrages are beyond all description. If you can increase your force, you are authorized to do so to any extent you may consider necessary.

I have just issued orders to Maj. Gen. Willock, of Marion County, to raise five hundred men, and to march them to the northern part of Daviess, and there unite with Gen. Doniphan, of Clay, who has been ordered with five hundred men to proceed to the same point for the purpose of intercepting the retreat of the Mormons to the north. They have been directed to communicate with you by express, you can also communicate with them if you find it necessary. Instead therefore of proceeding as at first directed to reinstate the citizens of Daviess in their homes, you will proceed immediately to Richmond and then operate against the Mormons. Brig. Gen. Parks of Ray, has been ordered to have four hundred of his brigage in readiness to join you at Richmond. The whole force will be placed under your command.

I am very respectfully,

Your ob't serv't, L. W. Boggs, Commander-in-Chief

Source: "Missouri State Archives: The Missouri Mormon War." n.d. Missouri Digital Heritage. Available online at https://www .sos.mo.gov/archives/resources/mormon.asp.

The Espionage Act (June 15, 1917)

The Espionage Act of 1917 passed a few months after the United States entered World War I. The law made it a crime for any person to convey information intended to interfere with the efforts of the U.S. Armed Forces to pursue the war or to promote the success of enemy countries. It made anyone guilty of such acts subject to a fine of $10,000 and a prison term of twenty years. It was aimed at socialists (such as Eugene Debs), pacifists, and other anti-war activists during World War I. Attorney General A. Mitchell Palmer and FBI director J. Edgar Hoover used the act to persecute left-wing political figures.

Section 1

That: (a) whoever, for the purpose of obtaining information respecting the national defence with intent or reason to believe that the information to be obtained is to be used to the injury of the United States, or to the advantage of any foreign nation, goes upon, enters, flies over, or otherwise obtains information, concerning any vessel, aircraft, work of defence, navy yard, naval station, submarine base, coaling station, fort, battery, torpedo station, dockyard, canal, railroad, arsenal, camp, factory, mine, telegraph, telephone, wireless, or signal station, building, office, or other place connected with the national defence, owned or constructed, or in progress of construction by the United States or under the control or the United States, or of any of its officers or agents, or within the exclusive jurisdiction of the United States, or any place in which any vessel, aircraft, arms, munitions, or other materials or instruments for use in time of war are being made, prepared, repaired. or stored, under any contract or agreement with the United States, or with any person on behalf of the United States, or otherwise on behalf of the United States, or any prohibited place within the meaning of section six of this title; or

(b) whoever for the purpose aforesaid, and with like intent or reason to believe, copies, takes, makes, or obtains, or attempts, or induces or aids another to copy, take, make, or obtain, any sketch, photograph, photographic negative, blue print, plan, map, model, instrument, appliance, document, writing or note of anything connected with the national defence; or

(c) whoever, for the purpose aforesaid, receives or obtains or agrees or attempts or induces or aids another to receive or obtain from any other person, or from any source whatever, any document, writing, code book, signal book, sketch, photograph, photographic negative, blue print, plan, map, model, instrument, appliance, or note, of anything connected with the national defence, knowing or having reason to believe, at the time he receives or obtains, or agrees or attempts or induces or aids another to receive or obtain it, that it has been or will be obtained, taken, made or disposed of by any person contrary to the provisions of this title; or

(d) whoever, lawfully or unlawfully having possession of, access to, control over, or being entrusted with any document, writing, code book, signal book, sketch, photograph, photographic negative, blue print, plan, map, model, instrument, appliance, or note relating to the national defence, wilfully communicates or transmits or attempts to communicate or transmit the same and fails to deliver it on demand to the officer or employee of the United States entitled to receive it; or

(e) whoever, being entrusted with or having lawful possession or control of any document, writing, code book, signal book, sketch, photograph, photographic negative, blue print, plan, map, model, note, or information, relating to the national defence, through gross negligence permits the same to be removed from its proper place of custody or delivered to anyone in violation of his trust, or to be list, stolen, abstracted, or destroyed, shall be punished by a fine of not more than $10,000, or by imprisonment for not more than two years, or both.

Section 2

Whoever, with intent or reason to believe that it is to be used to the injury or the United States or to the advantage of a foreign nation, communicated, delivers, or transmits, or attempts to, or aids, or induces another to, communicate, deliver or transmit, to any foreign government, or to any faction or party or military or naval force within a foreign country, whether recognized or unrecognized by the United States, or to any representative, officer, agent, employee, subject, or citizen thereof, either directly or indirectly and document, writing, code book, signal book, sketch, photograph, photographic negative, blue print, plan, map, model, note, instrument, appliance, or information relating to the national defence, shall be punished by imprisonment for not more than twenty years: Provided, That whoever shall violate the provisions of subsection:

(a) of this section in time of war shall be punished by death or by imprisonment for not more than thirty years; and
(b) whoever, in time of war, with intent that the same shall be communicated to the enemy, shall collect, record, publish or communicate, or attempt to elicit any information with respect to the movement, numbers, description, condition, or disposition of any of the armed forces, ships, aircraft, or war materials of the United States, or with respect to the plans or conduct, or supposed plans or conduct of any naval of military operations, or with respect to any works or measures undertaken for or connected with, or intended for the fortification of any place, or any other information relating to the public defence, which might be useful to the enemy, shall be punished by death or by imprisonment for not more than thirty years.

Section 3

Whoever, when the United States is at war, shall wilfully make or convey false reports or false statements with intent to interfere with the operation or success of the military or naval forces of the United States or to promote the success of its enemies and whoever when the United States is at war, shall wilfully cause or attempt to cause insubordination, disloyalty, mutiny, refusal of duty, in the military or naval forces of the United States, or shall wilfully obstruct the recruiting or enlistment service of the United States, to the injury of the service or of the United States, shall be punished by a fine of not more than $10,000 or imprisonment for not more than twenty years, or both.

Section 4

If two or more persons conspire to violate the provisions of section two or three of this title, and one or more of such persons does any act to effect the object of the conspiracy, each of the parties to such conspiracy shall be punished as in said sections provided in the case of the doing of the act the accomplishment of which is the object of such conspiracy. Except as above provided conspiracies to commit offences under this title shall be punished as provided by section thirty-seven of the Act to codify, revise, and amend the penal laws of the United States approved March fourth, nineteen hundred and nine.

Section 5

Whoever harbours or conceals any person who he knows, or has reasonable grounds to believe or suspect, has committed, or is about to commit, an offence under this title shall be punished by a fine of not more than $10,000 or by imprisonment for not more than two years, or both.

Section 6

The President in time of war or in case of national emergency may by proclamation designate any place other than those set forth in subsection: (a) of section one hereof in which anything for the use of the Army or Navy is being prepared or constructed or stored as a prohibited place for the purpose of this title: Provided, That he shall determine that information with respect thereto would be prejudicial to the national defence.

Section 7

Nothing contained in this title shall be deemed to limit the jurisdiction of the general courts-martial, military commissions, or naval courts-martial under sections thirteen hundred and forty-two, thirteen hundred and forty-three, and sixteen hundred and twenty-four of the Revised Statutes as amended.

Section 8

The provisions of this title shall extend to all Territories, possessions, and places subject to the jurisdiction of the United States whether or not contiguous thereto, and offences under this title, when committed upon the high seas or elsewhere within the admiralty and maritime jurisdiction of the United States and outside the territorial limits thereof shall be punishable hereunder.

Section 9
The Act entitled "An Act to prevent the disclosure of national defence secrets," approved March third, nineteen hundred and eleven, is hereby repealed.

Source: Pub.L. 65-24, 40 Stat. 217.

Lemon v. Kurtzman (1971)

In 1971, the U.S. Supreme Court decided the landmark case of Lemon v. Kurtzman, *overturning as unconstitutional the establishment of a Pennsylvania state law supporting the nonpublic (that is, parochial) religious-based studies passed through the Nonpublic Elementary and Secondary Education Act of 1968. This case set the precedent of the Lemon test, a three-part test the Supreme Court stipulated for states and for guidance to lower courts to use when assessing a law being challenged on the grounds of the Establishment Clause of the First Amendment.*

Syllabus

Rhode Island's 1969 Salary Supplement Act provides for a 15% salary supplement to be paid to teachers in nonpublic schools at which the average per-pupil expenditure on secular education is below the average in public schools. Eligible teachers must teach only courses offered in the public schools, using only materials used in the public schools, and must agree not to teach courses in religion. A three-judge court found that about 25% of the State's elementary students attended nonpublic schools, about 95% of whom attended Roman Catholic affiliated schools, and that to date about 250 teachers at Roman Catholic schools are the sole beneficiaries under the Act. The court found that the parochial school system was "an integral part of the religious mission of the Catholic Church," and held that the Act fostered "excessive entanglement" between government and religion, thus violating the Establishment Clause. Pennsylvania's Nonpublic Elementary and Secondary Education Act, passed in 1968, authorizes the state Superintendent of Public Instruction to "purchase" certain "secular educational services" from nonpublic schools, directly reimbursing those schools solely for teachers' salaries, textbooks, and instructional materials. Reimbursement is restricted to courses in specific secular subjects, the textbooks and materials must be approved by the Superintendent, and no payment is to be made for any course containing "any subject matter expressing religious teaching, or the morals or forms of worship of any sect." Contracts were made with schools that have more than 20% of all the students in the State, most of which were affiliated with the Roman Catholic Church. The complaint challenging the constitutionality of the Act alleged that the church-affiliated schools are controlled by religious organizations, have the purpose of propagating and promoting a particular religious faith, and conduct their operations to fulfill that purpose. A three-judge court granted the State's motion to dismiss the complaint for failure to state a claim for relief, finding no violation of the Establishment or Free Exercise Clause.

Held:

Both statutes are unconstitutional under the Religion Clauses of the First Amendment, as the cumulative impact of the entire relationship arising under the statutes involves excessive entanglement between government and religion.

MR. CHIEF JUSTICE BURGER delivered the opinion of the Court.

These two appeals raise questions as to Pennsylvania and Rhode Island statutes providing state aid to church-related elementary and secondary schools. Both statutes are challenged as violative of the Establishment and Free Exercise Clauses of the First Amendment and the Due Process Clause of the Fourteenth Amendment.

Pennsylvania has adopted a statutory program that provides financial support to nonpublic elementary and secondary schools by way of reimbursement for the cost of teachers' salaries, textbooks, and instructional materials in specified secular subjects. Rhode Island has adopted a statute under which the State pays directly to teachers in nonpublic elementary schools a supplement of 15% of their annual salary. Under each statute, state aid has been given to church-related educational institutions. We hold that both statutes are unconstitutional.

. . .

In the absence of precisely stated constitutional prohibitions, we must draw lines with reference to the three main evils against which the Establishment Clause was intended to afford protection: "sponsorship, financial support, and active involvement of the sovereign in religious activity."

Every analysis in this area must begin with consideration of the cumulative criteria developed by the Court over many years. Three such tests may be gleaned from our cases. First, the statute must have a secular legislative purpose; second, its principal or primary effect must be one that neither advances nor inhibits religion; finally, the statute must not foster "an excessive government entanglement with religion."

Inquiry into the legislative purposes of the Pennsylvania and Rhode Island statutes affords no basis for a conclusion that the legislative intent was to advance religion. On the contrary, the statutes themselves clearly state that they are intended to enhance the quality of the secular education in all schools covered by the compulsory attendance laws. There is no reason to believe the legislatures meant anything else. A State always has a legitimate concern for maintaining minimum standards in all schools it allows to operate. As in *Allen,* we find nothing here that undermines the stated legislative intent; it must therefore be accorded appropriate deference.

In *Allen*, the Court acknowledged that secular and religious teachings were not necessarily so intertwined that secular textbooks furnished to students by the State were, in fact, instrumental in the teaching of religion. The legislatures of Rhode Island and Pennsylvania have concluded that secular and religious education are identifiable and separable. In the abstract, we have no quarrel with this conclusion.

The two legislatures, however, have also recognized that church-related elementary and secondary schools have a significant religious mission, and that a substantial portion of their activities is religiously oriented. They have therefore sought to create statutory restrictions designed to guarantee the separation between secular and religious educational functions, and to ensure that State financial aid supports only the former. All these provisions are precautions taken in candid recognition that these programs approached, even if they did not intrude upon, the forbidden areas under the Religion Clauses. We need not decide whether these legislative precautions restrict the principal or primary effect of the programs to the point where they do not offend the Religion Clauses, for we conclude that the cumulative impact of the entire relationship arising under the statutes in each State involves excessive entanglement between government and religion.

Source: *Lemon v. Kurtzman*, 403 U.S. 602 (1971).

The American Indian Religious Freedom Act (August 11, 1978)

In 1978, Congress enacted the American Indian Religious Freedom Act to preserve and protect the right of Native Americans to believe and express their native religious traditions. The two key sections of that law are provided here in their entirety.

Section 1

On and after August 11, 1978, it shall be the policy of the United States to protect and preserve for American Indians, their inherent right of freedom to believe, express, and exercise the traditional religions of the American Indian, Eskimo, Aleut, and Native Hawaiians, including but not limited to access to sites, use and possession of sacred objects, and the freedom to worship through ceremonials and traditional rites.

Section 2

The President shall direct the various Federal departments, agencies, and other instrumentalities responsible for administering the relevant laws to evaluate their policies and procedures in consultation with native traditional religious leaders in order to determine appropriate changes necessary to protect and preserve Native American religious cultural rights and practices. Twelve months after August 11, 1978, the President shall report back to the Congress the results of his evaluation, including any changes which were made in administrative policies and procedures, and any recommendations he may have for legislative action.

[Note: One of the changes in administrative policy and procedure was Executive Order 13007, Indian Sacred Sites.]

Source: Federal Historic Preservation Laws, Act of August 11, 1978, 95-341, 42 U.S.C., 1996 and 1996a.

Denial of Equal Access Prohibited (1984)

In 1984, Congress added to the U.S. Code provisions prohibiting the denial of equal access to open public forums and spaces in public schools.

(a) Restriction of Limited Open Forum on Basis of Religious, Political, Philosophical, or Other Speech Content Prohibited.

It shall be unlawful for any public secondary school which receives Federal financial assistance and which has a limited open forum to deny equal access or for opportunity to, or discriminate against, any students who wish to conduct a meeting within that open forum on the basis of the religious, political, philosophical or other content of speech at such meeting.

(b) "Limited Open Forum" Defined

A public secondary school has a limited open forum whenever such school grants an offering to or opportunity for one or more noncurriculum related student groups to meet on school premises during noninstructional time.

(c) Fair Opportunity Criteria

Schools shall be determined to offer a fair opportunity to students who wish to conduct a meeting within its limited open forum if such school uniformly provides that (1) the meeting is voluntary and student-initiated; (2) there is no sponsorship of the meeting by the school, the government, or its agents or employees; (3) employees or agents of the school or government are present at religious meetings only in a non-participatory capacity; (4) the meeting does not materially and substantially interfere with the orderly conduct of educational activities within the school; and (5) nonschool persons may not direct, conduct, control, or regularly attend activities of student groups.

(d) Construction of Subchapter with Respect to Certain Rights

Nothing in this subchapter shall be construed to authorize the United States or any State or political subdivision thereof—(1) to influence the form or content of any prayers or other religious activity; (2) to require any person to participate in prayer or other religious activity; (3) to expend public funds beyond the incidental costs of providing the space for such student-initiated meetings; (4) to compel any school or agent employee to attend a school meeting if the content of the speech at the meeting is contrary to the beliefs of the agent or employees; (5) to sanction meetings that are otherwise unlawful; (6) to limit the rights of groups of students which are not of a specified numerical size; or (7) to abridge the constitutional rights of any person.

(e) Federal Financial Assistance to Schools Unaffected

Notwithstanding the availability of any other remedy under the Constitution or the laws of the United States, nothing in this subchapter shall be construed to authorize the United States to deny or withhold Federal financial assistance to any school.

(f) Authority of Schools With Respect to Order, Discipline, Well-being, and Attendance Concerns

Nothing in this subchapter shall be construed to limit the authority of the school, its agents or employees, to maintain order and discipline on school premises, to protect the well-being of students and faculty, and to assure that attendance of students at meetings is voluntary.

Source: *Denial of Equal Access Prohibited.* 20 U.S. Code §4071. Available online at https://www.law.cornell.edu/uscode/text /20/4071.

Edwards v. Aguillard (1987)

In 1987, the U.S. Supreme Court handed down its 7–2 decision in Edwards v. Aguillard *(482 U.S. 578), which decided a case that challenged a Louisiana "Creationism Act" on the basis of violating the Establishment Clause of the First Amendment. In this ruling, the majority opinion was written by Justice Brennan, and two dissents were written by Justices Scalia and Rehnquist.*

Syllabus

Louisiana's "Creationism Act" forbids the teaching of the theory of evolution in public elementary and secondary schools unless accompanied by instruction in the theory of "creation science." The Act does not require the teaching of either theory unless the other is taught. It defines the theories as "the scientific evidences for [creation or evolution] and inferences drawn from those scientific evidences." Appellees, who include Louisiana parents, teachers, and religious leaders, challenged the Act's constitutionality in Federal District Court, seeking an injunction and declaratory relief. The District Court granted summary judgment to appellees, holding that the Act violated the Establishment Clause of the First Amendment. The Court of Appeals affirmed.

Held:

1. The Act is facially invalid as violative of the Establishment Clause of the First Amendment because it lacks a clear secular purpose.

    (a) The Act does not further its stated secular purpose of "protecting academic freedom." It does not enhance the freedom of teachers to teach what they choose, and fails to further the goal of "teaching all the evidence." Forbidding the teaching of evolution when creation science is not also taught undermines the provision of a comprehensive scientific education. Moreover, requiring the teaching of creation science with evolution does not give schoolteachers a flexibility that they did not already possess to supplant the present science curriculum with the presentation of theories, besides evolution, about the origin of life. Furthermore, the contention that the Act furthers a "basic concept of fairness" by requiring the teaching of all of the evidence on the subject is without merit. Indeed, the Act evinces a discriminatory preference for the teaching of creation science and against the teaching of evolution by requiring that curriculum guides be developed and resource services supplied for teaching creationism, but not for teaching evolution, by limiting membership of the resource services panel to "creation scientists," and by forbidding school boards to discriminate against anyone who "chooses to be a creation scientist" or to teach creation science, while failing to protect those who choose to teach other theories or who refuse to teach creation science. A law intended to maximize the comprehensiveness and effectiveness of science instruction would encourage the teaching of all scientific theories about human origins. Instead, this Act has the distinctly different purpose of discrediting evolution by counterbalancing its teaching at every turn with the teaching of creationism.

(b) The Act impermissibly endorses religion by advancing the religious belief that a supernatural being created humankind. The legislative history demonstrates that the term "creation science," as contemplated by the state legislature, embraces this religious teaching. The Act's primary purpose was to change the public school science curriculum to provide persuasive advantage to a particular religious doctrine that rejects the factual basis of evolution in its entirety. Thus, the Act is designed either to promote the theory of creation science that embodies a particular religious tenet or to prohibit the teaching of a scientific theory disfavored by certain religious sects. In either case, the Act violates the First Amendment.

2. The District Court did not err in granting summary judgment upon a finding that the appellants had failed to raise a genuine issue of material fact. Appellants relied on the "uncontroverted" affidavits of scientists, theologians, and an education administrator defining creation science as "origin through abrupt appearance in complex form" and alleging that such a viewpoint constitutes a true scientific theory. The District Court, in its discretion, properly concluded that the postenactment testimony of these experts concerning the possible technical meanings of the Act's terms would not illuminate the contemporaneous purpose of the state legislature when it passed the Act. None of the persons making the affidavits produced by the appellants participated in or contributed to the enactment of the law.

Source: *Edwards v. Aguillard*, 482 U.S. 578 (1987).

Arizona Christian School Tuition Organization v. Winn et al. (2011)

In this case, the plaintiffs challenged a program of the State of Arizona on the grounds that it violated the Establishment Clause by providing tax credits to those who donate to private school tuition (including that of religious schools). In a 5–4 decision, the U.S. Supreme Court reversed a ruling by the court of appeals on the grounds that the plaintiffs lacked standing to bring the suit, arguing on the difference to bring a suit on the basis of a tax credit as opposed to a tax expenditure. The issue of whether taxpayers have any say in government spending would go unresolved.

Syllabus

Respondents, Arizona taxpayers, sued petitioner, Director of the State Department of Revenue, challenging Arizona Revised Statute Ann. 43-1089, on Establishment grounds. The Arizona law gives tax credits for contributions to school tuition organizations, or STOs, which then use the contributions to provide scholarships to students attending private schools, including religious schools. Petitioner, Arizona Christian School Tuition Organization and others, later intervened. The District Court dismissed the suit for failure to stake a claim (having standing to sue). Reversing, the Ninth Circuit Court held that the respondents had standing as taxpayers under *Flast v. Cohen* (392 U.S. 83) and had stated an Establishment Clause claim.

Held:

Because respondents challenge a tax credit as opposed to a government expenditure, they lack Article III standing under *Flast v. Cohen*. . . .

(a) Article III vests the Federal judiciary the "Power" to resolve "Cases" and "Controversies." . . . To obtain a ruling on the merits in federal court, a plaintiff must assert more than just the "generalized interest of all citizens in constitutional governance." . . . Instead, the plaintiff must establish standing, which requires "an injury in fact," "a casual connection between the injury and the conduct complained of," and a conclusion that it is "likely," as opposed to merely "speculative," that the injury will be "redressed by a favorable decision." . . .

(b) In general, the mere fact that someone is a taxpayer doesn't provide standing to seek relief in a federal court. . . .

(c) Respondents' suit does not fall within the narrow exception to the rule against taxpayer standing established in *Flast v. Cohen*. . . . To have standing under *Flast*, taxpayers must show (1) a "logical link" between the plaintiff's taxpayer status" and "the type of legislative enactment attacked," and (2) "a nexus" between such taxpayer status and "the precise nature of the constitutional infringement alleged." . . .

(d) Respondents' contrary position—that Arizonans benefiting from the tax credit in effect are paying their state income tax to STOs—assumes that all income is government property, even if it has not come into the tax collector's hands. That premise has no basis in standing jurisprudence. . . .

562 F.3d 1002, reversed.

Justice Anthony Kennedy delivered the opinion of the Court, in which Justices Roberts, Scalia, Thomas and Alito joined. Justice Elena Kagan filed a dissenting opinion, in which Justices Ginsburg, Breyer, and Sotomayor joined.

Source: *Arizona Christian School Tuition Organization v. Winn et al.*, 563 U.S. 125 (2011).

CONGRESS SHALL MAKE NO LAW *respecting an establishment of religion, or prohibiting the free exercise thereof; or abridging the freedom of speech, or of the press; or the right of the people peaceably to assemble, and to petition the Government for a redress of grievances.*

THE FIRST AMENDMENT TO THE U.S. CONSTITUTION
15 DECEMBER 1791

6 Resources

Introduction

This chapter lists and briefly annotates some major sources of information that the reader is encouraged to consult for further research and study on the topic. It begins with print resources, first discussing scholarly books that are cited and annotated. It cites and annotates government documents such as presidential executive orders and federal court rulings. Next, major scholarly journals that have published original research articles and book reviews on the subject are covered and described. Finally, the chapter discusses nonprint resources: feature-length films and videos available for viewing. These nonprint resources often dramatically depict the issues and people involved in the politics involving First Amendment freedoms politics, putting real faces to the numbers and statistics.

Print Resources

Books

Abanes, Richard. 2002. *One Nation under God: A History of the Mormon Church*. New York: Four Walls Eight Windows.

> Abanes discusses the political agenda at the core of Mormonism (LDS), its gradual transformation from a persecuted movement of radical zealots practicing polygamy and advocating a theocracy under a Mormon kingdom

A granite monument engraved with the First Amendment to the United States Constitution in front of Independence Hall in Philadelphia, Pennsylvania. (Berniephillips/Dreamstime.com) into a mainline Protestant denomination. In doing so, it reevaluates the LDS position on issues involving church and state relations.

Abraham, Henry J. 2008. *Justices, Presidents, and Senators: A History of the U.S. Supreme Court Appointments from Washington to Bush II.* 5th ed. Lanham, MD: Rowman & Littlefield.

This updated edition of Abraham's classic and comprehensive history of the court covers 110 justices and addresses why individual judges were nominated, how their nominations fared in the Senate, and whether they lived up to the expectations held for them and the legacy of their jurisprudence. It covers many judges and decisions that have impacted our understanding of the constitutional principles of the First Amendment. It provides insights into the history of the court, for example, how a fifth of the justices were seen as failures by the presidents who appointed them.

Abraham, Henry J., and Barbara A. Perry. 2013. *Freedom and the Court: Civil Rights and Liberties in the United States.* 9th ed. Lawrence: University Press of Kansas.

The authors portray the intriguing human stories behind landmark constitutional law cases, with a focus on fundamental issues of individual rights related to freedom of religion, separation of church and state, freedom of expression, due process, and political, racial, and gender equality.

Abrams, Paula. 2009. *Cross Purposes:* Pierce v. Society of Sisters *and the Struggle Over Compulsory Education.* Ann Arbor: University of Michigan Press.

Constitutional law professor Abrams has written this definitive study of the *Pierce v. Society of Sisters* landmark Supreme Court case. The book is a solidly researched and clearly written discussion that blends law, politics, and history, and it offers a captivating look at the clash between nationalism and religious pluralism.

Alley, Robert S. 1999. *The Constitution and Religion: Leading Supreme Court Cases on Church and State*. Amherst, NY: Prometheus Books.

This volume is a solid collection of original scholarly essays on the major Supreme Court cases dealing with church-state relations. It covers such issues as prayer in state legislatures, the Pledge of Allegiance, displays of the Ten Commandments in public buildings and public spaces, school prayer issues, vouchers for religious-based schools, religion in science classes, and the like. It is an objective presentation of the court's decisions.

Amar, Akhil Reed. 1998. *The Bill of Rights*. New Haven, CT: Yale University Press.

This award-winning history by Amar, a Yale Law scholar and a leading constitutional law scholar, provides deep insight into the impact, flexibility, and timeliness of the Bill of Rights that guarantees personal rights and shields society against authoritarianism. Amar emphasizes the counter-majoritarianism of the Bill of Rights and its impact over time, especially on state and local governments, as the courts have incorporated the Bill of Rights via the Fourteenth Amendment.

Belknap, Michael. 1994. *American Political Trials*. Westport, CT: Praeger.

This book examines the role of political trials and impeachments in U.S. history, from the early colonial era to the twentieth century. Its thirteen chapters each focus on a trial that is representative of a political era and the cases that resulted from political persecution. The book shows how defendants used the judicial process to advance their political objectives.

Belmas, Genelle, and Wayne Overbeck. 2019. *Major Principles of Media Law*. Boston: Wadsworth.

The authors provide a comprehensive summary of the current additions to, changes in, and development of media law and how they affect the constitutional understanding of freedom of the press in its complex permutations. The book reflects the authors' experiences in the courtroom and the classroom. It explores key issues in depth. Definitions of glossary terms help the reader understand the complex freedom of the press topics covered by the text.

Blanchard, Margaret A. 1992. *Revolutionary Sparks: Freedom of Expression in Modern America*. New York: Oxford University Press.

Blanchard's book presents an extensive discussion of freedom of expression in the United States, covering the period from the Civil War and Reconstruction up to that of the Reagan and Bush administrations. It is a comprehensive history of freedom of speech, covering topics such as national security, public morality, loyalty in times of war and social upheaval, and the right to preach on public street corners. She examines controversies over the press, the national government, the Supreme Court, and civil rights and liberties and presents a strong case for the right of Americans to speak their minds and to have access to the knowledge necessary for informed self-government.

Bonomi, Patricia U. 1986. *Under the Cope of Heaven: Religion, Society, and Politics in Colonial America*. New York: Oxford University Press.

Bonomi's book examines the role that religion played in American politics in shaping early American life and values. She focuses on the Middle and Southern Colonies as well as Puritan New England. She examines colonial clergy and churchgoers of diverse religious backgrounds and explores the relationship between religion and politics and the vital role religion played in the American Revolution and how that in turn shaped the complexities of religious freedom in American jurisprudence.

Butler, Jon. 2005. *Religion in Colonial America*. New York: Oxford University.

Butler narrates the state of religious affairs in both the Old and the New Worlds during the era of colonial times, from the failure of John Winthrop's attempt to establish "Puritan perfection," to the controversy over Anne Hutchinson, to the evangelism of the former slave and Methodist preacher Absalom Jones, to the spiritual resilience of the Catawba Indians. He explains how the meeting of these diverse groups produced an evolution of religious practice, including the birth of "revivals" and how they created a foundation for the First Amendment.

Byrd, James. 2013. *Sacred Scriptures, Sacred War: The Bible and the American Revolution*. New York: Oxford University Press.

Byrd presents a comprehensive analysis of how American revolutionaries defended their convictions through scripture; how many colonists saw the Bible as a book about war; and how God participated in combat, playing a decisive role on the battlefield. He details how, when war came, preachers and patriots alike turned to scripture for exhortations to fight. He shows how soldiers who died were given the halo of martyrdom and how a sense of divine providence was conferred on the revolutionary cause. The book describes how the Bible shaped the war and how the war shaped Americans' view of the Bible.

Chernow, Ron. 2004. *Alexander Hamilton*. New York: Penguin Press.

Chernow presents a landmark biography of Alexander Hamilton and how the Founding Father galvanized, inspired, scandalized, and helped to shape the United

States. His book is a full-length biography of Hamilton, the brilliant, charismatic, and dangerous founder. She recounts his turbulent life, from Washington's aide-de-camp, to his coauthoring of the *Federalist Papers*, to his role in founding the Bank of New York, to leading the Federalist Party, to serving as the first secretary of the treasury. It covers his impact on freedom of the press in regard to seditious libel and to his role in the Federalist Party's enactment of the Alien and Sedition Acts. She covers his friendships and titanic feuds with Thomas Jefferson, James Madison, John Adams, James Monroe, and Aaron Burr, including his duel to death with Aaron Burr in 1804.

Dreisbach, Daniel. 2002. *Thomas Jefferson and the Wall of Separation of Church and State*. New York: New York University Press.

Jefferson has had the most profound influence on church-state law, policy, and discourse. His concept of a "wall of separation between church and state" is broadly accepted as a concise description of the U.S. Constitution's church-state arrangements. Dreisbach offers an in-depth examination of the origins, controversial uses, and competing interpretations of the concept in American public policy.

Epp, Charles. 1998. *The Rights Revolution: Lawyers, Activists, and Supreme Courts in Comparative Perspective*. Chicago: University of Chicago Press.

Epp's book is the first comprehensive and comparative analysis of the growth of civil rights. He examines the high courts of the United States, Britain, Canada, and India within their constitutional and cultural contexts, thereby expanding our understanding of the relationship between courts and social change. Epp argues that civil rights and liberties rest on the democratization of access to the courts, the influence of advocacy groups, the growth of the financial and legal resources of ordinary citizens, and the planning of grassroots organizations. He shows that the shift in the rights of individuals is best understood as a bottom-up rather than top-down phenomenon.

Feldman, Noah. 2005. *Divided by God*. New York: Farrar, Straus and Giroux.

Feldman offers an appraisal of the profound conflict between religiously devout value voters and secularists over church-state matters. He shows how that conflict is as old as the country and how that complex history of the nation's past struggle with church-state relations shows how it might be resolved in today's religiously diverse society of Muslims, Hindu, Buddhists, Catholics, Protestants, and Jews. Feldman covers how people resolved conflicts over the Bible, the Pledge of Allegiance, the teaching of evolution, and similar issues through the shared values of liberty, equality, and freedom of conscience. He tells the story of a long-running conflict that has shaped the country and proposes a solution to the current iteration of that conflict while respecting the founders' view that religion and state should not mix.

Fitzgerald, Frances. 2017. *The Evangelicals: The Struggle to Shape America*. New York: Simon and Schuster.

Pulitzer Prize–winning author Fitzgerald presents a sweeping history of evangelicalism and the conflict between modernists and traditionalists. Her book includes vivid portraits of Billy Graham, Jerry Falwell, Pat Robertson, Jim Bakker, James Dobson, Rick Warren, R. J. Rushdoony, and Francis Schaeffer. In this outsider's book, she argues that evangelicals lost their way when they became a white-male reactionary force about saving the country by electing Republican politicians and fighting the culture wars begun in the wake of massive social changes of the 1960s. She argues that the movement became an unholy marriage between top evangelical leaders to the

Republican Party and conservative lobbyists and operatives. She concludes, however, that its influence is waning.

Flowers, Ronald B., Melissa Rogers, and Steven K. Green. 2008. *Religious Freedom and the Supreme Court.* 8th ed. Waco, TX: Baylor University Press.

This is a revised and updated edition of a classic text on the subject, with a new introduction on how the Supreme Court delineates the idea of religious freedom on a case-by-case basis. Clearly written, the text is aimed at the undergraduate market. It covers cases up to 2006.

Friedman, Leon, and Fred Israel, eds. 2013. *The Justices of the Supreme Court: Their Lives and Major Decisions.* 4th ed. 4 vols. New York: Facts-on-File.

This comprehensive four-volume set contains biographical sketches of all of the justices of the Supreme Court from 1789 to 2012. The edited volumes also present articles by leading legal historians on the landmark cases of the court, an updated appendix, revised statistics and charts, new tables, and a list of rejected and withdrawn nominees to the highest court. It offers a comprehensive chronology of the most significant moments in the court's history and fact boxes for each justice. It covers all the major Supreme Court cases dealing with First Amendment freedoms.

Gillman, Howard, and Cornell Clayton, eds. 1999. *The Supreme Court in American Politics: New Institutionalist Interpretations.* Lawrence: University Press of Kansas.

In this edited volume, Gillman and Clayton assemble a collection of distinguished contributors of essays using the new institutionalism in the social sciences to explore the court's institutional development and its relationship to broader political contexts, including party regimes, electoral systems, social movements, social change, legal precedents, political identities, and historically evolving economic structures. It examines the nature of the court's distinctive norms and how its decision-making in particular areas of law or periods of time is influenced by and in turn influences the social and political milieu of the court. The essays are provocative examinations of the court's role in maintaining or disrupting political, economic, and social structures and identities tied to ideology, class, race, gender, and sexual orientation.

Ginger, Ray, and Mike Davis. 2007. *The Bending Cross: A Biography of Eugene Victor Debs*. Chicago: Haymarket Books.
Historian and biographer Ginger and Mike Davis, the author of several books on politics, the environment, and urban issues present a moving and definitive account of the life and the legacy of arguably the most eloquent spokesman and leader of the labor and socialist movements in the United States. The book covers Debs's notable stands of freedom of the press and freedom of assembly and his persecution under the Espionage Act of 1917.

Green, Steven K. 2010. *The Second Disestablishment: Church and State in Nineteenth-Century America*. New York: Oxford University Press.
Green posits that the nineteenth century was the critical period in the history of church-state separation despite the dominance of evangelical Protestantism during that century. Green's study focuses on the period between the ratification of the Constitution and the Supreme Court decision in *Everson v. Board of Education* (1947), which mandated that the Establishment Clause applied to the states via the Fourteenth Amendment.

Hall, Kermit, and James W. Ely Jr., eds. 2009. *The Oxford Guide to United States Supreme Court Decisions*. New York: Oxford University Press.
The editors offer a collection of insightful accounts by eminent legal scholars of landmark cases before the Supreme Court, from *Marbury v. Madison*, to the Dred

Scott decision, to *Brown v. Board of Education* and *Roe v. Wade*. It includes more than four hundred cases, including more than fifty new landmark rulings, such as *Gonzales v. Planned Parenthood*.

Hamilton, Alexander. 2017. *The Essential Hamilton: Letters and Other Writings*. Edited by Joanne Freeman. New York: Library of America.

The book presents an unrivaled portrait of Alexander Hamilton using his own words. It details his meteoric rise, his controversial years as secretary of the treasury, and his scandalous final years. The book is one of a series on the Founding Fathers' public writings and includes private papers and correspondence. It offers his original writings on freedom of the press and speech.

Head, Tom. 2016. *The Religious Right in America: A Historical Encyclopedia*. Santa Barbara, CA: ABC-CLIO.

This encyclopedia approach examines the political influence of the religious right movement and its often cult-like appeal that at times seems to stand the idea of religious freedom on its head.

Holmes, David R. 2006. *The Faith of the Founding Fathers*. New York: Oxford University Press.

Religious historian Holmes of the College of William and Mary provides this clear and concise examination of the religious beliefs of the Founding Fathers, the state of religious culture in the late colonial era, and an account of the religious groups found in each colony. His book enlightens the topic of the various forms of Deism that flourished in the American colonies and the impact their ideas had on the American Revolution and establishment of the nation, including the concept of freedom of religion as eventually espoused in the U.S. Constitution.

Hudson, David L., Jr. 2017. *Freedom of Speech: Documents Decoded.* Santa Barbara, CA: ABC-CLIO.

> Hudson's book is a highly readable yet detailed exploration of essential and illuminating primary documents that provide insights into the history, development, and current conceptions of the First Amendment. It details key points in many Supreme Court cases and explains confusing legal terms and phrases in plain English for nonspecialist readers. A noted First Amendment scholar, Hudson brings his more than two decades of scholarship and teaching to the task of providing easy-to-follow explanations of these key documents.

Jefferson, Thomas. 1950. *The Papers of Thomas Jefferson.* Princeton, NJ: Princeton University Press.

> Since 1950, Princeton University Press has been publishing, in chronological order, the definitive scholarly edition of all of the correspondence and papers of Thomas Jefferson, including letters he received as well as those he sent. It totals seventy thousand items of quality, contextualized Jefferson source materials.

Jefferson, Thomas. 1977. *The Portable Thomas Jefferson.* Edited by Merrill Peterson. New York: Penguin Books.

> This edited volume of Jefferson's writings includes his "Summary View of the Rights of British America," his "Notes on the State of Virginia," seventy-nine letters, his opinion on the "Constitutionality of the Central Bank," his proposal for the Virginia Statute on Religious Liberty, and other writings.

Kluger, Richard. 2016. *Indelible Ink: The Trial of John Peter Zenger and the Birth of America's Free Press.* New York: W. W. Norton.

> Social historian Kluger presents, in rich detail, the dramatic clash during the colonial period of the powerful

antagonists marking the beginnings of freedom of the press in America. The book illustrates the vital importance of free public expression as the basis for democracy.

Kohut, Andrew, John C. Green, Scott Keeter, and Robert C. Toth. 2000. *The Diminishing Divide: Religions Changing Role in American Politics*. Washington, DC: Brookings Institution.
This new edition of a text that examines religion and politics shows the blunt, direct role of religion in U.S. politics, drawing on the extensive research of the Pew Research Center, the National Election Studies, and other data sets. It examines the historical relationship between religion and politics, and their changing role since the 1960s, and religious power in American political life in the twenty-first century.

Koppelman, Andrew, and Tobias Barrington. 2009. *A Right to Discriminate: How the Case of the* Boy Scouts of America v. James Dale *Warped the Law of Free Association*. New Haven, CT: Yale University Press.
Koppelman and Barrington demonstrate that the "right" to discriminate has a long and unpleasant history. The authors bring together legal history, constitutional theory, and political philosophy to analyze how the law might deal with discriminatory private organizations by a detailed examination of the *Boy Scouts of America v. Dale* case.

Laderman, Gary, and Luis León, eds. 2014. *Religion and American Cultures: Tradition, Diversity, and Popular Expression*. 2nd ed. 4 vols. Santa Barbara, CA: ABC-CLIO.
This revised and expanded edition of a four-volume work provides a detailed, multicultural survey of established and new American religions. It investigates the interactions between religion and ethnicity, gender, politics, regionalism, ethics, and popular culture in more than 140

essays that explore contemporary spiritual practices and cultures within a historical perspective.

Lambert, Frank. 2003. *The Founding Fathers and the Place of Religion in America*. Princeton, NJ: Princeton University Press. Lambert examines how the colonies, founded on explicitly religious experiments, came to be the first modern nation-state committed to the separation of church and state, as reflected in its constitution. He explains why it happened through a synthesis of American history, from the Puritan's arrival to Jefferson's presidency. He locates the shift in the mid–eighteenth century in the wake of evangelical revivalism and the arrival of new immigrants.

Lee, Jonathan H. X., Fumitaka Matsuoka, Edmond Yee, and Ronald Y. Nakasone, eds. 2015. *Asian American Religious Cultures*. 2 vols. Santa Barbara, CA: ABC-CLIO. This is a two-volume encyclopedia of Asian American religious cultures. It demonstrates their widely diverse groups and with equality discusses their heterogeneous religious beliefs and traditions. It provides authoritative data on their various religious experiences and includes critical essays on the intersection of race and religion among Asian Americans.

LeMay, Michael. 2017. *The American Political Party System: A Reference Handbook*. Santa Barbara, CA: ABC-CLIO. An in-depth look at American party system, the book examines the historical factors that transformed American politics, tracing the efficacy, sustainability, and popularity of political parties throughout six influential presidencies, from 1790 to the present day. It covers how major and minor political parties took critical stands on First Amendment freedoms, particularly on freedom of the press and freedom of assembly.

LeMay, Michael. 2018. *Homeland Security: A Reference Handbook*. Santa Barbara, CA: ABC-CLIO.

This volume details the creation of the U.S. Department of Homeland Security and how the law establishing the department and its enforcement of perceived threats to national security greatly impacted freedom of speech, assembly and association, and the right to petition grievances. It shows how the concern for national security clashed with freedom of religion and association.

Levy, Leonard W. 1994. *Establishment Clause and the First Amendment*. Chapel Hill: University of North Carolina Press.

Levy's classic work studies the circumstances leading to the writing of the Establishment Clause of the First Amendment. He argues that the founders intended to prohibit government aid for religion even on an impartial basis. This new edition incorporates new material and a discussion of Establishment Clause cases brought before the Supreme Court.

Levy, Leonard W. 1999. *Origins of the Bill of Rights*. New Haven, CT: Yale University Press.

In this history of the origins of the Bill of Rights, Levy offers a panoramic view of liberties secured by the first ten amendments. It explores behind-the-scenes machinations, public rhetoric, and the political motivations of James Madison and others. It is a terse and laconic study showing how the Bill of Rights evolved over time.

Lewis, Anthony. 2007. *Freedom for the Thought We Hate: A Biography of the First Amendment*. New York: Basic Books.

Anthony Lewis, a Pulitzer Prize–winning journalist, describes in detail how our free speech rights were established in five distinct areas: political speech, artistic expression, libel, commercial speech, and unusual forms of expression such as T-shirts and campaign spending.

Lewis describes the hard choices, heroic judges, and eccentric defendants who forced the legal system to confront one of nation's foundational ideas.

Lively, Donald E., and Russell L. Weaver. 2006. *Contemporary Supreme Court Cases: Landmark Decisions since* Roe v. Wade. Westport, CT: Greenwood Press.

The authors provide readers with an understanding of the significant role the Supreme Court plays in shaping the boundaries of government power and those of individual rights and liberties. From *Roe v. Wade* to 2005, the authors trace the court's impact on American society, examining the points and counterpoints of the Supreme Court's functions and how, among other issues, the court impacts the understanding of and implementation of First Amendment rights.

Mapp, Alf. 2003. *The Faith of Our Fathers: What America's Founders Really Believed*. Lanham, MD: Rowman & Littlefield.

Mapp's book cuts through the historical uncertainty to accurately portray the religious beliefs held by eleven of the Founding Fathers, including John Adams, Benjamin Franklin, Thomas Jefferson, and James Madison. He shows that they were men with religious beliefs as diverse as their political opinions. These profiles shed light on their lives and times as well as the role of religion in public life throughout American history.

McGarvie, Mark Douglas. 2004. *One Nation under Law: America's Early National Struggle to Separate Church and State*. DeKalb: Northern Illinois University Press.

Using an innovative perspective, McGarvie argues that the separation of church and state principle emerged as a result of the contract clause of the Constitution, not the First Amendment, and that the original intent of the framers was indeed separation. His book is a significant contribution to the vibrant scholarly debate on the subject.

McKenna, Marian. 2002. *Franklin Roosevelt and the Great Constitutional War: The Court-Packing Crisis of 1937*. New York: Fordham University Press.

McKenna presents a critical and revisionist portrayal of FDR's personal role in initiating a reorganization of the federal judiciary in an attempt to "pack" the court in 1937, increasing the number of justices from nine to fifteen. The book details his attempt to give the president the power to appoint new justices for every justice over the age of seventy who refused to resign or retire. The book chronicles the case histories and events that led to the crisis. It provides thorough documentation and reasoned criticism.

Merriman, Scott A. 2009. *Religion and Law in America: An Encyclopedia of Personal Belief and Public Policy*. 2 vols. Santa Barbara, CA: ABC-CLIO.

Merriman provides a comprehensive survey of one of the oldest and hottest debates in American history—the role of religion in public discourse. Using the encyclopedic approach, the two volumes cover 250 entries from A to Z that analyze specific court cases and offer short topical surveys. It offers thematic essays to analyze the Establishment Clause, the teaching of creationism and evolution, and the refusal of medical care on the grounds of religious belief. Its chronology traces the development of attitudes toward religious freedom and the complex relationship between church and state.

Merriman, Scott A. 2017. *When Religious and Secular Interests Collide: Faith, Law, and the Religious Exemption Debate*. Santa Barbara, CA: Praeger.

Merriman examines the countervailing arguments in the religious exemption debates and explains why it remains so heated and controversial a subject in modern politics. He uses up-to-date coverage as well as a full history of religious exemption cases from the nineteenth to the twenty-first centuries. The book explores the interplay between religion and law in the United States.

Parker, J. Wilson, Douglas Davison, and Paul Finkelman. 2003. *Constitutional Law in Context*. Vol. 1. Durham, NC: Carolina Academic Press.

This book puts major constitutional developments into historical perspective. It enables readers to better understand how doctrinal developments by the Supreme Court were shaped by historical developments and how developments shaping one doctrine sometimes influenced other doctrines. The book examines the commerce clause doctrine, substantive due process, and legal doctrine related to race and gender. The chapter on the doctrine of incorporation shows how the ideas of the founders were influenced by the denial of civil liberties during the crusade against slavery. It shows how the New Deal changed both the commerce clause and the substantive due process doctrine.

Parker, Richard, ed. 2003. *Free Speech on Trial: Communication Perspectives on Landmark Supreme Court Decisions*. Tuscaloosa: University of Alabama Press.

This volume presents contributions from twenty legal scholars of communication whose essays examine the constitutional guarantee of free speech and its symbolic relationship with communication practices by analyzing both case law and legal theory. The book reveals how the Supreme Court's free speech opinions have fashioned, reconstructed, and reformulated the contours and parameters of the Constitution's guarantee of free expression and how free speech shapes our government, culture, and American society.

Parrish, Michael E. 2002. *The Hughes Court: Justices, Rulings, and Legacy*. Santa Barbara, CA: ABC-CLIO.

Parrish presents an in-depth analysis of the workings and legacy of the Supreme Court under Chief Justice Charles

Evans Hughes. The book is one in a series on the Supreme Court. It offers a thoughtful discussion of the Supreme Court during one of the most tumultuous decades in the court's storied history. The book covers the key controversies, personalities, and case decisions handed down during the years of the Hughes court.

Peters, Shawn Francis. 2002. *Judging Jehovah's Witnesses: Religious Persecution and the Dawn of the Rights Revolution.* Lawrence: University Press of Kansas.

Peters offers a complete account of the personalities, events, and institutions behind the First Amendment rights claims and cases of the Jehovah's Witnesses. He relates the persecution against them and how the ACLU and liberal clergy stepped in to defend them. He examines strategies used to combat discrimination and, with respect to the Jehovah's Witnesses, freedom of religion, freedom of assembly, and freedom to petition the government for grievances.

Peters, Shawn Francis. 2003. *The* Yoder *Case: Religious Freedom, Education, and Parental Rights.* Lawrence: University Press of Kansas.

Peters tells the full story of the *Wisconsin v. Yoder* (1971) case. His book is a comprehensive, thoughtful, yet accessible examination of the events and personalities involved in the landmark case and the long battle of the Amish to secure their religious freedom rights.

Peterson, Merrill D., Robert C. Vaughan, and Robin Lovin, eds. 1988. *The Virginia Statute for Religious Freedom: Its Evolution and Consequences in American History.* Cambridge, England: Cambridge University Press.

The editors present a collection of essays from a symposium at the University of Virginia that provides a comprehensive examination of one of the most important primary documents on the religious freedom doctrine.

Powe, Lucas. 2000. *The Warren Court and American Politics*. Cambridge, MA: Harvard University Press.

Chief Justice Earl Warren led the Supreme Court during its most revolutionary and controversial period in American history. Powe revives the valuable tradition of looking at the Supreme Court in the wide political environment to argue the Warren court functioned as a partner in Kennedy-Johnson liberalism, imposing national liberal values on groups that were outliers: the white South, rural America, and areas of Roman Catholic dominance. Powe offers a learned and lively narrative to discuss more than two hundred significant rulings that changed the balance of American legislatures, gradually eliminating anti-communism in domestic security programs, reformed basic criminal procedures, banned school-sponsored prayer, and shaped new law on pornography.

Prados, John, and Margaret Pratt, eds. 2004. *Inside the Pentagon Papers*. Lawrence: University Press of Kansas.

The book examines in detail the legal and moral issues over government secrecy and democracy's need for truthfully informed citizens. It discusses the landmark decision over the Pentagon Papers and how the case influenced all subsequent freedom of the press jurisprudence and the impact of the court's principle of prior restraint. It shows how a close examination of the Pentagon Papers case illuminates the question of government responsibility at any time in history. It reexamines what happened, why it mattered, and why it remains relevant today. It focuses on the backstory of the Pentagon Papers and the resulting court case. It draws on oral history and previously classified documents to illustrate the consequences of the leak and of the litigation that followed, for the Vietnam War and, ultimately, for American history.

Ragosta, John A. 2013. *Religious Freedom: Jefferson's Legacy, American Creed*. Charlottesville: University of Virginia Press.
  A significant contribution to the extensive discourse on religious freedom, this is an engaging intellectual and legal history. Ragosta's core argument stands against both the preferentialist view and the view that the First Amendment was merely a jurisdictional mechanism to protect states' religious establishments. He makes a convincing case that Jefferson's strict separationist thought was and should remain at the center of the First Amendment.

Russo, Charles, ed. 2009. *Encyclopedia of Education Law*. 2 vols. Thousand Oaks, CA: Sage Publications.
  Russo's two-volume set provides contributions by more than one hundred contributors in an encyclopedia format. It helps readers to understand education law and how that law applies to issues today. It provides entries on persons, biographical sketches of important people, entries for 180 cases, and excerpts from the most important cases. It thereby touches on freedom of expression, access to assembly, and freedom of religion or limitations thereof with respect to students and the legal limitations of their freedom in the context of public and private schools.

Salvatore, Nick, ed. 2007. *Eugene V. Debs: Citizen and Socialist*. Champaign: University of Illinois Press.
  This classic biography of Eugene Debs provides a major reevaluation of Debs, the movements he launched and led, and his belief in American socialism as an extension of the democratic values and traditions on which the nation was founded. His life and work are especially relevant to freedom of association, freedom to petition grievances to government, and freedom of speech. It shows how the Espionage Act of 1917 so negatively affected those freedoms.

Schultz, David, and John Vile, eds. 2009. *The First Amendment Encyclopedia*. Washington, DC: CQ Press.

This reference volume presents more entries than any other work of its kind—the most exhaustive examination of the First Amendment Freedom. In 2016, Middle Tennessee University purchased the license to publish the work on a new website that created a searchable database of now more than fifteen hundred entries. The original volume has contributions from more than two hundred legal scholars in original essays and articles.

Schwartz, Bernard. 1992. *Freedom of the Press*. New York: Facts on File.

Schwartz's book is the first volume in the Facts on Files series on Supreme Court decisions in all the significant areas of constitutional law. This volume recounts the decisions, arguments, and unpublished drafts of opinions on First Amendment speech issues.

Sehat, David. 2011. *The Myth of American Religious Freedom*. New York: Oxford University Press.

In this historical review of religion in public life, Sehat traces the application of the First Amendment from the federal government to the states and local governments after 1940. He covers the culture wars of the last fifty years and the rise (and fall) of the Protestant establishment. Through a series of profiles of key actors, he questions the myths held by both the left and the right political beliefs in American politics.

Sheehan, Neil, Hedrick Smith, and E. W. Kenworthy, eds. 1971. *The Pentagon Papers*. New York: New York Times.

The definitive edition of the Pentagon Papers as published by the *New York Times*, this book provides a comprehensive archive for libraries, universities, and private citizens. It presents additional background materials related to the writing of the Pentagon Papers, their place in the history of U.S. policy since World War II, and the constitutional values raised by their publication in the *New York Times* and the *Washington Post*. It illuminates a landmark decision on the legal doctrine of prior restraint.

Siegel, Paul. 2007. *Cases in Communication Law*. 2nd ed. Lanham, MD: Rowman & Littlefield.
Siegel's book discusses sixty-one cases, of which forty-one are Supreme Court decisions, eleven are federal appellate decisions, and four are federal district court decisions. The casebook is designed as a companion to his basic textbook concerning communication law and is comprehensive in its discussion of freedom of speech and freedom of the press issues.

Simon, James. 2012. *FDR and Chief Justice Hughes: The President, the Supreme Court, and the Epic Battle over the New Deal*. New York: Simon and Schuster.
Simon examines the confrontation over the New Deal and FDR's resulting proposal to pack the court and reorganize the federal judiciary. He shows how FDR, despite losing the immediate battle over court packing, outmaneuvered the isolationist senators who had opposed his court-packing proposal, expedited aid to Great Britain and the Allies, and then led the United States into and through World War II.

Smith, Frank J., ed. 2016. *Religion and Politics in America: An Encyclopedia of Church and State in American Life*. 2 vols. Santa Barbara, CA: ABC-CLIO.
Organized alphabetically, this two-volume set offers insights into the contemporary controversies over religion and politics in the United States. Each entry places its topic in historical context and shows how religious beliefs and political ideals have always existed side-by-side, and often clashed, from colonial times to the present.

Tushnet, Mark. 2005. *A Court Divided: The Rehnquist Court and the Future of Constitutional Law.* New York: W. W. Norton and Company.

> Tushnet examines the Rehnquist court, arguing that the Supreme Court has always followed election returns. He notes that the Warren and Burger courts never got far out of line with the national political consensus. The Rehnquist court, Tushnet shows, reflected the 1980s and 1990s and the rise of conservatism. He shows how the court followed Congress' lead, striking down several symbols of the New Deal regulatory state. The court sided with more liberal positions at the margins of the social cultural wars—on gay rights, affirmative action, and early-term abortions. As Tushnet notes, in the arena of politics, economic conservatives were winning, and cultural conservatives were losing.

Urofsky, Melvin I. 2002. *Religious Freedom: Rights and Liberties under the Law.* Santa Barbara, CA: ABC-CLIO.

> Urofsky addresses the question of what constitutes "legitimate" constitutionally protected religious practice as it has been debated throughout American history. He offers a thorough, responsible, and evenhanded analysis to provide readers with a solid grounding in the complex constitutional issues that lie behind the headlines associated with controversial court cases.

Urofsky, Melvin I., and Paul Finkelman. 1987. *The March of Liberty: A Constitutional History of the United States.* 3rd ed. Vol. 1, *From the Founding to 1900.* New York: Oxford University Press.

> Urofsky and Finkelman's book blends cases and court doctrines with the political, economic, and social history of the United States. The book provides in-depth analyses of the intellects and personalities of the Supreme Court justices who wrote majority opinions, crafting landmark decisions. The book employs a holistic approach that integrates state and lower federal court cases with Supreme

Court decisions to better understand the complexity and development of legal doctrines.

Utter, Glenn H., and James L. True. 2004. *Conservative Christians and Political Participation: A Reference Handbook*. Santa Barbara, CA: ABC-CLIO.

Utter and True examine the involvement and influence of conservative Christians in American politics. They provide a historical overview of the interaction of religion and politics from colonial times to the present, exploring the demographics of conservative Christians, their major concerns, their goals, and the various political methods they employ to achieve them. It covers profiles of the major leaders and organizations of the movement.

Vile, John R. 2014. *Essential Supreme Court Decisions: Summaries of Leading Cases in U.S. Constitutional Law*. 16th ed. Lanham, MD: Rowman & Littlefield.

Vile's book has become a standard of the most important Supreme Court cases in U.S. constitutional law. His book includes every facet of constitutional law, including powers and privileges of the three branches of the national government, federalism, war powers, and extensive briefs on civil rights and civil liberties. This new edition is revised and updated. It covers cases by year, by the chief justices who presided over the cases, and by types of cases.

Vile, John R. 2015a. *Encyclopedia of Constitutional Amendments, Proposed Amendments, and Amending Issues, 1789–2015*. 4th ed. 2 vols. Santa Barbara, CA: ABC-CLIO.

In this fourth and updated edition, Vile presents a comprehensive review of constitutional amendments and proposed amendments, and he discusses the critical issues they deal with, from 1789 to the present. He covers each of the twenty-seven amendments as well as essays on proposed amendments, and he outlines proposals for more radical changes to the U.S. Constitution.

Vile, John R. 2015b. *Founding Documents of America: Documents Decoded.* Santa Barbara, CA: ABC-CLIO.

In this volume in ABC-CLIO's popular Documents Decoded series, Vile offers historic documents key to the foundation of the national government with introductions that supply the background information and analyses that highlight key provisions and provide historical context. It covers the Declaration of Independence, the Constitution, the Bill of Rights, private diary entries, and political polemics organized chronologically into four sections: antecedents, revolutionary and confederal periods, calling and convening the Constitutional Convention, and debating, ratifying, and implementing the Constitution. The book covers more than fifty primary source documents. It is aimed at high school and college students.

Wilcox, Clyde. 1992. *God's Warriors: The Christian Right in Twentieth-Century America.* Baltimore, MD: Johns Hopkins University Press.

Wilcox assesses the Christian right's mass base and electoral appeal using social science theories to account for their origins. He provides an overview of the Christian right and the interaction of religion and politics using survey data and a review of the recent literature on the topic.

Witte, John, Jr. 2012a. *No Establishment of Religion: America's Original Contribution to Religious Liberty.* New York: Oxford University Press.

Witte provides an in-depth analysis of the meaning of the Establishment Clause as an American innovation in the relation of church and state. He presents twelve original essays.

Witte, John, Jr. 2012b. *Religion and Human Rights: An Introduction.* New York: Oxford University Press.

This book is a comprehensive survey of religion and human rights, including both Eastern and Western traditions, and the category of indigenous religions. The book covers issues such as environmental sustainability; conflict transformation; world peace; group rights; self-determination of religious communities; and economic, social, and doctrinal rights; and the relationships between religion, culture, and ethnicity.

Wolbrecht, Christina, and Rodney E. Hero. 2005. *The Politics of Democratic Inclusion*. Philadelphia: Temple University Press. The authors contribute to our understanding of the processes and mechanisms by which underrepresented groups have and have not achieved political incorporation. They have collected essays from contributors that trace the issue of inclusion from colonial times to the present, giving particular emphasis to the institutions, processes, rules, and the context of the American political order that encourage, mediate, or hamper the representation and incorporation of disadvantaged groups.

Woodward, Robert, and Scott Armstrong. 1978. *The Brethren: Inside the Supreme Court*. New York: Simon and Schuster. The authors provide a detailed, behind-the-scenes account of the Supreme Court in action, piercing its secrecy to give an unprecedented view of the chief justice and associate justices and their maneuvering, arguing, politicking, compromising, and decision-making and how their decisions affect every major area of American life.

Zentner, Scot, and Michael LeMay. 2020. *Party and Nation*. Lanham, MD: Lexington Books. The authors examine immigration policy as a means to understand political party competition in American history. They show how the rise of President Donald Trump reflects an ongoing pattern of regime change in the United States, in which multiculturalism and nationalism have emerged as central aspects of the major parties' ideological and coalitional bases. They suggest a multi-culturalist Democratic Party and a nationalist Republican Party is a dramatic departure from the first American political regime, grounded in the founding generation's commitment to the principles of natural rights and shaping the national culture to support that principle. They discuss partisan debates over immigration set into relief the inherent tensions in that commitment and the permutations of regime change amid territorial expansion and the tragic conflicts over slavery and segregation. They show how industrialization and the immigration waves gave rise to the progressive administrative state and how the parties began a century-long transformation into the plebiscitary institutions they are today. They demonstrate how the debate over immigration not only illuminates party differences but has begun to define them.

Scholarly Journals

American Journal of Sociology was established in 1895 and is the oldest academic journal of sociology in the United States. It is attached to the Department of Sociology at the University of Chicago and is published bimonthly. It is a leading voice in all areas of sociology, with an emphasis on theory building and innovative methods, and is open to interdisciplinary contributions from anthropologists, economists, educators, historians, and political scientists. It publishes book reviews and commissioned book review essays.

Columbia Law Review has been published since 1901 and is a leading publication of legal scholarship. It is published in eight issues a year. It receives some two thousand submissions and publishes twenty to twenty-five manuscripts annually. Its online supplement, *Columbia Law Review Online*, has been available since 2008. It is edited by Columbia University Law School.

Emory International Law Review is a leading journal of international legal scholarship known for its excellence in scholarship, legal research, analysis, and professionalism. It publishes articles on a vast array of topics, from human rights to international intellectual property issues. It is published quarterly.

Emory Law Journal was founded in 1952 as the *Journal of Public Law*. It has been publishing academic, professional, and student-authored legal scholarship on the full range of legal subjects since 1978. It publishes six issues annually.

Georgetown Journal of Legal Ethics was founded in 1987. It is published quarterly. It publishes interdisciplinary scholarship related to the future of the legal profession, issuing cutting-edge articles on ethical issues from diverse practical areas.

Georgetown Law Review is headquartered at Georgetown University Law School in Washington, DC. It has published more than five hundred issues since its inception in 1912. It employs one hundred law students. It publishes its *Annual Review of Criminal Procedure* and articles across the full spectrum of legal issues and cases.

Harvard Law Review publishes eight regular annual issues of various legal articles by professors, judges, practitioners, and law students and leading case summaries. It is run by an independent student group at Harvard Law School. It also publishes an online Harvard Law Review Forum. One of the nation's oldest law reviews, it has been published since 1887. It is one of the most prestigious law reviews, with alumni that include Barack Obama, seven Supreme Court justices, including Ruth Bader Ginsburg who was its first female editor, and a host of federal court judges and other high-level federal government officials.

Hastings Law Journal has been published since 1949. It is the flagship law review of the University of California–Hastings. It is published six times per year. Its scholarly articles span a wide variety of legal issues and are written by experts in the legal community. It also publishes an occasional law symposium issue. It is run by ninety student members, and it reaches a large domestic and international audience.

International Journal for Religious Freedom is the journal of the International Institute for Religious Freedom of the World Evangelical Alliance. Published since 2012, it is issued twice per year. It provides a platform for scholarly discourse on issues related to religious freedom in general and on the persecution of Christians in particular. It is an interdisciplinary, international, peer-reviewed scholarly journal with research articles, documents, book reviews, and academic news in each issue.

Journal of the American Academy of Religion is a major academic journal in the field of religious studies. It is an international, interdisciplinary quarterly journal that covers the full range of world religious traditions, and it explores them with provocative studies of their methodologies. It has been published since 1967. It has a large and valuable book review section. It is published by Oxford University Press for the Department of Theological Studies at the Claremont Graduate University.

Journal of Church and State is a quarterly peer-reviewed academic journal of religious studies and political science covering First Amendment issues. It is published by Oxford University Press for the J. M. Dawson Institute of Church-State Studies at Baylor University. It was established in 1959. It publishes constitutional, historical, philosophical, theological, and sociological studies on religion and the body politic in various countries and cultures of the world. Each issue covers five or more major articles, thirty-five to forty book reviews, and occasional government or church documents as well as laws and court cases.

Journal of Law and Courts is a quarterly interdisciplinary journal for members of the law and courts community and section of the American Political Science Association (APSA). It features communications and fertilization across traditional boundaries. The journal publishes both theoretical and empirical articles employing rigorous arguments and methods. It is written in an accessible style.

Journal of Law and Religion is a peer-reviewed interdisciplinary journal edited by the Center for the Study of Law and Religion at Emory University and is published with the collaboration of the Cambridge University Press since 1982. It is a leading journal that publishes interdisciplinary and interfaith scholarship at the intersection of law and religion.

Journal of Religion is a quarterly peer-reviewed academic journal that publishes articles in theology, religion, ethics, and philosophy of religion as well as the role of religion in culture and society. Articles are written from a historical, sociological, psychological, linguistic, or artistic standpoint. It began in 1882 as the *Hebrew Student*, was changed to the *American Journal of Theology* in 1897, and since 1921 has been the *Journal of Religion*. It is published by the University of Chicago Press.

Law and Social Inquiry is a quarterly peer-reviewed journal that is multidisciplinary. It publishes original research articles and review essays that analyze law, legal institutions, and the legal profession from a sociological perspective. Its contributors include scholars from anthropology, criminology, economics, history, philosophy, political science, and sociology. It is published on behalf of the American Bar Association by Cambridge University Press.

Law and Society Review is a quarterly peer-reviewed journal that was founded in 1966 and is regarded by sociological scholars worldwide as a leading journal in the field.

It publishes original research on the relationship between society and the legal process, including articles, reviews, research notes, and new theoretical developments. It is published by Wiley for the Law and Society Association.

Liberty: A Magazine of Religious Freedom was founded in 1906 and is published by the Seventh-day Adventist Church. It covers issues involving the separation of church and state and current events in politics. It has a circulation of two hundred thousand. It is published bimonthly.

Northwestern University Law Review was founded in 1906 as the *Illinois Law Review*. It is published quarterly in print and online. It is student operated and features articles on general legal scholarship written by professors, judges, and legal practitioners as well as students. It hosts special symposium issues annually, such as *Ordering State-Federal Relations through Preemption Doctrine* (2007).

Notre Dame Law Review was founded in 1925 and known as the *Notre Dame Lawyer* until 1982. It is student edited and fosters scholarly discourse within the legal community that is mindful of its Catholic tradition. It is published in one volume annually, with five issues published between November and July. One issue of each volume focuses on Federal Courts, Practice & Procedure, as a forum for exploring civil practice and procedures in the federal courts.

Political Research Quarterly is a peer-reviewed academic journal that publishes original research on all aspects of politics across multiple fields. It is published by the University of Utah and is the official journal of the Western Political Science Association, with an emphasis on transcending the boundaries that conventionally separate subfields, methods, and specializations.

Religion and American Culture is a semiannual publication by the University of California Press for the Center for the Study of Religion and American Culture. Since 1991, it has been publishing scholarly discussion of the nature, terms, and dynamics of religion in the United States, embracing a diversity of methodological approaches and theoretical perspectives. It concerns the interplay between religion and other spheres of American culture.

Review of Politics publishes articles primarily on political theory, interpretive studies of law, and historical analysis on all aspects of politics: institutions, techniques, literary reflections on politics, and constitutional theory and analysis. It has been published quarterly since 1939 and is published by Cambridge University Press for the University of Notre Dame.

Social Work and Christianity publishes articles and book reviews related to the integration of faith and professional social work practices. It began publication in 1974. It is published quarterly and is the official publication of the National Association of Christians in Social Work.

Stanford University Law Review is published both in print (since 1948) and online (since 2011). It fosters intellectual discourse among student members and contributes to legal scholarship by addressing important legal and social issues. It is published in six issues per year, and its articles are contributed by *Law Review* members, other Stanford Law School students, professors, judges, and practicing attorneys.

Supreme Court Review has been published by the University of Chicago Law School since it first appeared in 1910. It provides a sustained and authoritative survey of the court's most significant decisions. It provides an in-depth critique of the Supreme Court and its work and the ongoing reforms and interpretations of American law. It is written by and for legal academics, judges, political scientists, journalists, and sociologists. It is published annually in the spring.

University of California Law Review is the preeminent legal publication of the University of California, Berkeley,

School of Law. It was founded in 1912. It is published six times annually and covers a wide variety of topics of legal scholarship. It is edited and published entirely by students at Berkeley Law. It publishes research by the Berkeley Law faculty, centers, students, judges, and legal practitioners.

University of Chicago Law Review was founded in 1933. It is edited by students and is one of the most prestigious and often-cited law reviews. Its authors include a host of Supreme Court justices, federal court judges, state supreme court judges, and preeminent legal scholars. It is published quarterly.

University of Minnesota Law Review has been published since 1917. It is solely edited by its board of thirty-nine student editors. It is published quarterly and covers the entire range of legal issues. It also publishes an annual symposium issue.

University of Pennsylvania Journal of Constitutional Law provides a forum for the interdisciplinary study and analysis of constitutional law. It cultivates legal scholarship, promotes critical perspectives, and reinvents the traditional study of constitutional law. It has twenty student editors. It has been published quarterly since 1998.

University of Pennsylvania Law Review focuses on a wide range of legal issues. It was founded in 1852 and published its 165th volume in seven issues in the 2016–2017 academic year. It serves the legal profession, the bench, the bar, and the legal academy by providing a forum for publication of legal research. From about two thousand submissions, it selects twelve articles in each volume and is cited with such peer organizations as Columbia, Harvard, and Yale.

University of Virginia Law Review has been one of the most prestigious publications in the legal profession since 1913—more than one hundred years. It is published eight times annually and covers law-related issues by and for judges, practitioners, teachers, legislators, students, and others interested in the law. The Virginia Law School was founded by Thomas Jefferson in 1819.

Yale Law Journal has been published since 1891. It has been at the forefront of legal scholarship and shapes discussion of the most important and relevant legal issues through rigorous scholarship. It is published eight times per year, and its online companion has been published since 2005. It is one of the most widely cited law reviews in the nation.

Nonprint Resources

Films

All the President's Men.

This 1976 feature-length film is a biography/drama/historical/political thriller about the 1972 presidential election, the Watergate scandal, and the investigative reporting by Bob Woodward and Carl Bernstein, portrayed by Robert Redford and Dustin Hoffman, with Hal Holbrook as the FBI agent known as "Deep Throat" and Jason Robards as the *Washington Post*'s Ben Bradlee, that brought about the downfall of President Richard Nixon. It coined the investigative reporting phrase, "Follow the money." It resonates with today's *Washington Post* and *New York Times* investigations of the Trump campaign and possible conspiracy with Russian interference in the 2016 election. It runs two hours and eighteen minutes and is in color (www.imdb.com/title/tt0074119).

The Birth of a Nation.

This 1915 movie depicts the Civil War, the assassination of President Lincoln, and the rise of the Ku Klux Klan. It is not historically accurate. It runs three hours and fifteen minutes and is in black and white. It was produced by the David Griffith Corporation and is available on DVD and IMDbPro.

Black Legion.

A disgruntled factory worker (played by Humphrey Bogart) joins a secret society (a thinly disguised KKK) that terrorizes foreigners. It was produced by Warner Brothers Studios and filmed in black and white, running eighty-three minutes. It is highly relevant today. It is available on DVD from Turner Classic Movies and has three stars on a four-star rating.

Bob Roberts.

This 1992 film is a mock documentary about a cynical conservative evangelical running for the U.S. Senate. It depicts his using all the new technologies of the modern era of politics and his ingratiating use of family values and nationalism. He campaigns around the state, singing protest songs such as "This Land Is Made for Me" and "Times Are Changing Back." He is depicted as a self-made multimillionaire with Gatsbyesque financial dealings. He is shown as a crafty, sleazy, but politically savvy politician who uses meaningless rhetoric and propaganda while accusing journalists of abusing freedom of the press. It stars Tim Robbins. It was produced by Miramax and PolyGram and distributed by Paramount Pictures. It is in color and runs 104 minutes and is available on IMDbPro.

The Crucible.

This 1996 film depicts a small group of girls in Salem, Massachusetts, who tell lies about how Satan has invaded them. It is based on the award-winning play by Arthur Miller, who wrote the screenplay. It is inspired by the Salem witch trials. It was nominated for two Oscars. It runs two hours and four minutes and is a masterpiece of a film. It was produced by the 20th Century Fox film corporation and is available on IMDbPro.

The Fourth Estate.

This Showtime television drama series by documentarian Liz Garbus delivers an astounding and intimate look at the inner workings of the *New York Times'* Washington bureau, where reporters and editors relentlessly pursue the constant chaos of the Trump administration. It is an example of the First Amendment in action.

Friendly Persuasion.

This 1956 film depicts a family of pacifist Quakers who struggle with their pacifism during the Civil War. It is set in 1862 Indiana. It stars Gary Cooper and Dorothy McGuire. It runs 137 minutes and is in color. It is an Allied Artist picture that was nominated for six Oscars and won five. It is rated 7.5/10 stars on IMDbPro.

The Gangs of New York.

This 2002 film stars Leonardo DiCaprio and Daniel Day-Lewis. It was directed by Martin Scorsese and was nominated for ten Oscars. Set in New York City's Manhattan in 1863, the film depicts the worst riot in U.S. history, when Protestant gangs terrorized Irish immigrants. In runs two hours and forty-seven minutes and is in color. It is a Miramax film and rated 7.5/10 on IMDbPro.

Hacksaw Ridge.

This 2016 film is a biography of a Seventh-day Adventist conscientious objector who served in World War II as an army medic. It is the true story of Desmond Doss, who saved the lives of seventy-five men during the battle of Okinawa. He is the only conscientious objector ever to win the Congressional Medal of Honor. The film was nominated for six Oscars and won two. It is in color and runs two hours and nineteen minutes. It was directed by

Mel Gibson, and is a Cross Creek Pictures production. It is rated 8.2/10 on IMDbPro.

Inherit the Wind.

This 1960 film stars Spencer Tracy and Gene Kelly. Tracy plays B. J. Cates, who is put on trial for teaching evolution. It is a thinly disguised depiction of the 1925 Scopes Monkey Trial. It runs two hours and eight minutes and is in black and white. It is a courtroom drama about evolution versus creationism. It was produced by MGM and is available on DVD. It is rated 8.2/10 on IMDbPro.

Ku Klux Klan: A Secret History.

This 1998 movie is a documentary that depicts the history of the Ku Klux Klan in the United States. It is in black and white and color. It is a Termite Art production and is available on DVD. It runs ninety-six minutes and is rated 7.5/10 on IMDbPro.

LBJ.

This 2016 film is a biographical drama in which Woody Harrelson stars as President Lyndon B. Johnson. It depicts his rise as a congressman from Texas to the White House. It is an Acacia Film Entertainment, Castle Rock Entertainment, and Savvy Media Holdings production. It runs one hour and thirty-eight minutes and is in color. It is rated 7.3/10 on IMDbPro.

Malcolm X.

This 1992 biographical feature film stars Denzel Washington as Malcolm X, for which he was nominated for the Academy Award for Best Actor. Angela Bassett plays Malcolm X's wife. It is based on the autobiography of Malcolm X by Malcolm and Alex Haley and was directed by Spike

Lee. It was distributed by Warner Brothers and internationally by Largo International. It is in color and runs three hours and twenty-two minutes. It is rated 7.7/10 on IMDb.

Mayflower: The Pilgrim's Adventure

This 1979 historical drama presents the story of the 1620 emigration of the Pilgrims from England to America, a journey of 103 religious "separatists." It depicts their religious persecution in England and journey to the Plymouth Colony. It stars Anthony Hopkins and Richard Crenna and is a Syzygy Productions film. It runs one hundred minutes and is in color. It was rated 6.4/10 on IMDb and is available on YouTube.

Monkey Trial.

This 2002 PBS documentary/biography/historical drama film is now available on Turner Classic Movies.com. It is a depiction of the famous John Scopes monkey trial in 1925 and the epic court battle between science and religion. It is in both color and black and white. It was part of the PBS series the American Experience and was broadcast in season 14 as episode 9. It runs one hour and is on IMDbTV. It was produced by the Nebraska ETV Network. It is rated 9.8/10 on IMDb.

Mormon Pioneers: The Great Trek West.

This film is a docudrama dramatization of the history of the Mormon pioneers traveling west on their one thousand–mile trek across the then western American wilderness. It is in color and was produced in 1996 by the Latter-day Saints production company, Trek West Productions. It runs one hour and five minutes. It is available on DVD and IMDbPro.

Salem.

This 2014 television series ran in thirty-six one-hour episodes. It is a drama/fantasy that explores what fueled the town's hysteria and infamous witch trials. It is distributed by 20th Television and WGN America. It is available on DVD from Fox Home Entertainment for the first season and on DVD from Amazon's CreateSpace MOD Program for the second season. It is rated 7.2/10 on IMDb.

The Scarlet Letter.

This 1995 film is a drama/romance depicting life in 1666 Massachusetts Bay Colony in which an affair between a young woman who is presumed to be a widow has an affair with the young Quaker pastor with disastrous consequences. It stars Demi Moore and Gary Oldman. It is a film by Allied Stars Ltd, Cinergi Pictures Entertainment, and Hollywood Pictures. It runs two hours fifteen minutes and is in color. It is rated 5.2/10 on IMDb.

Selma.

This 2014 film follows Martin Luther King Jr. and his movement through the violent, epic march from Selma, Alabama, to Montgomery, culminating in President Lyndon Johnson's signing of the Voting Rights Act of 1965. It won the NAACP Image Awards for Outstanding Actor (David Oyelowo) and Outstanding Picture. It is a British American–produced film distributed by Paramount Pictures. It runs 127 minutes and is in color. It was rated 8.7/10 on Rotten Tomatoes and 7.5/10 on IMDb. It is available on DVD.

Storm Warning.

This 1951 drama/film noir thriller is about a murder by the KKK. It stars Ronald Reagan, Ginger Rogers, Doris

Day, and Steve Cochran. Ronald Reagan plays the district attorney who pursues the murderers. Typical of movies in the 1950s, it depicts the KKK as thuggish criminals but avoids their racial hate message. It runs ninety-three minutes and is in black and white. It was distributed by Warner Brothers. It is rated 7.3/10 on IMDb.

Witness.

This 1985 film stars Harrison Ford, Kelly McGillis, and Lukas Haas. It was nominated for six Academy Awards and won two, for editing and writing. It is a gripping drama depicting a young Amish widow and her son, who witness a murder while changing trains in Philadelphia. Detective captain John Book (played by Ford) has to flee with them to protect them from the fellow police officers who were the murderers. They hide in Amish country. It is a good depiction of the Amish lifestyle and values. It is in color and runs one hour and fifty-two minutes. It was distributed by Paramount Pictures. It is rated 7.4/10 on IMDb.

Videos

Alleged: The Scopes Monkey Trial.

This video is an accurate portrayal of the Scopes monkey trial of 1925 (using the trial manuscripts for its screenplay). It stars Brian Dennehy as Clarence Darrow, Fred Thompson as William Jennings Bryan, and Colm Meaney as H. L. Mencken. It runs 28:50 minutes. It is available on DVD from Amazon.

Defining Religious Freedom in America

This is a video from the morning session of a daylong conference held by the First Amendment Center on March 18, 2013. The video covers a panel of distinguished scholars on the topic, discussing it from their various legal/religious traditions, backgrounds, and perspectives (e.g., Christian, Hindu, ACLU, Jewish). The video runs 1:38:45 and aired March 21, 2013. It is available on YouTube.

Freedom of Religion: A History of God in America

This YouTube video features a lecture by Randall Niles as he looks at the truth underlying the First Amendment and tries to answer the question, Where did the separation of church and state doctrine come from?

John Fea: Was America Founded as a Christian Nation?

In this video, Professor John Fea, of the History Department of Classics, Philosophy and Religion at the University of Mary Washington, lectures on his book of the same title. It aired August 31, 2012 as a Religious Freedom Lecture. It runs one hour and fifteen minutes and is available on YouTube.

The Liberty Threat: Attack on Religious Freedom in America

This is a video of a lecture by James Tonkowich on his book *The Liberty Threat*. In it, he covers court cases arguing that the doctrine of the rigid separation of church and state has led to a nation hostile to true faith, and he calls for Christian activism to oppose it. It well illustrates the conservative religious right's views on the separation of church and state doctrine. It aired October 20, 2014 and runs 34:56 minutes. In is available on YouTube.

"A Nation Reborn"

This fourth episode of the PBS Frontline history series *God in America* focuses on slavery and the conflict between abolitionists and slaveholders. It emphasizes President Lincoln's spiritual journey as he copes with the death of his young son and tries to make sense of the Civil War, showing how the war transformed his idea about God. It runs 51:09 minutes and is also available on DVD and YouTube.

"A New Adam"

This video is one episode from the PBS Frontline history series *God in America*, a six-part series of one-hour programs. It is the first episode of the series and explores the origins of Christianity in America and how the New World changed the faiths that settlers brought with them. It focuses on the alliance between Thomas Jefferson and evangelical Baptists and how that alliance served as the foundation of religious liberty. It runs 56:53 minutes. It is rated 6.6/7. It is available on DVD and YouTube.

"A New Eden"

This is the second episode of the PBS Frontline series *God in America*. It considers the origins of America's experiment in religious liberty and the competitive religious marketplace it unleashed. It discusses how upstart denominations raced ahead of traditional faiths, the wave of religious revivals, and the fierce political struggle with Catholic immigrants. It runs 56:45 minutes. It is available on DVD and YouTube.

"A New Light"

This is episode three of the PBS Frontline history series *God in America*. It covers the nineteenth-century United States and how forces of modernity challenged traditional faiths and drove a wedge between liberal and conservative believers. It aired October 12, 2010 and runs 56:07 minutes. It is rated 6.7/10 on IMDb.

"Of God and Caesar"

This is the sixth episode of the PBS Frontline series *God in America*. It discusses the moral crusade of evangelical conservatives and their efforts to change U.S. politics and culture. This episode reflects on the role of faith in public life in the country, from the ongoing quest for religious liberty to the early idea of America as the "city on a hill" envisioned by the Puritans four hundred years ago. It runs 55:19 minutes and is available on PBS DVD and YouTube.

The Pilgrims

This video is an Encyclopedia Britannica film and a historical and educational documentary. It deals with the Pilgrims and their journey from England to Holland and then to the Plymouth Colony on the *Mayflower*. Its emphasis is on their search for religious freedom. It is in black and white and runs twenty-two minutes. It is available on YouTube and is rated 4.5/5.

"Puritans and Religious Freedom"

In this C-SPAN video, which is part of the *Lectures in History* series, Professor Kevin Gooding, of the University of West Virginia, gives a talk about the Puritans in early colonial America and the idea of religious freedom and how the Puritans dealt (harshly) with those who dissented from their beliefs and codes. It aired September 16, 2015, and runs one hour.

"Religious Pacifists and the American Revolution"

This C-SPAN video covers Jared Burkholder, a Grace College professor, giving his lecture as part of C-SPAN's *Lectures in History* series. Burkholder speaks about religious pacifists during the American Revolution. He focuses on the diversity of responses to the war from Moravians, Mennonites, Brethren, and other "peace church" traditions rooted in Pietism. It aired February 19, 2015, and runs one hour.

"The Soul of a Nation"

This is the fifth episode of the PBS Frontline history series *God in America*. It focuses on evangelist Billy Graham's revivals that fused faith and patriotism. It covers the Reverend Dr. Martin Luther King Jr. and his emergence as a modern-day prophet. It runs 56:10 minutes and is available on PBS Video and on YouTube.

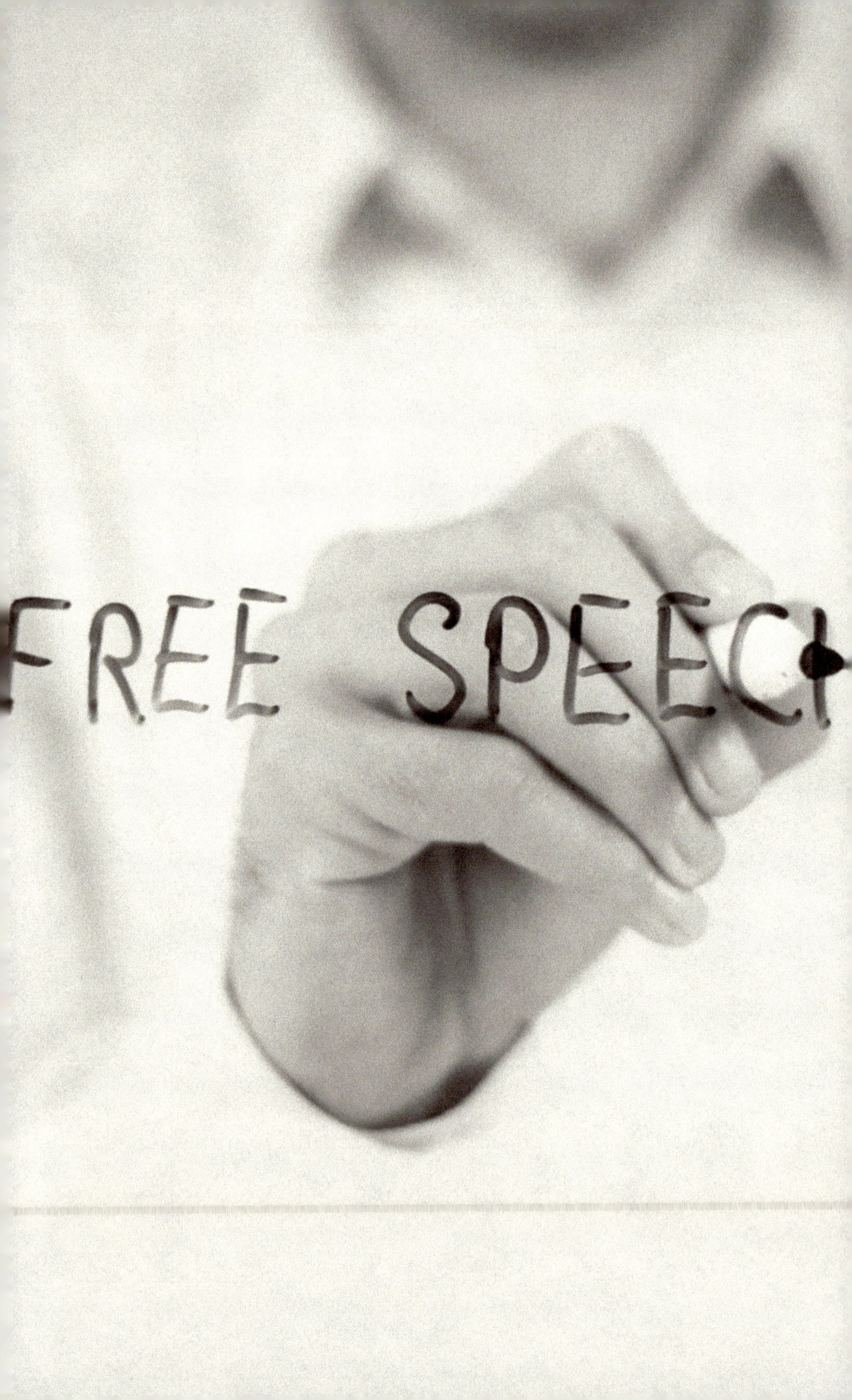
FREE SPEECH

7 Chronology

1649 The Maryland Colony enacts the Maryland Act of Toleration.

1674 William Penn and the Quakers settle in New Jersey and establish the colony as a "Holy Experiment" in religious tolerance.

1681 The Commonwealth of Pennsylvania is established by Pietist and Moravian communities. Religious tolerance, except for Catholics, is pronounced.

1691 Maryland's charter is revoked as well as the Act of Toleration. It becomes a royal charter colony.

1702 Maryland establishes the Anglican Church as its official religion.

1732 King George II allows the Georgia Colony, which seeks population to act as a buffer with Spanish and French colonies to its south, to accept various minority sects to freely practice their religion.

1735 The Moravian Brethren immigrate to the Georgia Colony.

1735 The New York Colony judiciary decides *Rex v. Zenger*.

1760 Old Order Amish and Mennonites move to Pennsylvania and start a mother colony there.

1774 The Shaker Quakers move to New York to freely practice their faith.

A visual representation of free speech. Free speech is only maintained by a citizen's use of it. (Stockbakery/Dreamstime.com)

1776   The Continental Congress declares independence from Great Britain. It first passes a resolution introduced by Richard Henry Lee, VA) on July 2 and then the more formal Declaration of Independence on July 4.

1776   The Constitutional Congress establishes a national government in the Articles of Confederation. The states ratify the Articles in 1781, and they remain in effect until the ratification of the U.S. Constitution in 1787. Under the Articles, there is no executive branch, and Congress has very little power. All laws require a super majority of state approval. There is no guaranteed Bill of Rights.

1785   The Protestant Episcopal Church of the United States is established.

1786   Virginia disestablishes the Anglican Church as its official state faith and enacts the Virginia Statute for Religious Freedom into the Virginia State Constitution.

1788   The U.S. Constitution is ratified.

1788   On June 21, the U.S. Constitution is adopted, and the Bill of Rights with its First Amendment rights is passed by Congress. The amendments are ratified in 1791.

1788   Congress passes the Judiciary Act establishing the U.S. Supreme Court, composed of five associate justices and one chief justice, and thirteen judicial districts.

1795   The Senate, exercising its advice and consent power, rejects the first Supreme Court justice nominee, John Rutledge.

1796   The Treaty of Tripoli is negotiated and ratified by the U.S. Senate with a statement that the United States is not a Christian nation.

1798   Congress enacts the Alien and Sedition Acts.

1800–1870   The Second Great Awakening movement takes place, reaches its high point in 1820, and is in decline by 1870.

1804   The Supreme Court of New York decides *People of the State of New York v. Harry Croswell.*

1812 The War of 1812 (with England) heightens fear of foreigners and brings doubts about the allegiance and loyalty of Catholics.

1813 The Mormon Church (LDS) begins; it is formally established in 1830.

1820 The Missouri Compromise is passed, admitting the slave state of Missouri and the free state of Maine to the Union. The act prohibits slavery in the new Louisiana Purchase north of latitude 36°30'. It is repealed in 1854 by the Kansas-Nebraska Act and is deemed unconstitutional in 1857 with the *Dred Scott* decision.

1821–1833 Increasing violence and conflict between Mormons and traditional Protestant denominations escalate to what is called the Mormon v. "Gentile" Wars.

1823 Massachusetts disestablishes its state church, the last state of the original thirteen to do so.

1831 The U.S. Supreme Court decides *Near v. Minnesota*.

1836 The Mormons move to Kirtland, Ohio.

1838 The Battle of Crooked River takes place between Mormons and a Missouri militia. Missouri governor Lilburn Boggs issues Executive Order 44, the "Mormon Extermination Order." The Mormons move to Nauvoo, Illinois.

1840 Brigham Young travels to England. In 1841, he returns with some ten thousand converts to the New Zion in Nauvoo.

1843 The Millerites movement begins. It formally becomes the Seventh-day Adventist Church in 1863.

1844 The Smith brothers (Joseph and Hiram) are martyred in Carthage, Illinois. Seventh-day Adventists is officially formed. The Nauvoo Charter is soon revoked and sets off the Mormons' great trek west.

1847 The Mormons move to Nebraska and then to the Salt Lake City area. Brigham Young begins his long term (1847–1877) as the president/prophet of LDS.

1848   The Treaty of Guadalupe Hidalgo is signed, ending the war with Mexico. It adds a huge territory to the United States, gives citizenship to former Mexican nationals living in new U.S. territories, and adds thousands of Catholic adherents to the U.S. population.

1848–1852   Approximately 1.2 million Irish Catholic immigrants arrive on the "famine ships."

1849   Secret Order of the Star- Spangled Banner is formed.

1858–1860   The Union Army occupies the Utah Territory.

1861   The Civil War begins in April at Fort Sumter.

1862   President Abraham Lincoln signs into law the Morrill Ant-Bigamy Act making polygamy illegal and limiting nonprofit ownership of land in any territory of the United States to $50,000.

1865   Congress passes and the states ratify the Thirteenth Amendment to the Constitution, which abolishes slavery in the United States.

1870   Senator Hiram Revels (R-MS) and Representative Joseph Rainey (R-SC) become the first African Americans to serve in Congress. Senate Democrats try to block Senator Revels from taking his seat; however, Senate Republicans defend him, and he is seated. Since then, 153 African Americans have served in the Congress.

1870s–1880s   The first wave of Hasidic Jews comes to the United States.

1872   The Jehovah's Witnesses is started by Charles Taze Russell.

1876   The LDS splinter group the Church of Christ ends.

1878   The U.S. Supreme Court rules, in *Reynolds v. United States*, that anti-polygamy law is constitutional. The Establishment Clause bans government from regulation of belief but allows it to regulate actions such as marriage.

1880s–1900   Sunni Muslims come to the United States in first big wave.

1890 Supreme Court decides *Davis v. Beason*, again upholding the ban on polygamy.

1890 Mormon Manifesto published by LDS president Woodruff announcing an end to practice of polygamy as official doctrine.

1913 Self-declared prophet Noble Drew Ali, of Newark, New Jersey, starts the Temple movement.

1913 The Seventeenth Amendment is ratified, which requires the direct election of senators rather than their being selected by state legislators. This followed years of bribery cases brought to the Senate, where members were bribing the state legislators to seat them and many states moving to a direct election system on their own.

1919 The International Peace Mission movement of Father Divine begins.

1919 The court rules on free speech cases *Schenck v. United States*; *Abrams v. United States*; and *Debs v. United States*. In *Debs v. United States*, the court upholds the conviction of Debs; his speech against draft laws was analogous to *Schenck* case.

1920 The Nineteenth Amendment is ratified, which allows women to vote in federal elections.

1924 Congress passes and President Calvin Coolidge signs the Indian Citizenship Act, which gives citizenship to all Native Americans born in the United States. They were not immediately given the right to vote, however, as that was left up to the states; it took thirty years for all Native Americans to have the right to vote in the United States.

1925 The court rules in *Pierce v. Society of Sisters* that parochial schools are constitutional and legal.

1925 The court decides the free speech case *Gitlow v. New York*.

1927 In *McGrain v. Daugherty*, the court establishes the power of congressional committees to compel witnesses to testify. Witnesses still retain their Fifth Amendment rights, however.

1930 The court issues the *Cochran v. Louisiana State Board of Education* decision.

1931   In *Near v. Minnesota*, the court holds that prior restraint violates freedom of press.

1932   The Nation of Islam (NOI) is started by W. Fard Muhammad.

1934   Fard Muhammad disappears, and Elijah (Poole) Muhammad takes over the Nation of Islam. NOI begins Chicago Temple 2 as its headquarters.

1935   The court rules in *Lynch v. Massachusetts*.

1937   The court rules in *De Jonge v. Oregon*.

1938   The court announces its opinion in *Lovell v. Griffin*.

1938   The Fair Labor Standards Act is passed by Congress and signed by President Roosevelt. It is considered the last major piece of the New Deal legislation. It creates a forty-hour workweek, makes child labor illegal, and sets a minimum wage.

1939   The court announces the "access to public forum" doctrine in *Hague v. Committee for Industrial Organization*.

1940   The court issues its ruling in *Cantwell v. Connecticut* that government cannot require permits to solicit for religious groups if it does not for secular groups.

1940   In *Minersville School District v. Gobitis*, the court upholds the flag salute law.

1940   The Lubavitch Hasidic Jewish sect moves to Crown Heights, New York.

1941   The court weighs in on religious solicitation in *Cox v. New Hampshire*.

1941   On December 8, following a joint address to both chambers of Congress by President Roosevelt regarding the attack on Pearl Harbor, Congress votes on a war resolution declaring war on Japan. Representative Rankin (R-MT) is the lone "no" vote against the war.

1941   On December 11, Congress declares war on Germany and Italy. Representative Rankin votes "present" on these two votes. No member in either chamber votes against the declarations.

1941 The court decides *Chaplinsky v. New Hampshire* and announces its "fighting words" doctrine.

1941 The court decides *Jones v. City of Opelika* and *Marsh v. Alabama*.

1942 The court establishes a "religious test" for public benefits in *Chaplinsky v. New Hampshire*.

1943 The court decides the landmark case of *West Virginia State Board of Education v. Barnette* that overturns the flag salute decision in *Gobitis*.

1943 The court decides *United States v. Ballard* and *Prince v. Massachusetts*.

1945 The court rules on prior restraint to assemble in *Thomas v. Collins*.

1946 The court hands down its opinion in *Estep v. United States*.

1947 The *Everson v. Board of Education* decision is announced; the court ruling provides the Everson test for when aid to parochial schools is permissible.

1948 *McCollum v. Board of Education* is decided.

1948 Congress passes the Displaced Persons Act of 1948 in response to millions of people in Eastern and Central Europe who were left homeless and destitute following World War II. It allows for four hundred thousand people to come to the United States for resettlement over the next four years. Hearings on the matter were televised and became one of the most infamous House hearings.

1948 The House Committee on Un-American Activities begins a public hearing looking into the allegations by Whittaker Chambers, a former communist spy, that Alger Hiss, a former State Department official, was a spy for the Soviet Union.

1952 Malcolm Little is released from prison, during which time he had converted to Islam, joined NOI as Malcolm X.

1952 The *Zorach v. Clauson* and *Kedroff v. Saint Nicholas Cathedral* decisions are announced.

1953   The court issues opinions in four major cases: *West Virginia v. Barnette*; *Murdock v. Commonwealth of Pennsylvania*; *Niemotkov v. Maryland*; and *Fowler v. Rhode Island*.

1954   The Wicca neo-pagan religion starts; it comes to the United States around 1960.

1954   U.S. Senator Lyndon B. Johnson writes a bill, later called the Johnson Amendment, that mandates Internal Revenue Service rules be changed regarding charitable religious nonprofit exemptions from federal taxes. They are to be cancelled if the church advocates voting for a particular party or candidate from the pulpit or participates in the campaign on behalf of or against a candidate for public office; the religious exemption is for 501(c)(3) nonprofit organizations.

1954   Four Puerto Rican nationalists open fire on the House floor from the visitor's gallery while the House is voting to reauthorize a bill allowing Mexican farmworkers to work in the country. Five members were wounded, but, miraculously, no one was killed. The Army-McCarthy hearings begin. The televised hearings were set up by Senator Joseph McCarthy (R-WI) to investigate army security, which followed his allegations that communists had infiltrated American government. The army responded by accusing Senator McCarthy of using his influence to give special treatment to one of his aides who had been drafted. Senator McCarthy's popularity plummets after these hearings, and he is censured by the Senate on December 2, 1954.

1957   Senator Strom Thurmond (R-SC) carries out the longest filibuster in Senate history, holding the floor for twenty-four hours, eighteen minutes. He was delaying passage of the Civil Rights Act of 1957.

1957   In *Watkins v. United States*, the court determines that Congress can investigate individuals but cannot in the process expose their private affairs without justification.

1958   The court announces its decision in *NAACP v. Alabama*, a freedom of association case, in favor of NAACP and its desire to keep its membership list private.

1959   The *Murray v. Curlett* opinion is announced.

1960   Malcolm X leaves the NOI and founds the Organization of Afro-American Unity (OAAU).

1960   The court announces the NAACP's right to air grievances in *Bates v. Little Rock*.

1960   In *Braunfeld v. Brown* and *Gallagher v. Crown Kosher Super Market of Massachusetts, Inc.* the court hands down rulings on Sunday blue laws.

1960   The court decides the case of *McCullum v. Maryland*.

1961   The *McGowan v. Maryland* Sunday blue law decision is handed down.

1961   The court rules state law requiring any kind of religious test as unconstitutional, even requiring swearing an oath to assume a public office. It rules on religious aid in *Torcaso v. Watkins*.

1962   The American Atheists Organization is formed.

1962   The landmark *Engle v. Vitale* case is decided; it bans required prayers in schools as unconstitutional.

1963   The *Abington School District v. Schempp* decision is rendered by the court; it bans required reading of the Bible in public schools.

1963   *Sherbert v. Verner* overturns the state law denying unemployment benefits to people who refuse to work on their Sabbath.

1963   The court decides *Murray v. Curlett*, another ban on school prayers, and announces decisions in *Edwards v. South Carolina*.

1964   The Civil Rights Act of 1964 is passed after more than fourteen hours of filibuster by Senator Robert C. Byrd (D-WVA). After being on the floor for sixty days, cloture is taken, with a vote of 71 to 29, the first cloture invoked on a civil rights bill. Senator Engle of California, although very ill with brain cancer and unable speak, is on the floor for the vote; he points to his eye to vote for cloture. The act provides for minority voting rights, outlaws discrimination at public facilities, and creates equal employment protections. The act is a key component of the Great Society legislation.

1964   The court rules on free press rights in *New York Times v. Sullivan*.

1964   In *Garrison v. Louisiana*, the court overturns the conviction of District Attorney Jim Garrison, holding criminal libel law used to convict him unconstitutional.

1965   Malcolm X is assassinated.

1965   Internal Revenue Service (IRS) issues rule on Social Security exempting Old Order Amish and Mennonites.

1965   The Voting Rights Act of 1965 is passed by Congress and signed into law by President Lyndon Johnson. It bans "Jim Crow" laws, which were primarily used in the South, specifically literacy tests and poll taxes. The act also requires the Judiciary Department to approve state and county voting practices in the South.

1965   The court strikes down Louisiana's "breach of peace" law in *Cox v. Louisiana*.

1966   Congress passes and President Johnson signs the Freedom of Information Act (FOIA), which gives the American people and press access to federal executive records.

1967   The court rules in *Curtis Publishing v. Butts* and *AP v. Walker*.

1968   The court rules in *Board of Education v. Allen*; in *Epperson v. Arkansas*, which bans the state law forbidding the teaching of evolution; and in *Flast v. Cohen* on standing to sue.

1968   The court rules against use of ten-day injunction against the National States Rights Party of white supremacists in *Carroll v. President and Commissioners of Town of Princes Anne*.

1968   In *United States v. O'Brien*, the court rules that the law against burning a draft card does not violate the First Amendment.

1969   The court decides for the national Presbyterian Church in *Presbyterian Church v. Hull Church*.

1969   The court decides *Tinker v. Des Moines Independent Community School District* and *Brandenburg v. Ohio*.

1969   The court strikes down the Birmingham parade ordinance in *Shuttlesworth v. Birmingham*.

1969   Representative Shirley Chisholm (D-NY) becomes the first African American congresswoman. She was the only female in her freshman class of members of the House. She went on to serve seven terms in Congress.

1969   In *Gregory v. City of Chicago*, the court holds against the Chicago Police Department's overzealous actions to "quell an anticipated civil disorder."

1970   *Walz v. Tax Commission of the City of New York* is decided.

1971   The court issues the landmark decision in *Lemon v. Kurtzman*, which allows state aid to sectarian schools meeting a three-point test.

1971   The court decides *Tilton v. Richardson* and *Committee for Public Education and Religious Liberty v. Nyquist*.

1971   The court rules in the Pentagon Papers case, *New York Times v. United States*, and the free speech case of *Cohen v. California*.

1971   In *Coates v. City of Cincinnati*, the court strikes down a loitering ordinance on basis that the "annoying conduct" wording is too vague.

1971   The Twenty-Sixth Amendment is ratified, lowering the voting age to eighteen in federal elections.

1972   The court issues the *Yoder v. Wisconsin* landmark decision, ruling that states must provide exemptions from certain compulsory education attendance laws to Amish and Mennonites.

1972   Congress enacts the Indian Education Act.

1972   The court announces a decision in *Lloyd Corporation v. Tanner*.

1973   The Senate Select Committee on Presidential Campaign Activities, better known as the Watergate Committee, begins open public hearings. The committee is tasked with investigating campaign activities during the 1972 presidential campaign, including the break-in at the Democratic National Committee headquarters in the Watergate Hotel. The hearings lead to the unprecedented action of the committee suing President Nixon for access to his White House tapes. The House Judiciary Committee eventually passes three articles of impeachment. President Nixon resigns on August 9, 1974, before the full House can vote on impeachment.

1974   Congress enacts the Indian Self-Determination and Education Assistance Act.

1974   The court reaches a decision in *Meek v. Pittenger.*

1975   Elijah Muhammad dies, and his son, Wallace Dean Muhammad succeeds him. He moves from the NOI to form the American Society of Muslims and becomes a Sunni Imam.

1975   The court rules in *Nebraska Press Association v. Stuart.*

1975–1990   A wave of Palestinian and Lebanese refugees arrives in United States.

1976   Minister Louis Farrakhan revives the NOI.

1976   The court decides *Roemer v. Board of Public Works of Maryland* and *Buckley v. Valeo,* which is on campaign spending by a candidate or family.

1976   In *Virginia Board of Pharmacy v. Virginia Consumer Council,* the court rules that commercial speech is protected under the First Amendment.

1977   *Wolman v. Walter; Trans World Airlines v. Hardison;* and *Zacchini v. Scripps-Howard Broadcasting* are decided.

1977   In *Bates v. State Bar of Arizona,* the court rules that lawyers have right to advertise.

1978   Congress passes the American Indian Religious Freedom Act, the Tribally Controlled Community College Assistance Act, and the Indian Child Welfare Act.

1978   The court decides *McDaniel v. Paty,* which overturns the state law banning clergy from serving in public office.

1978   The court decides *Village of Skokie v. National Socialist Party*, upholding the Nazi Party adherents' right to parade in public protest in Skokie, Illinois.

1979   The Indian Archaeological Resources Protection Act is passed by Congress. The court decides the case of *Jones v. Wolf.*

1980   The *Committee for Public Education and Religious Liberty v. Regan* decision is rendered.

1980   *Stone v. Graham* bans the display of the Ten Commandments in public schools as an unconstitutional violation of the Establishment Clause.

1981   The court decides *Widmar v. Vincent*; *Thomas v. Review Board of Indiana Employment Security Division*; *Heffron v. International Society for Krishna Consciousness*; and *Gallagher v. Crown Kosher Super Market.*

1982   The court decides *Larkin v. Grendel's Den*; *Valley Forges and People Christian College v. Americans United for Separation of Church and State*; *Larson v. Valente*; and *Mueller v. Allen.*

1982   The court's verdict in *Marsh v. Chambers* allows states to hire a chaplain to open legislative sessions.

1982   In *Bob Jones University v. United States*, the court rescinds the university's tax-exempt status because of its racial discrimination policies.

1983   Supreme Court rules in *Island Tree School District v. Pica;* and tax exemption case *Bob Jones University v. United States.*

1984   Congress passes the Equal Access Act.

1984   *Lynch v. Donnelly* is decided, upholding a nativity scene in a public park if it is among other holiday displays.

1984   The *Marsh v. Chambers* decision allows military chaplains.

1985   *Aguillard v. Felton*; *Grand Rapids School District v. Ball*; *Board of Trustees of Scarsdale v. McCreary*; *Thornton v. Caldor*; and *Wallace v. Jaffree* are decided.

1986   *Ohio Civil Rights Commission v. Dayton Christian Schools* is decided in favor of the school.

1986   *Goldman v. Weinberger* upholds air force regulations against wearing a skull cap on duty. The court decides *Bowen v. Roy* and decides the free speech case of *Bethel School District v. Fraser*.

1987   The court rules on the "creationism" case *Edwards v. Aguillard* and *Corporation of the Presiding Bishop of the Church of Jesus Christ of the Latter-Day Saints v. Amos*.

1987   The court rules that Rotary Clubs have to open membership to women in *Rotary International v. Rotary Club of Duarte*.

1988   Congress enacts the Indian Gaming Regulatory Act.

1988   The court decides *Bowen v. Kendrick*; *Lyng v. Northwest Indian Cemetery Protection Association*; *Hustler v. Falwell*; and *Hazelwood School District v. Kuhlmeier*.

1989   The *County of Allegheny v. American Civil Liberties Union, Greater Pittsburgh Chapter* decision is handed down, banning a nativity scene placed alone in a courthouse staircase as unconstitutional.

1989   The court delivers its tax exemption opinion in *Texas Monthly, Inc. v. Bullock* and decides *Texas v. Johnson*.

1990   Congress passes the Native American Graves Protection and Repatriation Act.

1990   The court renders its opinion in *Board of Education of the Westside Community Schools v. Mergens* that requiring public schools to provide equal access to religious groups as they do to secular groups.

1990   In *Employment Division v. Smith*, the court allows Oregon to fire an employee for smoking peyote during a religious ceremony.

1992   *Lee v. Weisman* is decided that an officially sanctioned prayer at graduation is unconstitutional, but the public school can provide a sign language interpreter to a deaf child at a religious school.

1992   The court issues a verdict in *R. A. V. v. City of St. Paul,*

1993   The court announces verdicts in *Lamb's Chapel v. Center Moriches Union Free School District*; *Church of Lukumi Babalu Aye v. City of Hialeah*; and *Zobrest v. Catalina Foothills School District*.

1994   *Board of Education of Kiryas Joel Village School v. Grumet* overturns a New York law benefiting a single religious group, a special school for disabled Orthodox Jewish children.

1994   Congress enacts the Religious Freedom Restoration Act to ensure that religious freedom is protected, and rules that the Government must show compelling state interest to restrict any religious practice.

1994   The court upholds women's right to abortion access in *Madsen v. Women's Health Center*.

1994   The court decides *Rosenberger v. University of Virginia*.

1994   *Capitol Square Review and Advisory Board v. Pinette* allows for a cross by a private group in a public forum near the statehouse as the space is open to all on equal terms.

1996   The court rules in *Agostini v. Felton* and *City of Boerne v. Flores*.

1997   The Supreme Court rules on the case of *Hurley v. Irish-American Gay, Lesbian and Bisexual Group of Boston* on the rights of gays and lesbians to demonstrate in public.

1997   The court decides the free speech case *Reno v. American Civil Liberties Union* and the free exercise versus eminent domain issue in *City of Boerne v. Flores*.

2000   The court decides *Santa Fe Independent School District v. Doe*, striking down the use of prayer voted on by students to be read at football games as subtle religious coercion of the minority by the majority.

2000   In *Mitchell v. Helms*, the court rules the federal government can provide computer equipment to all schools under the Elementary and Secondary Education Act.

2000   The Boys Scouts of America must open their membership to openly gay leaders in the *Boy Scouts of America v. Dale* decision.

2001   The 9/11 terrorist attacks and an anthrax contamination threat cause alarm about Islamic terrorism. In October, Congress passes the USA PATRIOT Act in response.

2001   The court decides religious clubs are allowed to meet in public schools in *Good News Club v. Milford Central School.*

2002   The court approves a voucher system for private schools in *Zelman v. Simmons-Harris* decision.

2002   The court rules in the free speech case of *Watchtower Bible and Tract Society v. Village of Stratton.*

2002   In direct opposition to the wishes of President George W. Bush, Congress creates a new cabinet-level department, the U.S. Department of Homeland Security (DHS).

2003   The court decides the free speech cases *United States v. American Library Association*; *Virginia v. Hicks*; and *Virginia v. Black.*

2004   The court decides *Elk Grove Unified School District v. Newdow*, ruling on narrow "standing to sue" technical grounds.

2004   *Locke v. Davey* allows the state to refuse scholarship funds to college students pursuing divinity degrees.

2004   The court decides the free speech case *Ashcroft v. American Civil Liberties Union.*

2005   The court announces decisions on *McCreary County v. American Civil Liberties Union of Kentucky*; *Van Orden v. Perry*; and *Cutter v. Wilkinson* in regard to monuments displaying the Ten Commandments on the State Capitol grounds or in Kentucky courthouses.

2006   The court renders its decision in *Gonzales v. O Centro Espirita Beneficente Uniao do Vegetal*, allowing a small religious sect to use a hallucinogenic herbal tea in religious ceremonies.

2007 Mitt Romney runs for president on the Republican Party ticket.

2007 The court rules taxpayers cannot bring Establishment Clause cases against the Office of Faith-Based and Community Initiatives created by the President George W. Bush administration in the case of *Hein v. Freedom from Religion Foundation*.

2007 The court decides *Morse v. Frederick*.

2008 Senator Barack Obama (D-IL) is the first African American to be elected president of the United States. He is also only the third sitting senator to be elected president, after Warren Harding in 1920 and John F. Kennedy in 1960.

2010 The court rules that student organizations at a public university cannot limit their membership to those who share their belief system if doing so results in discrimination on the basis of sexual orientation in *Christian Legal Society v. Martinez*.

2010 In *Citizens United v. Federal Election Commission*, the court holds that unlimited spending by independent organizations is protected free speech.

2011 The *Arizona Christian School Tuition Organization v. Winn* and *Christian Legal Society v. Martinez* decisions are announced.

2012 In *Hosanna-Tabor Evangelical Lutheran Church and School v. Equal Employment Opportunity Commission*, the court decides for the church.

2014 The *Town of Greece v. Galloway* opinion is rendered by the court.

2016 President Obama directs the U.S. Department of Education to issue a "guidance" to state and local schools to allow transgender students the right of access to bathrooms that match their gender identity.

2017 In February, newly appointed secretary of education Betsy DeVos, under direction from the President Trump White House, rescinds the Obama "guidance."

2017   President Trump and Attorney General Sessions also announce that the new administration will seek to rescind the Johnson Amendment rules for the IRS that ban religious organizations from political endorsements from the pulpit.

2017   The White House announces a flurry of executive orders that rescind Obamacare rules and the Deferred Action for Childhood Arrivals (DACA) and Deferred Action for Parents of Americans and Lawful Permanent Residents (DAPA) executive actions regarding Dreamers.

2017   Acting attorney general Sally Yates is fired for her refusal to defend the constitutionality of the Trump executive orders on a travel ban for everyone seeking to enter the United States from seven predominantly Muslim countries. Within the month, two federal courts, a district court, and an appellate court place stay orders on the travel ban. The Trump administration then announces it will rewrite the travel ban executive order to clarify it is not a Muslim ban, which is unconstitutional on its face.

2018   The court decides *Janus v. American Federation of State, County, and Municipal Employees*, ruling that public sector unions cannot charge "agency fees" on members who decline to join the union, overturning the 1977 decision in *Abood v. Detroit Board of Education*.

Glossary

Advocacy   The support given by interest groups who act as stakeholders in the politics of First Amendment freedoms, often by supporting court adjudication through amicus briefs to assist persons or groups who are directly challenging the constitutionality of federal, state, or local laws or government regulations that may impinge on or limit one of the First Amendment freedoms.

Amicus Curiae   Latin for "friend of the court," it is a legal brief submitted by a person or group who is not a party to the legal dispute or case but who argues a particular legal position for the court's consideration. Most Supreme Court cases that are challenging government action on constitutional grounds have amicus briefs associated with them.

Amish   A group of traditionalist Christian fellowship arising in eighteenth-century Europe, named after Jacob Amman, that share with Mennonites an origin in the Swiss Anabaptist movement. They are known for simple living, plain dress, and a reluctance to adopt modern technology and lifestyle. They have sometimes been a party to cases challenging laws, such as state compulsory education laws, on religious freedom grounds, such as in *Wisconsin v. Yoder* (406 U.S. 205, 1972).

Annabaptists   A Christian movement arising out of the Radical Reformation, known as Rebaptizers. It was an offshoot of Protestantism in sixteenth-century Europe that advocated strongly for the separation of church and state.

Appellant/Appelle The two parties to an appeal case. An appeal is a procedure by which an appellant (a person or entity) seeks review of a lower court's ruling. The appellee is the respondent to an appeal.

Arguendo A Latin phrase sometimes used in Supreme Court opinions that means "for the sake of argument."

Articles of Confederation The confederal government (1781–1789) created by the Second Constitutional Congress to replace British rule. It was replaced by the U.S. Constitution in 1789. It had no Bill of Rights.

Bill of Rights A bill or declaration of rights delineated as fundamental rights; the first ten amendments to the 1789 U.S. Constitution.

Certiorari A writ or order by which a higher court reviews the decision of a lower court.

Citizenship The legal concept identifying a member of a society tied to the right to vote, to be eligible to hold political office, and other fundamental rights contained in the Bill of Rights.

Civil Rights and Liberties The protections afforded by law, especially those extended to citizens, and generally embodying the protection of natural rights and natural justice within a nation's laws and the commitment to enforce them fairly.

Cognitive Speech Speech that is the expression of ideas.

Commercial Speech Speech that promotes some type of commerce and is a form of protected communication under the First Amendment; that is, speech that proposes a commercial transaction.

Common Schools The term used in the nineteenth century to refer to public schools.

Contemporary Community Standards A standard used by courts to test descriptions or depictions of sexual matters that was first adopted by the U.S. Supreme Court in *Roth v. United States* (354 U.S. 476, 1957). The community standard may be used without reference to a precise geographical area.

Criminal Syndicalism   Syndicalism is defined as a doctrine of criminal acts for political, industrial, and social change. Such acts include advocating crimes of sabotage, violence, and other unlawful methods of terrorism. Criminal syndicalism laws were enacted to oppose economic radicalism by criminal or violent means.

Cult   A system of belief and religious veneration directed toward a particular figure or object; usually a small group having beliefs and practices that others see as strange or sinister.

De Facto   A Latin phrase meaning "by action."

De Jure   A Latin phrase meaning something being done "by law."

Defamation   The oral or written communication of a false statement about another person that unjustly harms the person's reputation or livelihood and usually constitutes a tort.

Denomination   A recognized, autonomous branch of the Christian church.

Deportation   A legal process by which a nation forcibly ejects or sends individuals who are in a country illegally or are believed to be threats to health or safety back to their countries of origin after refusing them legal residence. During wartime, it was used against noncitizens (e.g., World War I) who adhered to a political ideology, such as anarchism, communism, or socialism, considered at the time to be dangerous to society and was used to suppress the freedom of speech of persons advocating such ideology.

Dicta   (plural for dictum) Legal terminology; a statement of opinion considered to be authoritative, although not binding, given the recognized authoritativeness of the person who pronounced it.

Doctrine of Incorporation   The legal theory allowing the Supreme Court to apply the Bill of Rights to the states under the Fourteenth Amendment's Due Process Clause.

Due Process of Law   Constitutional limitation on government behavior to deal with an individual according to prescribed rules and procedures. Based on British common law, it prohibits government from depriving an individual of "life, liberty, or property," as protected by the Fifth Amendment to the Constitution with respect to the national government and by the Fourteenth Amendment against such violations by the states.

Emotive Speech   Speech that is the expression of emotion.

Equal Protection of the Law   The constitutionally guaranteed right that all persons be treated the same before the law.

Establishment Clause   A provision of the First Amendment that prevents the establishment of religion; along with the Free Exercise Clause, it protects religious liberty.

Executive Orders   Actions issued by a president that are assigned numbers and published in the *Federal Register*, akin to laws passed by Congress, that direct members of the executive branch to follow a new policy or directive. They have been used against minority religion adherents, such as the Trump administration's "Muslim travel ban."

Exempt   An individual, class, or category of individuals to whom a certain provision of the law does not apply.

Expedited Removal   A stipulation in law changing the procedures by which persons in the United States without legal status may be deported with fewer judicial protections to do so.

Expulsion   The decision of a sovereign nation to legally compel an individual to permanently leave its territory. It was used against radical political ideologues who used free speech to protest government, and states and the federal government used that advocacy as grounds to expel them.

Federal Abstention Doctrine   Any of several doctrines that a court of law in the United States may (and in some cases, must) apply to refuse to hear a case if doing so would potentially intrude upon the powers of another court.

Fighting Words Doctrine   In U.S. constitutional law, the doctrine is used by courts as a limitation to protected free speech under the First Amendment. The doctrine was established, in a 9–0 decision, in *Chaplinsky v. New Hampshire* (315 U.S. 568, 1942). It allows government to limit speech when it is likely to incite immediate retaliation, as in the Jehovah's Witnesses case.

Fourteenth Amendment The post–Civil War amendment, ratified in 1868, that declares that all persons "born or naturalized in the United States" are citizens. It overturned the 1857 decision in *Dred Scott v. Sandford* (60 U.S. 393), which had declared that blacks were not and could not be citizens. In subsequent decisions, the Supreme Court gradually applied most of the first ten amendments to the states via the Fourteenth Amendment.

Inadmissibles Persons encountered at ports of entry who are seeking lawful admission into the United States but are determined to be inadmissible, individuals presenting themselves to seek humanitarian protection under U.S. laws, and individuals who withdraw their application for admission and return to their countries of origin within a short time frame. It has been used against persons seeking admission as refugees on the grounds of religious persecution in their country of origin.

Injunctive Relief A writ or court order stopping an agency or governmental official from taking an action that petitioners argue before a court would be harmful.

Judicial Review A power, exercised by U.S. courts, to examine legislation and to strike down those laws that judges believe violate the U.S. Constitution.

Jurisprudence Taking legal action in courts of law or the system of applying judicial judgments (reviews, for example).

Jus Sali Citizenship based on place of birth.

Jus Sanguinis Citizenship based on blood or parentage.

Landmark Decision A Supreme Court decision that sets a precedent or distinguishes tests or other guidelines that determine subsequent court cases on a legal matter.

Libel   A written or published defamatory statement.

Magna Carta   An act signed in 1215. It is the first written document presented to and signed by King John of England (1166–1216) that limited the monarch's powers. It was the basis of English citizens' rights, for example, the right to assemble to protest a grievance against the government.

Millennial Movement   The belief by a religious, social, or political group or movement; it means "containing a thousand."

Ministerial Exception Rule   A court or congressional rule that exempts ministers of churches from suing their church in civil court, for example, on personnel matters, rights to employment compensation, hiring, and firing.

Nativism   Individuals who favor citizens over noncitizens based on their ethnic identity or religious affiliation. American nativists have often been particularly hostile to Roman Catholics and are currently hostile to Muslims.

Naturalization   The legal act of making an individual a citizen who is not born a citizen.

Papist   A pejorative term used by Protestants for the Roman Catholic Church and its teachings, practices, and adherents.

Per Curiam   A legal term for an action taken by a higher court reviewing the decision of a lower court in which the decision is rendered by the court (or at least a majority of the court and often by a unanimous court) collectively rather than being authored and signed by an individual jurist.

Permanent Resident   A noncitizen who is allowed to live permanently in the United States, who can travel in and out of the country without a visa, and who can work without restriction; such person is allowed to accumulate time toward becoming a naturalized citizen.

Prior Restraint   In First Amendment jurisprudence, government action (censorship) that prohibits speech or expression before the speech happens or in advance of publication. It is usually considered unconstitutional subject to a small number of exceptions.

Privileges and Immunities   Fourteenth Amendment–based aspects of citizenship designed to protect citizens from government; there is widespread disagreement on their actual scope and the relationship to the privileges and immunities conferred by state citizenship.

Proselytize   To convert or attempt to convert someone from one religion, belief, or opinion to another.

Public Forum Doctrine   The Supreme Court established three types of public forum in *Perry Education Association v. Perry Local Educators' Association* (460 U.S. 37, 1983). It is an analytical tool used in First Amendment jurisprudence to determine the constitutionality of a speech restriction implemented on government property.

Racial Profiling   A pattern of behavior by police officers that is based on racial appearance.

Refugee   An individual who has fled his or her own country, usually because of war, upheaval, or political or religious persecution, who is seeking sanctuary, refuge, or asylum in another country.

Remand   An action taken by a higher court reviewing the decision of a lower court by which a case is sent back to the lower court for new action following the dicta or guidance of the higher court as to some point of law, often involving a constitutional question or issue.

Rights   Legitimate claims that an individual can make against government, the most extensive of which apply to citizens. Rights are thought to be correlative with duties. A citizen who has the right to seek governmental protection thus also has the obligation to serve in the military when needed.

Sabbatarianism   A religious law, norm, or customary practice as to which day, Saturday or Sunday, a religious group/denomination/cult/sect holds to be the holy day.

Sanctuary   A place of safety and protection, especially sought by refugees.

Sanctuary City   A city in the United States that follows certain procedures that shelter illegal immigrants that may be by de jure or de facto action. The designation has no legal meaning and is most commonly used for cities that do not permit municipal funds or resources to be applied in furtherance of enforcement of federal immigration laws; that is, they do not allow police or municipal employees to inquire about one's immigrant status. It is typically used by city governments to protect "unpopular" ethnic or religious minority members and is often justified by religious freedom First Amendment rights.

Scapegoat   In the Bible, a goat sent out into the wilderness after the Jewish chief priest had symbolically laid the sins of the people on it. To make a scapegoat of someone or some group is to blame them for the sins of others.

Schism   A split or division between strongly opposed sectarians or parties caused by differences of opinion or belief.

Sect   A group of people with somewhat different religious beliefs (typically regarded as heretical) from those of a larger group to which they belong.

Seditious Libel   The act or crime of publishing a seditious statement. It was a crime under English common law first established in 1606 by the Star Chamber.

Slander   Defamation that is spoken by the defendant.

Stakeholder   A person or organization with an interest or concern in something, especially a business; one who is involved or is affected by a policy or course of action.

Stare Decisis   Latin meaning "let the decision stand"; a doctrine or policy of following the rules or principles of determining points in litigation according to precedent.

Statutory Interpretation   The right, especially by U.S. courts, to interpret the meaning of acts of legislation.

Symbolic Speech   A legal term in the United States used to describe action that is purposefully and discernably used to convey a particular message or statement to those viewing it, such as the wearing of black armbands, burning a draft card or a flag, or refusing to salute the flag or recite the Pledge of Allegiance, often on religious or political ideological grounds.

Tax Exemption A rule of a tax code excusing a person or group from having to pay a tax, for example, exempting churches from property taxes.

Tort A wrongful act or an infringement of a right (other than under contract) leading to civil liability.

Unitarianism The liberal religion characterized by free and responsible search for truth and meaning.

Universalism Christian universalism is a school of Christian theology that holds the belief in universal reconciliation, that all human beings are already reconciled to God, even if they are unaware of it.

Wall of Separation Doctrine Thomas Jefferson, echoing Roger Williams, described it as "between the garden of the church and the wilderness of the world"; it refers to the American constitutional principle of the separation of church and state.

Writ A form of legal command in the name of a court or other legal authority to act or abstain from acting in some way.

Xenophobia An intense or irrational dislike or fear of people from other countries—a "fear of the foreign." It is often the basis upon which a person's exercise of his or her First Amendment rights is denied or suppressed, often by violence or by de facto or de jure means.

Index

Note: Page numbers followed by *t* indicate tables.

About the Author

Michael C. LeMay, PhD, is professor emeritus from California State University–San Bernardino, where he served as director of the National Security Studies Program, an interdisciplinary master's degree program, chair of the Department of Political Science, and assistant dean for student affairs for the College of Social and Behavioral Sciences. He has frequently written and presented papers at professional conferences on the topic of immigration. He has also written numerous journal articles, book chapters, published essays, and book reviews. He is published in the *International Migration Review, In Defense of the Alien, Journal of American Ethnic History, Southeastern Political Science Review, Teaching Political Science,* and the *National Civic Review.*

He is the author of thirty academic books, nineteen of which are academic volumes dealing with immigration history and policy. His prior books on the subject are *Party and Nation: Immigration and Regime Politics in American History* (2020); *The Immigration and Nationality Act of 1965: A Reference Guide* (ABC-CLIO, 2020); *Immigration Reform: A Reference Handbook* (ABC-CLIO, 2019); *Homeland Security: A Reference Handbook* (ABC-CLIO, 2018); *Religious Freedom in America: A Reference Handbook* (ABC-CLIO, 2018); *U.S. Immigration Policy, Ethnicity, and Religion in American History* (Praeger, 2018); *Illegal Immigration: A Reference Handbook,* 1st and 2nd editions (ABC-CLIO, 2007; 2015); *Doctors at the Borders: Immigration and the Rise of Public Health* (Praeger, 2015); editor and contributing author of the three-volume set *Transforming*

America: Perspectives on U.S. Immigration (Praeger, 2012); *Guarding the Gates: Immigration and National Security* (Praeger Security International, 2006); *U.S. Immigration and Naturalization Laws and Issues: A Documentary History*, edited with Elliott Robert Barkan (Greenwood, 1999); *Anatomy of a Public Policy: The Reform of Contemporary Immigration Law* (Praeger, 1994); *The Gatekeepers: Comparative Immigration Policy* (Praeger, 1989); *From Open Door to Dutch Door: An Analysis of U.S. Immigration Policy since 1820* (Praeger, 1987); and *The Struggle for Influence* (1985).

Professor LeMay has written two textbooks that have considerable material related to these topics: *Public Administration: Clashing Values in the Administration of Public Policy*, 2nd edition (2006) and *The Perennial Struggle*, 3rd edition (2009). He frequently lectures on topics related to immigration history and policy.

He loves to travel and has lectured around the world, visiting more than 150 cities in 51 countries. His previously authored books in the ABC-CLIO Contemporary World Issues series are *U.S. Immigration* (2004); *Illegal Immigration*, 1st edition (2007), 2nd edition (2015); *Global Pandemic Threats* (2016); *The American Political Party System* (2017); *Religious Freedom in America* (2018); *Homeland Security* (2018); *The American Congress*, with Sara Hagedorn (2019); *Immigration Reform: A Reference Handbook* (2019); and *The Immigration and Nationality Act of 1965* (2020).